Managing Organizational Change in Public Services

Forming part of the Understanding Organizational Change series, *Managing Organizational Change in Public Services* focuses on the organizational dimension of change management in public services. Combining aspects of change management theory with 'real life' practice in the form of organizational cases from different regions and sectors, this edited collection identifies and analyzes significant issues regarding the development, implementation and evaluation of public service change initiatives. Featuring contributions from leading authors in the field, this text provides an overview of organizational change management with a focus on leadership, management and strategies for change.

Looking at cases from Europe and North America, *Managing Organizational Change in Public Services* offers both a global, as well as a cross-sector analysis of this complex and challenging process. Different sectors that are examined include:

- Transport
- Health
- Education

This book offers an excellent introduction to change management and how it works within public service organizations internationally. It will be vital reading for all those engaged with the study or practice of this dynamic subject.

Rune Todnem By is a Lecturer at the School of Business, Enterprise and Management at Queen Margaret University, Edinburgh, UK. He is the editor of the Journal of Change Management and founder of the International Change and Improvement Leadership Network.

Calum Macleod is Senior Research Fellow within UHI Policyweb, the University of the Highlands and Islands Research Institute for Remote and Rural Regions, based in Inverness, UK.

Understanding Organizational Change

Series editor:
Dr Bernard Burnes

The management of change is now acknowledged as being one of the most important issues facing management today. By focusing on particular perspectives and approaches to change, particular change situations, and particular types of organization, this series provides a comprehensive overview and an in-depth understanding of the field of organizational change.

Titles in this series include:

Managing Organizational Change in Public Services

International issues, challenges and cases

Edited by Rune Todnem By
and Calum Macleod

Routledge
Taylor & Francis Group

LONDON AND NEW YORK

First published 2009
by Routledge
2 Park Square, Milton Park, Abingdon, Oxon OX14 4RN

Simultaneously published in the USA and Canada
by Routledge
270 Madison Ave, New York, NY 10016

Routledge is an imprint of the Taylor & Francis Group, an informa business

Typeset in Times by
Keystroke, 28 High Street, Tettenhall, Wolverhampton
Printed and bound in Great Britain by
Antony Rowe, Chippenham, Wiltshire

British Library Cataloguing in Publication Data
A catalogue record for this book is available from the British Library

Library of Congress Cataloguing in Publication Data
Managing organizational change in public services : international issues,
challenges and cases / edited by Rune Todnem By and Calum Macleod.
p. cm.
Includes bibliographical references and index.
1. Public administration. 2. Civil service–Management. 3. Administrative
agencies–Management. 4. Organizational change–Management.
5. Organizational effectiveness–Management. I. By, Rune Todnem.
II. Macleod, Calum, 1969 Apr. 15–
JF1351.M349 2009
352.3'67–dc22
2008036303

ISBN: 978–0–415–46758–2 (hbk)
ISBN: 978–0–415–46759–9 (pbk)
ISBN: 978–0–203–88183–5 (ebk)

Contents

List of illustrations and tables

Figures

Tables

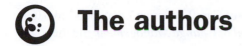

The authors

Bernard Burnes is Professor of Organizational Change at Manchester Business School, University of Manchester. His teaching and research cover organizational change in its broadest sense. Bernard is the author of over 80 journal articles and book chapters, and some 15 books, including *Managing Change*, which is in its fourth edition. His current research includes a study of the contribution of Kurt Lewin to organizational change.

Rune Todnem By is Lecturer at the School of Business, Enterprise and Management, Queen Margaret University, Edinburgh. He is the editor of *Journal of Change Management* and founder of the *International Change and Improvement Leadership Network* (www.iciln.com). Rune's main research interests are organizational change leadership and management with a focus on change readiness and capacity.

Raymond Caldwell is Professor of Organizational Change at Birkbeck College, University of London. His research interests cover organizational change theory and practice, with a specific focus on change agency and distributed leadership in organizations. At present his central research concern is with rethinking concepts of agency and change in organizational theory. Raymond is the author of *Agency and Change: Rethinking Change Agency in Organizations*.

Esther Cameron is Director of Cameron Change Consultancy, a niche consultancy offering organization development, change management coaching and leadership development to public and private sector organizations. She has published two books, including the top-selling *Making Sense of Change Management*, co-written with Mike Green. Esther is also a regular contributor to the (London) *Guardian*'s public management column.

Colin Carnall is Chief Executive of Cass Executive Education Ltd. He is the Founding Editor of the *Journal of Change Management* and the author of *Managing Change in Organizations*, now in its fifth edition.

Fariborz Damanpour is Professor of Management at Rutgers University. His primary area of research is management of innovation and change. Fariborz served as chairman of the Department of Management and Global Business of the Rutgers Business School and Department Editor of the Technology and Innovation Management Department, *IEEE Transactions on Engineering Management*. Currently he is on the editorial boards of the *Journal of Engineering and Technology Management* and *Journal of Management Studies*.

Thomas Diefenbach is Lecturer in Management at University of Strathclyde Business School. His main areas of expertise are management, organization theory, change management, strategy, intangible assets, and critical management studies – all as socio-philosophical interrogations of the relations between the individual, organizations and society, with the focus on power, interests and ideology. Thomas is the author of the book *Management and the Dominance of Managers*.

Mike Green runs his own consultancy, Transitional Space, specializing in individual, team and organizational development. Mike also tutors and coaches as a Visiting Executive Fellow at Henley Management School. His two books, *Making Sense of Change Management* (with Esther Cameron) and *Change Management Masterclass* are guides to the models, tools and techniques of individual, team and organizational change.

David Lewin is the Neil Jacoby Professor of Management, Human Resources and Organizational Behavior at the UCLA Anderson School of Management. A specialist in human resource management and industrial relations, David has published 19 books and more than 150 articles. Prior to joining UCLA, he served as Professor, Director of the Ph.D. Program, Director of the Human Resources Research Center and Director of the Senior Executive Program at the Columbia University Graduate School of Business.

Rune Lines is Professor in Strategy at the Norwegian School of Economics and Business Administration (NHH). Current research interests include causes, content and consequences of individual reactions to planned organizational change, relationships between organizational change and organizational learning, and links between organizational change, individual emotions and organizational learning.

Eric Lofquist is Associate Professor in Strategy at the Norwegian School of Economics and Business Administration (NHH). Current research interests include strategic organizational change in high-risk environments, and the effects of mismatching change and culture types on strategic business outcomes such as safety in high-reliability organizations.

Calum Macleod is Senior Research Fellow within UHI Policyweb, The University of the Highlands and Islands Research Institute for Remote and Rural Regions, based in Inverness, UK. Calum's research interests are in public policy implementation, change management and sustainable development.

Katarina Østergren is Associate Professor at the Norwegian School of Economics and Business Administration (NHH). She has a special interest in studies of management control, governance, and organizational change and learning in the public sector. Katarina is also associated with HEB, the Programme for Health Economics in Bergen, Norway.

Bruce E. Perrott is Senior Lecturer at the University of Technology, Sydney. Bruce is concerned with how business and marketing strategies are formulated, formalized and managed through to the implementation phase. Bruce has over 20 years' experience as a consultant advising senior managers on business and marketing strategies for growth, working internationally with both private and public sector organizations.

Harry Sminia is Lecturer in Strategic Management at University of Sheffield Management School, and previously worked as Lecturer in Strategic Management at the Vrije University, Amsterdam. Harry has published in several journals, including *Journal of Change Management*, *Journal of Management Studies* and *Strategic Change*.

Inger Stensaker is Associate Professor in Strategy and Management at the Norwegian School of Economics and Business Administration (NHH). Her research interests are within strategic and organizational change, change management and responses to change. Her work has appeared in *Human Relations*, *Research in Organizational Development and Change*, *Organization Dynamics*, the *British Journal of Management* and the *Journal of Applied Behavioral Science*.

Antonie Van Nistelrooij is Associate Professor at the Nijenrode Business University. He is also Senior Lecturer in Organization Behavior and Organization Development at the Vrije University, Amsterdam, Management of Change at the University of Groningen, and Management of Conflict at the University of Maastricht.

Richard M. Walker is Professor of Public Management and Policy at the Kadoorie Institute, University of Hong Kong and the School of City and Regional Planning, University of Cardiff. His research agenda is empirical and explores the determinants of performance in public organizations, innovation, red tape and environmental policy. Richard is on the editorial boards of *Administration and Society*, the *Journal of Public Administration Research and Theory* and *Public Administration*. His forthcoming co-edited book published by Cambridge University Press is titled *Public Management and Performance: Research Directions*.

Series editor's preface

In the past, and to an extent even today, the literature on organizational change has tended to focus on the private sector. There are many reasons for this, not least the twin assumptions that all the interesting changes were taking place in the private sector and that the public sector was composed of relatively monolithic and unchanging bureaucracies. If this ever was the case, the past 25 years have shown that it is no longer. The rise of New Public Management with its emphasis on 'marketization' and 'customer' focus has led to rapid, innovative and radical transformation of public organizations across the globe. Though the balance of services that constitute the public sector may vary from country to country, its importance is crucial for people's everyday lives in all countries. Therefore, the ability of the public sector to be able to manage change effectively and efficiently is also crucial to all of us.

I am, therefore, particularly pleased to welcome this book to the series. Rune Todnem By and Calum Macleod have assembled an impressive cast of contributors from different countries who each provide a valuable insight into managing change in the public services. As well as making a considerable contribution to the debate on the changing nature of public services, this book also makes a significant contribution to the Routledge book series Understanding Organizational Change. It is an accepted tenet of modern life that change is constant, of greater magnitude and far less predictable than ever before. For this reason, managing change is acknowledged as being one of the most important and difficult issues facing organizations today. Consequently, both practitioners and academics, in ever-growing numbers, are seeking to understand organizational change. As a result, the range of competing theories and advice has never been greater and never more puzzling.

Over the past 100 years there have been many theories and prescriptions put forward for understanding and managing change. In the 1940s, Kurt

Lewin created perhaps the most influential approach to managing change. His *planned* approach, encapsulated in his three-step model, became the inspiration for a generation of researchers and practitioners, mainly – though not exclusively – in the United States. Throughout the 1950s, Lewin's work was expanded beyond his focus on small groups and conflict resolution to create the Organization Development (OD) movement. From the 1960s to the early 1980s, OD established itself as the dominant Western approach to organizational change.

However, by the early 1980s more and more Western organizations found themselves having to change rapidly and dramatically, and sometimes brutally, in the face of the might of corporate Japan. In such circumstances, many judged the consensus-based and incrementally focused OD approach as having little to offer. Instead, a plethora of approaches began to emerge that, while not easy to classify, could best be described as anti-OD. These newer approaches to change were less wary than OD of embracing issues of power and politics in organizations; they did not necessarily see organizational change as clean, linear and finite. Instead, they saw change as messy, contentious, context dependent and open-ended. In addition, unlike OD, which drew its inspiration and insights mainly from psychology, the newer approaches drew on an eclectic mix of sociology, anthropology, economics, psychotherapy and the natural sciences, not to mention the ubiquitous post-modernism. This has produced a range of approaches to change, with suffixes and appellations such as emergent, processual, political, institutional, cultural, contingency, complexity, chaos, and many more.

It is impossible to conceive of an approach that is suitable for all types of change, all types of situations and all types of organizations. The aim of this series is to provide both a comprehensive overview of the main perspectives on organizational change, and an in-depth guide to key issues and controversies. The series investigates the main approaches to change, and the various contexts in which change is applied. The underlying rationale for the series is that we cannot understand organizational change sufficiently, nor implement it effectively, unless we can map the range of approaches and evaluate what they seek to achieve, how and where they can be applied, and, crucially, the evidence that underpins them.

Series editor
Bernard Burnes
Professor of Organizational Change
Manchester Business School
The University of Manchester

Editors' preface

Academic and practitioner interest in how to successfully manage organizational change in public services has never been higher. 'Change management' modules are a common feature of undergraduate and postgraduate social sciences programmes internationally, both in relation to generic business management and related programmes and, increasingly, in relation to public policy and management programmes. Meanwhile, public service practitioners are engaged in either initiating or responding to a constant stream of change initiatives of frequently bewildering complexity, which all too often fail to achieve what they set out to do.

This book is about both the study and the practice of organizational change in public services. It does not claim to offer definitive grand theories to somehow best explain that phenomenon. Nor does it provide a handy checklist to be consulted and ticked off to enable change initiatives to proceed serenely and seamlessly towards securing their objectives. Instead, the contributions that make up this edited collection invite the reader into the rather more complex world of public services organizational life – one in which the initiation and management of change unfolds in often highly contested theoretical and practical terrain and which is shaped by almost endless permutations of macro- and micro-level variables, the significance of which are highly context dependent.

There are four parts to the book. Part I is contextual and enables us to sketch some of the background detail in terms of discourses on public goods and services and consider the links between public administration, public management and the modernization of public services. In Part I we also map some of the key dimensions of change as they are identified in the somewhat theoretically fragmented organizational change management literature.

Part II is primarily theoretical in focus. It examines leadership, management and strategies for change in public service organizations. In Chapter 2, Esther Cameron and Mike Green consider issues relating to contextual leadership for change in the public sector. Bruce E. Perrott, in Chapter 3, then discusses the application of strategic management and strategic issues management in public sector organizations experiencing varying degrees of environmental turbulence. In Chapter 4, Thomas Diefenbach's intellectual assault on the ideological use of New Public Management (NPM) concepts during organizational change initiatives serves as a timely reminder that the role of the scholar is to question as well as to explain. In Chapter 5, Raymond Caldwell questions whether there is theoretical and practical space for middle managers to transform themselves from what he calls the notorious 'change-resistant lump in the middle' to actors for positive organizational change in public services. In Chapter 6, Colin Carnall's discussion of his convergence model of strategic change points to the need to view specific organizational change initiatives within the shifting sands of simultaneously occurring change, while attempting to engineer a degree of organizational synthesis. In the final chapter of Part II, Bernard Burnes makes a compelling case for planned change, drawing on the UK National Health Service's efforts to shape development and delivery of services in line with NPM concepts of the 'empowered consumer' to illustrate his analysis.

In Part III the focus moves from the primarily theoretical to the empirical as various contributors examine the implementation and evaluation of public service change initiatives. David Lewin's account of change management in relation to public sector compensation contained in Chapter 8 provides insights into key constituencies' views on the introduction of incentive pay policies in the US public sector and discusses strategies for undertaking such initiatives in practice. Eric Lofquist and Rune Lines' analysis of a failed change initiative in the Norwegian civil aviation sector in Chapter 9, and Antonie Van Niestelrooij and Harry Sminia's account of structural and process change in administering Dutch collective employee benefit regulations in Chapter 10, both portray approaches to change that were originally viewed as participative and inclusive, but which produced tensions and conflict as they transmuted towards a top-down orientation. Next, Katarina Østergren and Inger Stensaker's analysis of strategic change management in the Norwegian higher education sector in Chapter 11 charts and explains the proactive and offensive organizational repositioning that occurred within the sector in the face of changing market conditions. Then, in the penultimate chapter, Richard M. Walker and Fariborz Damanpour's longitudinal study of the impact of the public service modernization agenda in the United Kingdom suggests that – in the context of English local government at least – local authorities are placed under institutional pressure to conform to national government public services objectives but that adoption of aspects of that reform agenda occurs more quickly in relation to organizational values than organizational behaviours.

Finally, in Part IV, conclusions are drawn in relation to the study of public service organizational change, and key findings and emerging themes are discussed. The diverse dimensions of change and change management contexts make us hesitant to make overly ambitious claims regarding the scope for directly comparative analysis contained in this volume. Indeed, the concluding chapter includes a section on the limits of comparative international analysis in the field of organizational change management generally and that relating to public services in particular. Thus, on one level this book can be treated as a 'reader' in public service organizational change management in which the individual chapters stand on their own merits as challenging both theory and practice in the field. Yet these collective contributions also leave us sufficiently emboldened to claim that there are issues and challenges relating to the phenomenon of change that transcend tightly defined theoretical and geographical boundaries in public service management. It is clear from the following contributions, for example, that there has been a general trend towards reconfiguring what public services do and how they should do it in which the managerialist elements of NPM have been to the fore in many developed liberal democracies. Making the public sector and public services more 'business-like' in terms of flexibility and customer orientation in pursuit of greater efficiencies, economy, effectiveness and equity has had profound impacts on public services in Europe, North America and Australasia, and some of the ripples of that agenda – welcome or otherwise – can be felt in the change cases encountered in Part II and especially Part III of this volume. While we go to some length to stress the vital significance of context in analysing and undertaking change, it is clear that certain issues such as values, power, authority, legitimacy, control and empowerment have a general theoretical and practical resonance regarding their mediation within and across public service organizational boundaries. To a large extent, then, the current volume is about these broader issues and how they impact upon the change contexts presented in the chapters that follow.

Rune Todnem By and Calum Macleod

Acknowledgements

We would like to extend our gratitude to all our colleagues who contributed, both directly and indirectly, to the realization of this book, and to the series editor and publisher for their encouragement and assistance. Furthermore, we would like to thank our families, friends and colleagues for their continuous support, and our students for their constant sharing of knowledge and experience.

Part I
Context

1 An overview of managing organizational change in public services

Calum Macleod and Rune Todnem By

- **Introduction**
- **The public sector and public goods and services**
- **Public administration, public management and the 'modernization' of public services**
- **The key dimensions of organizational change**
- **Conclusions**

Introduction

As with organizational change management in general, academic and practitioner interest in the management of organizational change in public services has never been higher. It is not difficult to see why. How public services are organized and what they provide in terms of order and opportunity makes these services lightning rods for shaping key aspects of the relationship between citizen and state and in maintaining the social cohesion of civil society at large. Little wonder, then, that when political parties in advanced liberal democracies seek to convince the electorate that the future they offer will be distinctive from and somehow better than that which went before, their plans for reforming public services become touchstones for that 'better' society. However, the gulf between the promise of change in public services and its delivery can be frustratingly wide for even the most self-assured of political leaders. In 1997 the United Kingdom Labour Party swept to power accompanied by the soundtrack of a vacuously anodyne, yet persuasively catchy, pop song titled 'Things Can Only Get Better', and a determination to demonstrate its credentials for change by reforming, or 'modernizing', the United Kingdom's public services. Yet a mere two years later, much of the initial optimism that underscored Labour's ambitions for public services and their recipients appeared to have dissipated, as the then prime minister, Tony Blair, made all too clear in a speech to the British Venture

Capitalists Association in July 1999: 'You try getting change in the public sector and public services. I bear the scars on my back after two years of government' (quoted in Seldon, 2005:423).

Why is instigating and managing change in public service organizations apparently so challenging? Are there specific strategies that can fruitfully be applied in pursing change in public services organizations and are particular leadership styles suited to particular change contexts? What factors have the capacity to shape – and in many cases stall – change in public services organizations? And when change does penetrate the structures and processes of public service organizations, what difference does it actually make to public servants' actions and behaviour?

This edited collection seeks to address these and related issues. As such, it is mainly a book about what happens *within* public services organizations when change is pursued in its various manifestations. That is not to say that 'bigger-picture' socio-economic and political factors driving change are ignored. In many instances, such factors exert significant influence in shaping and colouring the context for change discussed in the chapters that follow. However, it is primarily at the micro level, relating to the flow of interaction between individuals, units and departments, that the analytical focus of the collection is situated.

The contributions that follow are set against the backcloth of a public services reform agenda which, some academic writers claim, has an increasingly *international* dimension (Pollitt and Bouckaert, 2004). That is not to suggest that the experience of public services reform in every developed liberal democracy has been the same. Neither, by extension, is it to suggest that off-the-peg 'solutions' for public services change management issues in one country can necessarily be transferred and integrated successfully in another, for a variety of socio-economic, cultural and political reasons that emphasize the vital importance of context in applying change management tools and analysing change management processes. We return to these issues in the concluding chapter.

At the same time, an undeniable concentration of intellectual and political energy has been directed towards importing a swathe of managerialist techniques under the rubric of New Public Management (NPM) into the public services of a number of countries, most notably the United Kingdom, the United States, New Zealand and Australia since the 1980s. Even countries where NPM has been largely eschewed for less abrasively generic approaches to public management have shared with their more

NPM-fixated counterparts a continuing concern for achieving the four 'Es' of efficiency, effectiveness, economy and equity from the scarce financial resources pumped into public services. Indeed, internationally, 'modernization' of public services is an established political mantra and the four Es are ingrained in its watchwords of customer choice, flexibility in delivery and responsiveness to demand.

This first chapter conceptualizes themes revisited in subsequent sections of the book by providing a (necessarily brief) account of aspects of public services management and by considering key characteristics of the change management literature. It begins with a discussion of the public sector and of public goods and services that outlines their significance to society. From there the chapter moves on to consider significant developments in shaping the public services reform agenda as it has evolved over the past 30 years. The chapter then examines the key dimensions of change as discussed in the change management literature before providing some concluding remarks.

The public sector and public goods and services

The public sector can be defined as that part of the economy controlled by national, state or local government to provide a range of critical public goods and services to members of society. As such, the administration of these goods and services represents a vital conduit for shaping the relationship between the state and civil society. As Massey and Pyper (2005:2) note,

> It is through the public administration of goods and services that societies (as represented by their governments) decide how to order, reward, punish and structure the interaction between the state and individuals, interest groups, professions, regions, big issues and the day-to day-realities of life.

The range of public goods and services varies from country to country but may generally be said to include homeland defence, law and order, education, environmental protection, health care, transportation and a range of social welfare programmes. Goods and services controlled via government are said to be 'public' in that they provide both individual and *collective* benefits to people in society. For example, the regular collection and disposal of household refuse has obvious benefits for the individual householder and for everyone else living in the vicinity, in terms of health and sanitation. Similarly, high levels of education are often linked to wider economic benefits for society arising from a highly skilled workforce. Public goods and services are also distinguished by their *non-exclusivity*, in the sense that their benefits can be accessed by all members of society (for example, street lighting, clean air, and so on). Flynn expands on these points in his discussion of differentiating characteristics between the public and private sectors. He identifies the key defining characteristic between the sectors as involving 'whether goods and services are sold only to people who pay for them and whether anyone with money can access them while other people are excluded' (2002:14).

Generally speaking, if the answer to either of the above propositions is 'yes', then the goods and services in question are not 'public' in nature. Indeed, as Flynn (2002) also notes, a prime justification for the existence of the public sector is the need to provide such goods and services on a collective basis as a consequence of the market's inability to do so.

Other characteristics identified by Flynn (2002) as having traditionally distinguished the public sector from the private sector relate to *financing arrangements*, *ownership of facilities* and *employment arrangements* for the provision of services. Essentially, public services are funded by government via taxation rather than by direct payments made by individual customers and, in general, publicly owned facilities have tended to be used to provide services by public employees.

However, certain features that traditionally distinguished the public sector from its private sector counterpart have become increasingly blurred over time in important respects. There are less clear lines of distinction in terms of *ownership* of public goods. For example, in the United Kingdom the traditionally state-owned industries of steel, energy and telecom were all privatized in the 1980s. There are new ways of delivering and financing public services with public–private partnerships (PPPs), an established mechanism in these regards in the United Kingdom, Australia and elsewhere. Thus, in the United Kingdom, for example, public transport, in the form of rail and bus services, is contracted out to private sector providers who compete to run these services on a franchised basis for set periods of time. The United Kingdom was also in the vanguard of developing private finance initiatives (PFIs) in the early 1990s. Such initiatives transfer the risks associated with public service capital projects (such as the construction of schools and hospitals) to the private sector, which owns and maintains these 'public' assets for an agreed time.

The next sections consider key factors that have contributed to the blurring of public and private sector distinctions and that drive the processes of public services change management.

Public administration, public management and the 'modernization' of public services

The contemporary agenda for managing change in public services is rooted in shifting perspectives on the relationship between politics, administration and management in determining 'who gets what, when, how', to use Lasswell's (1936) memorable phrase. From the birth of the modern welfare state in the mid-twentieth century to the mid-1970s these distinctions seemed relatively clear-cut in terms of public services. Elected officials in government decided on policy objectives, legislated as appropriate and allocated resources to appointed public officials in publicly owned state bureaucracies to seamlessly turn these objectives into reality through the provision of public goods and services. As such, there lay a clear distinction between 'politics' and 'administration', one that is amplified by Massey and Pyper in their review of theories and debates concerning public management and modernization. They state:

> The notion of public administration suggests a clear division between elected and appointed officials with the former making strategic policy decisions based upon their election manifesto, while the latter, the bureaucrats, administer these decisions in a disinterested way, according to clear public interest rules and procedures. Its principal organising mode is through hierarchically organised bureau or bureaucracy.
>
> (2005:15)

However, by the 1970s the prevailing orthodoxy of public administration was beginning to creak under the weight of first academic and then ideologically driven political assault. Initial academic concern with how public services were administered had many of its roots in an influential set of economic theories concerning the relationship between liberty, the individual and the state that were formulated by neo-liberal economists of the 'New Right'. Neo-liberalism espoused the virtues of the capitalist economy and the free market as the safeguards of, and drivers for, economic and individual liberty. Thus, it was held that people should be free to live their lives on the basis of individual choices available to them with the minimum of intervention from the state (see Massey and Pyper

(2005:31–35) for an outline of the main schools of neo-liberal economic theory).

A second academic front of inquiry with implications for the future direction of public services opened up in the early 1970s as the nascent field of policy implementation studies began to question what public policy actually delivered in practice. What they found was not encouraging. Many of the initial studies that shifted the focus of inquiry from policy formulation to implementation were prompted by the perceived disappointing results of governments' effort to translate ambitious public service intent into action matching the scale of that ambition. The United States in particular provided fertile ground for inquiry in light of the apparent failure of President Lyndon B. Johnson's administration to initiate many of the profound changes that large parts of its 'Great Society' programmes had promised in the 1960s. Indeed, in one of the very earliest of these studies, Derthick (1972) documented the meagre policy outputs of a programme that had been the brainchild of the President himself. In chronicling the obstacles facing policy actors in attempting to implement a programme of urban renewal, she noted that such impediments included a lack of responsiveness from the federal bureaucracy to presidential initiatives, the conflicting agendas of conservationists and urban planners, racial issues, and objections from Capitol Hill.

Somewhat ironically, given how managerialism would subsequently be inculcated within the public services domain of a number of countries, the managerialist prescriptions that emerging 'top-down' implementation studies advocated as an antidote to perceived 'implementation gaps' in public services delivery served only to reinforce the rigidly controlling distinction between 'politics' and 'administration' which was the underpinning characteristic of the traditional model of 'public administration'.

The mid-1970s in particular marks the beginning of a decisive political shift from traditional notions of public administration – with its emphasis on political control, collectivism and bureaucracy – towards the embracing of quite different public management techniques and principles in many countries. In part, this shift was prompted by concerns regarding 'economic overload' (King, 1975) whereby, in the United Kingdom and United States at least, an expanding public sector seemed in danger of outpacing taxpayers' capacity to pay for the costs of the public services provided in a climate of increasing fiscal crisis. At the same time, the 'neo-liberal' theories of the 'New Right', emphasizing the primacy of the individual over the collective in organizing the economic aspects of society, were gaining political currency, nowhere more so than in the United Kingdom and United States. Following its election to office in 1979, Prime Minister Margaret Thatcher's Conservative government pledged to 'roll back the frontiers of the state', while in 1980 the new Republican administration of President Ronald Reagan declared an end to 'big government'.

In the United Kingdom, the United States and elsewhere the public sector became the inevitable test-bed for reformulating the relationship between state and individual in line with 'New Right' thinking, while simultaneously attempting to wring greater efficiency, effectiveness and economy from resources allocated to public services. Within that context, the doctrine of NPM (emphasizing flexible *management*, rather than rigid *administration*, of the public sector) became the dominant set of organizing principles driving public services reform. Indeed, the growing influence of NPM in the 1980s introduced features not previously encountered in the public sphere to the design, structure and delivery of public services, many of which continue to shape the provision of contemporary public services. Hood (1991:4–5, quoted in Massey and Pyper, 2005:37) notes these features as including the following:

1 a move to 'let managers manage' with the development of hands-on professional management that elevated the role of managers above that of professionals in some parts of the public sector;
2 the implementation of explicit standards and measures of performance;
3 greater emphasis on output controls, with resources being directed to areas according to measured performance indicators;
4 a move to disaggregate units in the public sector, through privatization and agencification;
5 a shift to greater competition through the use of contracts and public tendering procedures;
6 a stress on private sector styles of management and flexibility in the hiring and rewarding of staff;
7 a stress on greater parsimony and discipline in resource use, cutting costs and resisting interest group and public sector union demands for favorable treatment.

For some commentators (Ranson and Stewart, 1994; Rose and Lawton, 1999), the importing of generic management techniques from the private to the public sector remains problematic. In particular, they argue that the public sector is distinctive from the private sector in three important respects. In terms of *purpose*, the public sector has multiple (sometimes incompatible) social objectives, underpinned by collective values determined by need and resource availability. Regarding the *conditions of its strategic and operating environment*, the public sector has multiple stakeholders, greater public accountability, complex and contested performance indicators, and complex implementation processes to navigate. In terms of *tasks*, the public sector is said to afford less discretion to public officials, while there is difficulty in measuring outcomes derived from the execution of these tasks. For others, the similarities between the public and private sectors outweigh their alleged differences and thus the basic principles of management are the same whether applied in the public or the private sphere of the economy.

Unpicking the definitional threads of public management, Pollitt and Bouckaert highlight some of the intellectual tensions associated with migrating generic techniques to the specifics of public services management. They state:

> Generic management studies tend to be fairly functional/instrumental in orientation: management is about getting things done as quickly, cheaply and effectively as possible – and usually about getting things done through other people ('staff', 'the workforce', 'personnel', 'human resources'). The study of public administration, by contrast, although sharing a concern with effectiveness, was typically also focused on 'public sector values' such as democracy, accountability, equity and probity.

(2004:9)

Some observers may well argue that the injection of managerialism to public services within many countries over the past 25 years, together with the emphasis on consumers, markets and choice that permeates the contemporary 'modernization' agenda, renders the 'public–private' debate obsolete in any practical sense. Others are more sceptical. For example, Pollitt and Bouckaert (2004) acknowledge that the wave of public management reform sweeping through liberal democracies in the first decade of the twenty-first century under the auspices of 'modernization' has an explicitly international dimension. However, that shared vocabulary does not necessarily denote shared international purpose or meaning. They write:

> Terms such as 'privatization', 'agentification' , 'contractualization', 'continuous quality improvement', 'efficiency gains', 'activity-costing', 'regulatory impact assessment' and 'performance management' are part of this international lexicon. Their repeated use seems to confirm that everyone is involved in basically the same

enterprise, a global shift in the direction of modern management. This is by no means necessarily the case. This special vocabulary may serve to conceal and constrain the nature of beneficial change as well as aid it.

(Pollitt and Bouckaert, 2004:200)

The use of language in relation to public services change management is revisited in the next part of the book. Prior to that, we pause to consider key dimensions of organizational change.

The key dimensions of organizational change

It is clear from the preceding discussion that public services in developed liberal democracies have been subject to considerable change over the past 30 years. In some instances (most notably in relation to the use of NPM techniques and principles) reform has had a strong ideological tail wind. Yet even when it has not, all public service reform – outwardly at least – has arguably been driven by the pursuit of best value from these services through pursuit of greater economy, efficiency, effectiveness and equity from the resources allocated to them while maintaining political support. For the most part, such change as has occurred can be characterized as that relating to *structure* (primarily organizational restructuring) or *process* (e.g. service provision systems, standards of individual and service performance, budgeting procedures). In this penultimate section we consider the dimensions along which specifically *organizational* change can be analyzed, as detailed in the change management literature.

The significance of change management, both as a growing area of academic inquiry and more generally in organizational life, is well rehearsed. Indeed, for many academics writing in the field, change – and the need to manage it – is an almost permanent characteristic of organizational life, whether that organization resides in the public or the private sector (Burnes, 2004b). This impression is reinforced in Moran and Brightman's (2001:111) definition of change management as 'the process of continually renewing an organization's direction, structure and capabilities to serve the ever-changing needs of external and internal customers'. The ability to successfully steer organizations through change is therefore increasingly seen as an important managerial skill (Senior, 2002). Indeed, Graetz (2000:550) goes further, stating:

> Against a backdrop of increasing globalisation, deregulation, the rapid pace of technological innovation, a growing knowledge workforce,

and shifting social and demographic trends, few would dispute that the primary task for management today is the leadership of organisational change.

Graetz (2000) may be referring to a litany of factors commonly associated with instigating change in private sector organizations. However, such factors also resonate strongly with change management within public services contexts. In developing their general model of public management reform, Pollitt and Bouckaert (2004:25–37) identify five sets of broad forces driving or restraining change in public services. These include *socio-economic forces* (global economic forces; socio-demographic change; socio-economic policies); the *political system* (new management ideas; pressure from citizens; party political ideas); *elite decision-making* (regarding what is desirable and feasible); *chance events* (such as scandals and disasters); and the *administrative system* (content of reform package; implementation process; results achieved).

The pervasive influence of change in organizational life means that there is no shortage of management literature, both generic and increasingly focusing on change in the public services, that examines the phenomenon. As with many other areas of academic inquiry in the social sciences, the field of change management studies contains analytical schisms offering differing explanations as to how organizational change can be characterized. Where there does seem to be consensus is in the view that there is no one 'best' way to manage organizational change (Burnes, 1996). This point has particular relevance to the study of change in public services. As the wide-ranging clusters of forces contained in Pollitt and Bouckaert's (2004) public management reform model suggest, any search for a definitive set of variables with which to explain change in public services is likely to end in disappointment. Such variables are too diverse, complex and, above all, too dependent on socio-economic, cultural and political *contextual* factors at play within specific national public services arenas for a unifying theory of public services change management to be constructed.

While a unifying grand theory of organizational change management remains equally elusive in the general field of organizational studies, some inroads have been made towards tidying the analytical boundaries of change by, for example, categorizing it in terms of first- and second-order change (Burke, 2002; Wischnevsky and Damanpour, 2005) (see Chapter 12) or by '*rate of occurrence*', '*how it occurs*' and '*scale*' (Senior, 2002; By, 2005). Each of these latter three categories is considered briefly next.

Rate of occurrence of change

The rate of organizational change can be categorized as *discontinuous, incremental, bumpy incremental, continuous* and *bumpy continuous* (By, 2005). *Discontinuous change* is defined by Grundy (1993:26) as 'change which is marked by rapid shifts in either strategy, structure or culture, or in all three'. It can be instigated by major internal problems or by considerable external shock (Senior, 2002). According to Luecke (2003:102), *discontinuous change* relates to 'single, abrupt shift[s] from the past' that occur through large, widely separated initiatives followed by long periods of consolidation and stillness. Burnes (2004b) identifies *incremental change* as relating to an ongoing process whereby individual parts of an organization deal increasingly and separately with one problem and one objective at a time. *Bumpy incremental change* on the other hand is characterized by 'periods of relative peacefulness punctuated by acceleration in the pace of change' (By, 2005:372). In contrast, Burnes (2004b) suggests that *continuous change* relates to ongoing, organization-wide strategies and the ability to change quickly and perpetually to anticipate and respond to the demands of the environment. By (2005) then argues the case for the fourth and final category of *bumpy continuous change*, acknowledging that the difference between *incremental change* and *bumpy incremental change* also applies to organization-wide change.

How change occurs

Analysis of how organizational change occurs is dominated by the concepts of *planned* and *emergent* change (Bamford and Forrester, 2003) (see Chapter 7). The *planned* approach to change, first developed by Lewin (1946), emphasizes the importance of understanding the different states that organizations have to go through in order to move from an unsatisfactory state to an identified desired state (Eldrod and Tippett, 2002). As such, the planned approach advocates the discarding of old behaviour, structures, processes and culture before successfully adopting new approaches. The approach is captured in a three-stage process of unfreezing, moving and refreezing.

In contrast to the top-down-oriented planned approach, proponents of *emergent* change advocate this essentially bottom-up approach on the grounds that the pace of change is so rapid that it is impossible for senior management teams to identify, plan and implement the necessary organizational responses effectively (Kanter *et al.*, 1992). Consequently, the responsibility for organizational change must become increasingly devolved (Wilson, 1992). A key feature of the emergent approach is that change should be seen not as a series of linear events unfolding over a set time period, but rather as an open-ended, ongoing process of adaptation to changing circumstances and conditions (Burnes, 1996, 2004b; Dawson, 1994). In this context, change becomes an unpredictable process developing through the interplay of relationships between multitude variables within an organization.

Other change management theorists have sought to chart more of a middle way in undertaking organizational change by emphasizing the significance of contingency. For example, Dunphy and Stace (1993:905) assert that 'managers and consultants need a model of change that is essentially a "situational" or "contingency model", one that indicates how to vary strategies to achieve "optimum fit" with the changing environment'. In this respect it is argued that an organization's structure and performance are dependent upon the particular situational variables it encounters and that change strategies need to be modulated accordingly.

Scale of change

There is evidence of greater consensus in the change management literature regarding the scale of change. Dunphy and Stace (1993) provide four classifications in this respect: fine-tuning, incremental adjustment, modular transformation and corporate transformation. Fine-tuning involves a process of matching the organization's strategy, processes, people and structure (Senior, 2002) and normally takes place at the departmental or divisional level. As such, fine-tuning is designed to develop personnel suited to the organization's present strategy and to refine its policies, methods and procedures (Dunphy and Stace, 1993). *Incremental adjustment* involves distinct modifications to management processes and organizational strategies without including radical change (Senior, 2002).

In contrast to the above, *modular transformation* is characterized by major shifts in one or several departments or divisions and, as such, can constitute radical change. However, it focuses on instigating change in part of the organization. Alternatively, *corporate transformation* occurs at the organization-wide level and is characterized by radical alterations to the business strategy (Dunphy and Stace, 1993). Examples of such change include altered power and status, reorganization, reformed organizational core values and mission, and revision of interaction patterns (Dunphy and Stace, 1993).

Conclusions

The contemporary public services reform agenda has been shaped and driven by a complex range of socio-economic, cultural and political factors that have blurred the distinctions between the public and the private sectors in the design and delivery of these services. In particular, the introduction of a range of techniques associated with the managerialist philosophy of what is broadly termed New Public Management has exercised significant influence on the contours and content of public services in a number of countries. Even when this has not been so, public services organizations have by no means remained immune from pressures to recalibrate their structures and/or processes in response to demands from various quarters to modernize public services. At the same time, contextual factors, together with an appreciation of the dimensions of organizational change being analysed, are clearly significant in the evaluation of any specific public services change management process and in relation to drawing lessons of wider intellectual and practical applicability from that process.

Part II
Leadership, management and strategies for organizational change in public services

2 Contextual leadership and change in the public sector

Esther Cameron and Mike Green

- Introduction
- The broad differences between the public and the private sector
- What change outcomes are UK organizations aiming for?
- Two assertions about leadership
- Five leadership roles
- Which roles work best in different contexts?
- Implications for public sector managers
- Conclusions

Introduction

This chapter explores the hypothesis that different patterns of leadership behaviour are more successful in different change management contexts. A critical literature review, the authors' practitioner experience and the authors' own recent research involving experienced United Kingdom managers are all used to make sense of, identify and recommend how public sector organizations can more successfully manage change.

We will first examine the broad differences between the way public and private sector organizations work, and explore some of the governing variables and the difficulties encountered strategically, operationally and culturally. Then, more specifically, we look at the type of leadership needed to create particular change outcomes, whatever the broader context. This leads to several key conclusions about the management of change in public sector organizations.

The broad differences between the public and the private sector

The first question to ask is whether public and private sector organizations differ sufficiently from each other to require different types of leadership. To answer this question, it is important to establish whether the inherent qualities of these two types of organization are so dissimilar in specific, identifiable ways that tasks cannot be completed, and strategy cannot be set, in the same way.

An examination of existing research shows that there are various dimensions on which public sector organizations appear to differ from private sector ones, some of which were referred to in Chapter 1 in terms of purpose, conditions of strategic and operating environments, and tasks. Rainey *et al.* (1976) further summarize the literature on differences between public and private organizations by grouping the terrain into three areas:

- environmental factors, including the degree of market exposure, legal formal constraints and number and type of political influences;
- organizational–environment transactions, including level of coerciveness (the unavoidable nature of many government activities), breadth of impact, amount of public scrutiny and the existence of unique public expectations;
- internal structures and processes, including complexity of objectives, number of evaluation and decision criteria, type of authority relations and the role of the administrator, measures of organizational performance, incentives and incentive structures and personal characteristics of employees.

Although this research was completed over 30 years ago, many readers will instinctively say that Rainey *et al.*'s (1976) list still holds true for many public sector organizations in comparison to most private sector organizations. This original research concluded that public sector managers are likely to experience the following:

- less flexibility and autonomy in defining purpose;
- objectives that are more diverse;
- objectives that are harder to specify;
- planning which involves a more complex set of influences;
- more difficulty in long-term planning;
- greater constraints to select and manage subordinates;
- more difficulty in measuring results and also, partially as a consequence of that difficulty, finding it harder to attain results and effective performance.

Almost 25 years later, Rainey and Bozeman (2000) still conclude that public sector organizations have more goal complexity and ambiguity. Interestingly, they also conclude that in their more recent studies, managers across the two sectors do not have widely different perceptions about levels of bureaucracy within their organizations, although public sector managers still perceive constraints in terms of policy and procedures around things such as people management and procurement.

However, Boyne (2002), in his study of public–private differences in the United Kingdom, found that there were limitations on this type of research because most of the statistical evidence uses narrow measures of 'publicness'. He came to only three clear conclusions. These were that public sector organizations are more bureaucratic, that public sector managers are less materialistic and that public sector managers have weaker organizational commitment than their private sector counterparts.

Both Rainey and Bozeman's (2000) and Boyne's (2002) conclusions describe the broad behavioural fallout of some of the basic differences between the way the sectors are governed. It seems important to dig a bit deeper if we want to discover how change can be more effectively managed in the public sector.

Let us look specifically at UK local government organizations to illustrate some of the differences between the basic tenets of private and public sector (see box). A fundamental difference is of course ownership, and therefore locus of control. Local authorities are controlled by central government policy and the local government democratic process. They are accountable to the electorate, to central government and to various regulatory bodies. To gain control over its profits, a private firm may wish to charge a higher or lower price for a product or service of particular quality. Contrastingly, local government services can be dramatically enhanced or depleted in their perceived value by what the ruling party decides. This factor is under the control of the local government leaders, which makes leadership of change more about being flexible and 'in touch' with political movements, and less about making clever strategic decisions.

UK local government

Over 20,000 democratically elected local councillors (Members) in England and Wales represent local communities and local people on the 410 local authorities of England and Wales. Employing over 2 million people, these local councils undertake an estimated 700 different functions. Local government employs 2.1 million people in England and 164,000 in Wales and is one of the largest employers in England and Wales. Local councils spend over £70 billion a year. Education, leisure and social

continued

services are just some of the areas in which people are employed within local authorities. An estimated 400 occupations and thousands of different job titles exist – for example, officers work in environmental health, planning, surveying, legal work, accountancy, IT, personnel, policy and research. Fifty-eight per cent of jobs in local government are in education (teachers and support staff) while 14 per cent work in social services.

Source: www.lga.gov.uk

There is also a vast array of continually fluctuating central government targets and performance indicators that local authorities have to achieve or aspire to. This makes the context in which people work bewilderingly uncertain at times in the most basic way – more so than is generally felt with the sometimes unpredictable changes in the marketplace that exist for private sector organizations. However, there are some private sector organizations for which competition is so active, especially if the cost of entry into a particular market is quite low, that the level of uncertainty about the organization's continued success is just as high.

Reward is also handled very differently. In the private sector, when a company gets into trouble, people tend to lose their jobs as a direct result. In the public sector, although there are increasing incidences of job losses, it is harder for individuals to trace this outcome back to their own performance, and job losses are more likely to be connected with political decision-making and broader reviews of costs across the board. Likewise, if a public sector organization is doing well, its success is unlikely to be translated into staff rewards. This means that performance management is a less immediate, less powerful way of motivating staff in the public sector, as performance does not directly affect reward or employability.

The economic fundamentals are also different. In the public sector, as funding is mainly through local taxation and central government funding, very few parts of local authorities have to make a profit. They just have to balance their budgets. However, local authorities are constrained by the amount of tax they can raise and have a mixed ability to increase or decrease discretionary services (non-statutory requirements) and increase or decrease discretionary charges. In some ways this can distort the strategy-making process as the degrees of freedom are fewer than for private sector companies. In the private sector, organizations can enter or exit particular markets; local authorities only have the ability to change how they operate within the market. In many areas, market forces are not at play. This makes the task of leadership in public sector less about growth and winning, and more about balancing and improving.

The political process itself is a dominant factor in public sector life, at both national and local levels. Typically, in the United Kingdom, those in power will need to seek re-election every four years, which means that on the one hand some changes need to be enacted very quickly towards the beginning of tenure, while on the other hand some decisions – the large-scale, longer-term, more complex challenges – may never be addressed at all. Politicians are conscious of the electoral calendar, and so are public sector organizational managers. However, this can be paralleled in private sector life with combinations of short-term commercial deadlines and longer-range strategic initiatives.

The management of operations is also an area of difference between the private and public sectors. We have established that there is a high degree of goal complexity in the public sector. In the private sector there is often a simpler agenda such as profitability, return on capital employed (ROCE) or shareholder value. However, delivering social outcomes, with scarce resources, to a community that has a seemingly insatiable desire for consuming the services is an incredibly difficult challenge. Satisfying one section of the community can directly cause dissatisfaction in another section of the community. The difficulty of defining outcomes is partly a result of the massive task that local authorities have (for example, creating a 'healthy city') and partly as a direct result of politicians attempting to construct goals that please everyone all the time by being all things to all people. Consequently, measurement can be more difficult in the public sector; working out whether something is working or not can be extremely difficult because of the complexity of the overall system. Operational management in the public sector therefore needs to focus more on a sense of purpose, and inspiring staff to do a few good things, and meeting a small number of important goals. This is more obvious in the private sector, and the focus is more on speedy implementation at low cost.

Consultation is a difficult area for public sector organizations. They are required to demonstrate equity and openness and transparency, so some decision-making processes have to be relatively long-winded and drawn out. The presence of the public purse means that risky options and innovations, especially where lives are at risk, fairness is in doubt, or large amounts of money are being spent, have to be tempered. In the private sector, risk-taking is not quite so visible, and not quite so closely scrutinized. Managers in the public sector need to be alert to the risks, and able to lead people through those risks calmly and with reassurance.

The differences between the public and private sector, however, are not static. As is noted in Chapter 1, the public sector is changing in many ways. There are many debates concerning the modernization agenda for public services – for example, regarding customer focus, performance management, accountability and delivery arrangements. More and more services are being market-tested, and the number of public–private initiatives and social enterprises is increasing dramatically.

To take one highly representative example in the United Kingdom, the Welsh Assembly has developed a model of making connections across all stakeholder groupings to deliver a much-enhanced customer focus. Sue Essex, Minister for Finance, clearly states the position (Welsh Assembly, 2007):

> Our research shows that the public feel that the way in which organizations shape and deliver services is as important as the content. This is why our public services need to be more citizen-centred and why the way that public service bodies manage their customer service is so important for the public. . . . Services are changing fast as we move into the 21st century . . . concerted action is needed now. We need to be more ambitious and innovative in making public services more customer-focused, going right to the heart of the way we lead and manage our public service bodies. This is about change and culture throughout the organization, not just the front desk.

> Achieving the service outcomes we all want also depends on effective co-operation and partnership between service providers and with service users – both have their part to play. High quality customer service is an essential part of building that strong sense of trust between services and citizens, which underpins our ambition to transform public services in Wales.

This type of approach incorporates cross-sector and multi-agency working, and greater accountability and performance management, with the overarching emphasis on improving customer service (see Figure 2.1).

The differences between the sectors are certainly being blurred in some places. At the same time, there are some tremendously difficult challenges facing local authorities, such as the need to ensure community cohesion, to deal with an ever more erratic climate and to tackle highly contentious issues such as recycling. All these challenges require local authority managers to lead well in these highly complex and highly visible circumstances. Private sector managers do not necessarily have an

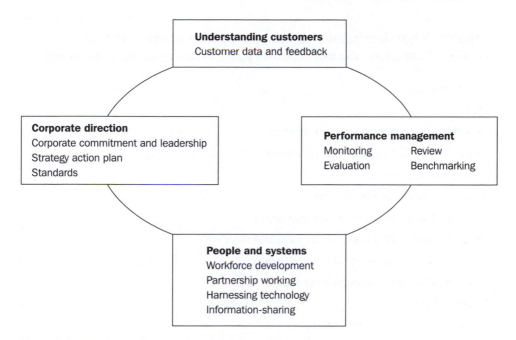

Figure 2.1 *The key elements of an organizational approach to improving customer services*
Source: Cameron and Green (2008).

explicit social responsibility, though clearly the whole area of corporate social responsibility and corporate governance suggests that they too need to be factoring these issues into their strategic analyses. Of course there is the added dimension of a political overlay on many of the publicly provided services that complicates the leadership picture.

What change outcomes are UK organizations aiming for?

Having looked at the inherent difference between the sectors and commented on the blurring of the edges between these sectors, we now turn our attention to the types of change outcomes desired by United Kingdom organizations. We recently created a list (see box) of the most prevalent organizational changes required in the United Kingdom, based on our experience of working with a wide range of organizations across both private and public sectors.

Typical organizational changes across all sectors in the United Kingdom (The most common public sector types are emboldened)

Restructuring

Crisis

Working towards new five-year strategy

Technology-led change, e.g. new computer system/handhelds, etc.

Process re-engineering

Merger or acquisition or takeover

New product or service to be designed/launched

Need to work with a range of partners/stakeholders

Focus on improving supply chain management

Complex whole-organizational change

Cultural change

New legislation to be implemented

Tighter compliance regime being brought in

Growing a new enterprise

Workforce unhappy/resistant

Critical project to deliver

The first thing that was very striking was that when we asked private and public sector managers, they both came up with roughly the same types of change. It appears to be true that both private and public sectors are facing the same types of organizational changes. In the private sector, in our experience, the most common types of change that managers are facing are restructuring, working towards a five-year strategy, implementing technology-led change and creating cultural change. In the public sector, in our experience the most common types of change that managers are facing are restructuring, working towards a five-year strategy, an increasing need to work with a range of partners and stakeholders, creating complex whole-organizational change and creating culture change. Of course, in reality the details vary greatly from organization to organization.

This very basic list would imply that public sector organizations experience many of the same changes as private sector organizations, but probably have a slightly shorter-term focus and a broader, and very often more complex, remit. This would be mainly due to the ongoing democratic political process and the multiple goals of public sector organizations. Some organizations, of course, are private sector organizations delivering public services, such as rail services or refuse collection. These organizations are often more able to be very focused about what they do, although just as prone to being influenced by current political thinking.

Two assertions about leadership

Having examined the difference between the context for change between the public and the private sectors, we now want to discuss the relationship between leadership and change, exploring the hypothesis that some forms of leadership are more successful in obtaining some change outcomes than others.

We wish to first make two assertions about leadership and change. The first assertion is that leadership in the twenty-first century is an extremely complex social phenomenon. Our notions of what leadership is and who does it are shifting and changing as society shifts and changes. The leadership 'archetypes' that we use today in the Western world are very different from the command and control ideas that existed in the 1960s. The rise of the leader as a visionary and charismatic presence throughout the 1980s (Bass and Avolio, 1990) and the development of ideas of leaders as containers for emergence of change (Wheatley, 2001) have left us holding myriad seemingly contradictory notions of what leadership actually is.

The second assertion is that organizational context matters. We believe strongly that there are different ways to manage change, and that what is the best way depends on both the existing circumstances and the outcome desired. Some changes are best approached through a controlled pilot, some need to be managed top-down, some emerge from good ideas on the ground, others need to be carefully designed in the mind of one visionary. Various researchers and writers promote their own approaches. Senge *et al.* (1999) advocate the 'start small' approach, whereas Kotter (1996) prefers a top-down leader-led change process. Other writers, such as Wheatley (2001) and Shaw (2002), talk about emergence, and leaders creating the conditions for change rather than managing the process. Rather than follow one theory of how leaders need to lead, our work has been to investigate the collective wisdom among experienced organizational managers about what approaches to change work best for achieving the various outcomes and starting points associated with different change contexts.

Much useful research has been done already. Bass and Avolio (1990) examined the effects of transformational leadership. This work revealed the power of leadership behaviour such as 'charismatic leadership' and 'individual consideration' to make a difference to their subordinates' motivation levels, no matter what the situation is. These results, however, were never linked to outcomes such as successful organizational change or improved team performance. Effort has also been put into finding out what leaders need to do to make effective change happen (Kotter, 1996). This work has been helpful in letting leaders know how best to manage top-down change. However, this approach assumes that a top-down change process is the right approach, and that the context of the organizational change required is irrelevant.

Five leadership roles

We have been pioneering a model of change leadership that clusters leadership behaviour around an area of focus, rather than meticulously listing competences or isolating particular behaviours. These roles are flexible and dynamic, and, we believe, represent modern, commonly understood archetypes of leadership. They also conform more closely to our beliefs about how managers learn to lead: namely, that this is done through social learning – for example, imitation and role-play (Bandura, 1977) – as well as through behavioural routes such as working out observable behaviours that are needed to get the required rewards. In many ways, they are reminiscent of the Belbin (1981) team roles, which, as he was at pains to point out, are not personality types but are instead roles that we can actively decide to take up. It is the intuitive characteristics and typical focus that are important for managers to recognize and role-model, not merely the specific behaviours.

Our research indicates that the five role clusters have very high face validity. In our workshops with managers, participants understand these roles very quickly, as if they are natural ways of being that everyone can identify with. Using these roles as our tool, we have begun to explore change leadership contexts in an attempt to uncover the leadership roles that give the best results in those specific contexts (Cameron and Green, 2008).

The five roles are:

- the Edgy Catalyser; focuses on creating discomfort to catalyse change;
- the Visionary Motivator; focuses on engagement and buy-in to energize people;
- the Measured Connector; focuses on a sense of purpose and connectivity across the organization to help change to emerge;
- the Tenacious Implementer; focuses on projects, plans, deadlines and progress to achieve results;
- the Thoughtful Architect; focuses on frameworks, designs and complex fit between strategies and concepts to ensure that ideas provide a sound basis for change.

Figure 2.2 *Summary of the five leadership roles*
Source: Cameron and Green (2008).

Which roles work best in different contexts?

In our recent research into what successful managers focus on (Cameron and Green, 2008), we invited 83 experienced UK managers to tell us which of these five leadership roles were used by successful managers they have worked with or for. The respondents were a mix of 50 per cent public, 40 per cent private and 10 per cent voluntary sector managers. The vast majority of respondents live and work in the United Kingdom, with a very small percentage living and working elsewhere.

Seventy per cent of the respondents were male and 30 per cent were female.

The first striking message from the data we gathered is that there was no significant difference between the views of public, private and voluntary sector managers when it came to judging what type of leadership is needed to address a particular context.

The second strong conclusion from these initial data is that all five roles are needed when leading change, to varying degrees. In 80 per cent of the responses, all five roles were used to some degree, and when we averaged the frequency of use of each of the five roles over all the responses, all roles were used to almost exactly even extents.

We then invited these managers to tell us about which roles work best in different contexts. We asked respondents to select the two leadership roles from the list of five that they thought would be most successful in a particular scenario. The summary of results appears in Figure 2.3, and the

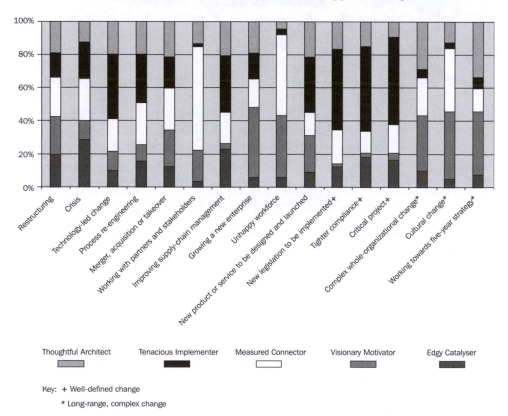

Key: + Well-defined change

   * Long-range, complex change

Figure 2.3 *Roles most important for managers to adopt in various organizational situations*

most popular change contexts are discussed in the following paragraphs and compared with our experiences as change consultants of successful leadership of change in a range of organizations.

Leadership when working with partners and stakeholders

The need to work with a wide range of partners and stakeholders – suppliers or purchasers, or collaborative business partners – is very high on the agenda for most organizations. This need is particularly complex and constantly shifting for those who work in the public sector in the United Kingdom across the health, education and social care sectors, and beyond.

Unsurprisingly, the Measured Connector was named by almost all respondents as one of the most important leadership roles to use in this context. Working with stakeholders and partners is not just about getting people together, but also about jointly arriving at a crisp, clear sense of purpose. The Measured Connector role is perfectly attuned for this type of work.

The Visionary Motivator and Thoughtful Architect roles came second and third in the list, but a long way behind the Measured Connector, with the Edgy Catalyser and Tenacious Implementers being selected only a couple of times each. Respondents seemed to think that creating discomfort and paying attention to good planning were far less important than establishing a sense of connection. Our experience with public sector organizations trying to knit together partnerships across health and social services in the United Kingdom is that the latter two roles are important but will not prove effective without some sound connectivity in place.

Complex whole-organizational change

Complex whole-organizational change can be a long and gradual process, so it is not surprising that the Visionary Motivator is seen as the most important role for sustaining a sense of direction and energy. The Measured Connector and Thoughtful Architect roles are seen as the next most important, presumably to keep people connected, keep information flowing and to ensure that there is a sensible and workable framework for change in place. The Tenacious Implementer and Edgy Catalyser roles are seen as necessary, but not to such large extents.

Cultural change

Cultural change is seen to require a great deal of both the Visionary Motivator role and the Measured Connector role. The Thoughtful Architect role is seen as more important for tackling complex whole-organizational change than it is for achieving cultural change. The Tenacious Implementer and Edgy Catalyser roles were seen as necessary for cultural change, but to smaller extents than the other three roles. Perhaps this is because cultural change is more about addressing what is beneath the surface and may be harder to change than about addressing broad strategic direction, or changing tactics. Cultural change is seen and experienced as something much deeper that cannot be wholly designed or implemented but needs to grow from within. Visionary Motivators help people to see what is attractive and motivating about a new type of approach, and Measured Connectors ensure that people are brought together to develop new ideas and new partnerships to enable cultural change to really happen.

Working towards a five-year strategy

What leadership roles are required when the organization wishes to develop and work towards a five-year strategy? The Visionary Motivator role is consistently the most frequently selected role for working towards such a strategy, followed closely by the Thoughtful Architect role, with the other three roles present but seen as less important to have in large quantities. Perhaps this is because the establishment of a five-year strategy takes quite a bit of strategic thinking, as well as a lot of enthusiastic and engaging communication.

Leading a restructuring process

A quarter of all those completing our questionnaire named restructuring as one of the top current change priorities for their organization. This chimes with our own experience particularly with public sector organizations, where restructuring is a common solution to seemingly intractable organizational problems.

Our survey suggests that a balanced leadership approach is required when tackling restructuring, with contributions from every one of the five roles. The Edgy Catalyser role is needed to let everyone know why the restructure is happening, and to enable those involved to experience the discomfort of current problems. Less successful restructurings in our experience seem to happen in a cloud of mystery, without any clear rationale or existing problem being outlined. The Visionary Motivator role is needed to begin to engage people in the future. Restructurings are tough to get through because they often have to be drawn-out processes if the leadership wants to be seen to be fair and above board. This is especially true in the public sector, where rules about fair processes for staff are generally adhered to. The more successful restructuring exercises that we know about have been led by people who have been good at inspiring people to believe that once the change process is all over, a hopeful future will begin to emerge.

The Measured Connector role is especially important once the new structure is in place because new relationships and a sense of purpose are extremely important to sustained success. New connections have to be established and new goals have to be agreed. Bringing these about is something that seems harder in organizations where there are mechanistic assumptions about the remit of each division, and a lack of natural connectivity.

During a restructure the Tenacious Implementer role is important in ensuring that plans are doable and deadlines are achieved. Restructurings that feature repeated delays and missed deadlines take a lot of performance energy out of an organizational system; people need to talk to each other over the water cooler to cope with the uncertainty. This unsteadiness often interferes with even the most dedicated individual's productivity.

The Thoughtful Architect role is also needed to think through and explain any new processes or ways of working. This leadership role is often undervalued because Thoughtful Architects do not operate at top speed, and may be comfortable with a level of complexity that leaves others feeling confused or anxious. Nonetheless, the Thoughtful Architect is vital when thinking through and explaining a new structure as, in our experience, people get into the new posts with absolutely no idea how the new organization is 'supposed' to work.

Implications for public sector managers

What are the change leadership lessons that arise for public sector managers from our examination of the differences between the public and the private sector, in terms of their inherently different governing variables? The public sector appears to be characterized by goal complexity, ambiguity, a need for flexibility, and a difficulty with 'driving change' by cutting through red tape or decreasing consultation. Performance management is less effective in the public sector because rewards are less easily traceable to any one team's performance. In the public sector it appears to be helpful if managers establish a crisp sense of purpose and help their teams to focus on the few critical things that need to be achieved, while maintaining flexibility as regards longer-term goals, which in some cases may never be achieved before there is a change in the political atmosphere. This implies that public sector managers need to be excellent masters of the Measured Connector role, and able to use the Tenacious Implementer role extremely well when necessary.

When it comes to looking at specific change outcomes, what are the implications for public sector managers? If restructuring, process re-engineering, mergers, partnership working and culture change continue to be the key change challenges facing the public sector, then the leadership roles that will be most in demand are the Measured Connector, the Tenacious Implementer and the Visionary Motivator.

The Measured Connector role needs to be used increasingly inside, outside and across the boundaries of public sector organizations. Many of the restructurings in local government in recent years have been focused on joined-up thinking and cross-council working. Managers who can connect people across the inevitable silos that have established themselves, and will continue to form, will become invaluable. Similarly, influencing across organizational boundaries with partner organizations, outsourcing companies, local businesses, the voluntary sector and local communities is a critical role for effective working, economic prosperity and social cohesion. It is important to note that the Measured Connector is not only good at connecting, but also very clear about core purpose and the hard rules of engagement.

The Tenacious Implementer role, as indicated above, is an important role in the types of change usually associated with project management such as business process engineering, technology-led change, compliance and legislative change, etc. Given the vagaries of politicians, it is important that managers in the public sector continue to hold the searchlight on those critical projects that will take time to implement, and will require attention to milestones and details, as well as the energy to keep on going. This task needs to be underpinned by sound planning skills and, more importantly, an ability to endlessly follow up on progress and insist on keeping to timescales, and replanning only when absolutely necessary.

The Visionary Motivator role is the third most important role for public sector managers. This role is needed when such a manager is faced with long-range or complex change, or an unsettled workforce. Given that the sense of change initiative overload and consequent fatigue in the public sector is quite prevalent, with no sign of the pace-setting government agenda letting up, the Visionary Motivator is one role that needs to be convincingly mastered, and used well. Our research shows that this role is most effective when used to help people to gain energy and a feeling of commitment when imagining a new future, especially when the manager believes in it. However, unless the political horizon is fairly predictable, this role is not always convincing or usable, except with shorter-range projects.

Given the more turbulent times ahead in the United Kingdom and elsewhere, in terms of being exposed to market testing and having to deal with major social and environmental changes, the Thoughtful Architect is one role whose importance cannot be overestimated. There will be a real need for public sector managers to think long and hard about the future, and generating new strategies and frameworks that fit together and make sense of the new world is clearly important. For example, in the area of individualized budgets in social care, an area that is becoming more and more important in the United Kingdom.

The Edgy Catalyser also continues to be important in enabling change, and will perhaps increase in importance over the next few years. Our research suggests that the Edgy Catalyser role is one role that is best used in small doses, but is highly effective when done well. By (2007) makes a convincing case for the need for organizations to focus on change readiness, rather than expending all their energy on defining and implementing change. Many argue that we lack a sense of urgency, and are therefore not at all 'ready', as regards the really big looming issues such as our ageing population, the potential effects of global warming, and what we need to start doing now about all this. There does need to be a sense of urgency inserted into many of the important challenges that we face. In some ways the compliance regime (in the United Kingdom the Comprehensive Performance Assessment, for example), the effectiveness of the overview and scrutiny function, market testing, and the continuing rise in citizen expectations all help. Nonetheless, managers inside public sector organizations will need to learn how to create discomfort and mobilize dissatisfaction with the status quo. However, the role of the

Edgy Catalyser is one that is not a traditional stance for a public sector manager to take, as it involves making waves and being troublesome.

Table 2.1 summarizes our findings, and identifies the leadership roles that are best suited to the identified public sector organizational change situations.

Conclusions

In summary, all five roles are important in making change happen in the public sector (see Table 2.1). It might be worthwhile for those responsible for developing public sector managers to consider which of these five roles are being developed by current training or learning provision, and which are not. HR professionals might also consider which roles are

Table 2.1 *Public sector change situations and leadership roles*

Public sector drivers for change	Change situation	Primary role	Secondary roles
The need to span public and private sectors in the delivery of public services; increased multi-agency working; more permeable organizational boundaries	Leadership when working with partners and stakeholders	Measured Connector	Visionary Motivator and Thoughtful Architect
The government's continuing modernization agenda coupled with the increasing turbulence and rates of change in the wider economy and environment	Leading complex whole-organizational change and cultural change, and working towards a five-year strategy (long-range complex change)	Visionary Motivator	Thoughtful Architect (leading complex whole-organizational change and five-year strategy) and measured connector (cultural change)
Increasing customer, citizen and end-user expectation for the delivery of tailored solutions in a resource-scarce situation	Leading a restructuring process	Edgy Catalyser, Visionary Motivator, Measured Connector, Tenacious Implementer and Thoughtful Architect	

encouraged through performance review arrangements and which are perhaps unwittingly discouraged.

The Measured Connector role is seen as an especially important role when building partnerships between organizations. This partnership-building cannot happen automatically and needs people to talk and work things out together: it is a job that takes time and patience to carry out well.

Our experience is that the connecting aspects of the Measured Connector role are often done well in the public sector, but the ability of managers to help teams to focus on the important few issues, and to encourage people to worry less about the hundreds of other issues that they could be looking at, is rarer. This kind of purposeful, containing, patient, focused leadership is not always encouraged or emphasized by performance indicator-based leadership assessment. Researchers and practitioners might explore how best to develop more of this kind of leadership within organizations, especially at the top.

The Visionary Motivator and Thoughtful Architect roles are important when the organization is looking further ahead and attempting to put a long-range strategy in place, but the longevity of any strategy in a public sector organization will often rely on the political temperature and the strength of relationships between politicians and public sector managers as much as on the quality of the managers in place.

The Visionary Motivator role is hard to sustain in public sector organizations because of political changes, and fluctuations in the government's intentions. Just when you think you have settled on a five-year strategy, a new initiative or priority comes along and derails your plans at their very foundation. This can make the Visionary Motivator look rather shallow or, at worst, duplicitous. Responding to this type of situation demands a great deal of flexibility and self-management. Academics might look into successful long-range strategies within local government, and examine what factors contributed to this working well. How much of this was due to what sort of behaviour by public sector managers, and what skills can be developed?

The Tenacious Implementer role also seems significant, because the role is seen as important in tackling public sector change challenges, although not to any very great extent. Implementation is an area that public sector managers regularly say they struggle with and yearn to do better. Tenacious Implementers are often brought into public sector organizations from the outside, for example, as interims or consultants or high-profile recruits from well-respected commercial operations. These people may struggle to understand the culture, become very frustrated and often have disappointing results. This thirst for 'getting things done' is very real, but perhaps this is a role that the public sector could encourage in homoeopathic quantities in its own managers, rather than bolting on large doses of it.

The Edgy Catalyser is the other essential element of leadership of change that might be missing in a public sector organization, because it requires a high level of commitment to a particular goal or cause, plus a slightly risk-taking attitude – both qualities that are slightly rarer in the public sector because of the type of person who is attracted to work in that sector. Those involved in public sector manager recruitment, and in HR roles within the public sector, might reflect on how best to begin to develop and embrace the Edgy Catalyser role within public sector organizations.

3 Managing public sector organizations in environmental turbulence

Bruce E. Perrott

- Introduction
- The public sector
- Operating environment
- Measuring environmental turbulence
- Strategic management
- Strategic issue management
- Conclusions

Introduction

As in the private sector, public sector organizations face increasingly turbulent operating environments. To succeed and survive, public sector managers need to progressively adapt and change in order to maintain an alignment between conditions of the environment and their organizational direction and capabilities. Strategic issue management is one discipline that, when practised effectively, can facilitate the ongoing management of this alignment process and of organizational change. This chapter will examine aspects of strategic issues management as one useful component of the change management process when applied to public sector organizations. First, the chapter will discuss general conditions facing the public sector, and explore the current operating environment. Second, it will provide suggestions on how to measure environmental turbulence in order to inform managers and prepare them for organizational change. Third, the chapter will look at strategic management, and in particular strategic issue management, as sets of tools and processes that can be effective and appropriate in the process of managing change in public sector organizations operating in high levels of turbulence.

The public sector

As discussed in Chapter 1, the public sector is generally perceived as that section of a society that provides services from the three levels of government, namely national, state or region, and local. These services usually include education, health, security, law and order, infrastructure management, monitoring and maintenance of the environment, and watching over underprivileged sections of the community (Fredrickson, 1980; Starling, 2005).

A review of values on how resources are allocated in the public sector took place in many Western countries during the 1970s. This gave rise to the movement known as New Public Administration (NPA) (Wilenski, 1988). The underlying philosophy of this movement added social equity to the classic objectives of public sector organizations. In turn, this development introduced the rationale of efficiency, economy and the coordinated management of services provided. NPA has continued to evolve with increasing emphasis on matters such as ensuring equality in government service availability, management accountability, and increased responsiveness to the needs of citizens. The primary focus of the NPA was concerned with executing public mandates as effectively and economically as possible, and with influencing and executing policies that more generally improve the quality of life.

A number of reasons for this change in public sector philosophy were suggested by Wechsler (1989):

- reductions in state and federal grant programmes;
- electorates' aversion to increased taxes;
- increasing acceptance of financial self-reliance;
- a new emphasis on raising revenues without increasing taxes;
- diminished fiscal capacity;
- an increased demand for services.

Increasing and changing demands concerning what public sector organizations did, and how they did it, required changes in how these organizations were managed. This pressure for change led to the development and introduction of New Public Management (NPM) (Exworthy and Halford, 1998). The themes informing the reforms introduced under the heading of NPM in the United Kingdom have been summarized as follows (Bovaird and Russell, 2007):

- stronger leadership with a clear sense of purpose;
- better business planning;

- sharper performance management;
- a dramatic improvement in diversity;
- a more open service that allows for new talent;
- a better deal for staff.

In their assessment of the UK public services reforms initiated between 1999 and 2005, Bovaird and Russell (2007) identified a further wave of reforms that took place after October 2003. Here there is more emphasis on the strategic and market orientation aspects of public management:

- strategy focus on the top four or five priorities;
- more rigorous challenge on the achievement of government targets;
- better understanding of customers – make them the heart of policy design;
- improved connections between departments and the front-line delivery point;
- better leadership;
- better human resource management;
- a better understanding of the management of risk;
- improved efficiency.

Projections made by an OECD symposium suggest that governments of the future face a number of further challenges if they are to keep up with changing societies (Lau, 2000). They must learn how to understand the needs of increasingly diverse, mobile, complex and fragmented constituencies, and be able to provide appropriate action in response to these needs (Lau, 2000). Changing demands on government translate into responsive changes of the various public sector organizations vested with the responsibility of delivering a range of public services.

Operating environment

A model of the operating environment and dynamics of Western public sector organizations is proposed in Figure 3.1 (based on Perrott, 1996, figure 1). In this model a public sector organization's primary focus and *raison d'être* is to effectively deliver a range of services to nominated consumer groups. Strategies regarding the nature, pricing, distribution and communication of the services offered initially stem from policy formulated by the ministers in charge of the particular service portfolio. Ministers are elected representatives of the people and supervise a

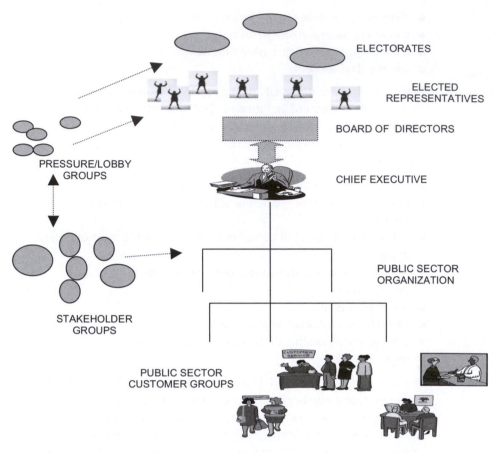

Figure 3.1 *Public sector operating environment*
Source: Based on Perrott (1996).

specified portfolio of public services under an Act of Parliament, such as Consumer Affairs or Education.

Most public sector organizations are now required to gain approval of their strategic plans from the appropriate minister. Plans set policy and strategic direction together with performance criteria within the terms of the legislative framework controlling the portfolio (Bovaird and Russell, 2007). The performance of senior public sector managers is judged against the criteria agreed to in the plans.

Although consumers of public services are of primary importance, there are other stakeholders whose interests must be considered if an organization is to pursue a reasonable level of social responsibility (Preston and Post, 1975). Stakeholders have been defined as those individuals or groups who have an interest in the organization or who are affected by its actions (Ansoff, 1965). They may also take a proactive role around certain issues and form pressure groups in an attempt to influence decision-makers and outcomes. This is most likely to occur in the public sector setting through approaches to the elected representatives or minister in charge of the portfolio of interest, thus impacting on the mandates, strategies and/or priorities of the public sector organization concerned.

The nature and frequency of interaction between the public service organization and its key constituents in its operating environment create a turbulence that in turn impacts on internal strategy and structure. It has been suggested that contemporary governments are exposed to a much greater array of outside forces in a number of ways (Lau, 2000). These include:

• greater economic interdependence among organizations;
• a decrease in government monopoly status, hence greater competition for the services they offer;
• increasing liaison and interaction with international entities;
• progressive government reforms with increased governance and accountability;
• the changing nature and range of public services offered;
• linkage, communication and coordination between government at sub-national, national and international levels.

One useful tool with which to review the expected dynamics of the public management in the twenty-first century is the principal–agent framework (PAF) (Lane, 2005). This framework places the government as principal facing different agents in the form of service providers to the public. Public management differs from the private sector in that the public sector has two logics that must be adhered to: efficiency and accountability. Hence, in public sector management it matters not only what is accomplished, but also how it is accomplished (Laffont, 2001).

In addition to the contractual arrangement between government and agent, there are reforms and changes to these agreements – hence the acceleration of the practicalities of the new public administration as the reform agenda continues to gain momentum (Lane, 2005). The reforms that continue include emphasis on outputs and outcomes, productivity and effectiveness, customer service, downsizing or economy, deregulation or reregulation, decentralization, privatization or public–private partnerships, contracting out, and leaner and flatter organizations.

The public reform agenda has, however, been inhibited by the absence of a self-inventing mechanism, which is the ability to transform public systems and organizations to create dramatic increases in their effectiveness, efficiency, adaptability and capacity to innovate (Osborne and Plastrik, 1997). Prevailing wisdom in political science was that government bureaucracies were immortal and that the status quo was difficult to change as they showed strong resistance to change.

Going forward, a whole new set of values have been recommended to estimate the value of public services (Lane, 2005:34):

● benchmarking and Total Quality Management;
● results-based budgeting and accrual budgeting;
● user charging;
● privatization;
● outsourcing.

The conditions making way for the accelerated adoption of public management change are seen to be fourfold. First, there is a maturing of the public sector, owing to imposed limits on available funds and the reluctance to increase taxes to fund expansion of activities (Lane, 2005). Second, the information revolution is increasing both the quality and the quantity of information available to agencies. This also impacts upon the ability to network, reduce service operating costs and make services more accessible to target audiences. Third, globalization impacts on government through accelerated policy diffusion such as deregulation, global public procurement and migration from one state to another. Fourth, there is the growth in public services during the twentieth century, which are said to have grown, on average, faster than the private sector (Lane, 2005).

These changes in conditions for public service organizations can be viewed as an increase in operating environmental turbulence that will be discussed in the next section.

Measuring environmental turbulence

Based on perceptions, estimates can be made of the level of turbulence of various factors in the operating environment. The variables used would be selected to suit the type of public sector function and purpose under review, and may include the following environmental factors:

- customers;
- competition;
- shareholders;
- lobby and pressure groups;
- trade unions;
- social and demographic trends and change;
- government policy;
- relevant legislation;
- economic trends and change;
- industry dynamics;
- technology.

The scale prepared by Ansoff and McDonnell (1990) can be used to estimate the level of turbulence for each of the environmental variables selected. Each variable may be assessed according to a five-point environmental turbulence scale made up of the following increments:

- Level 1: Repetitive;
- Level 2: Slow Incremental;
- Level 3: Fast Incremental;
- Level 4: Discontinuous Predictable;
- Level 5: Discontinuous Unpredictable.

Level 1 environments are seen to be repetitive. Here there is little change over time, with events tending to move in cycles rather than changing. Level 2 indicates change that is incremental but slow. Generally it is easy to predict the nature and rate of change in Level 2 environments. Level 3 is also incremental, but change occurs in the various environmental factors at a faster rate. Level 4 describes an environment that introduces new dimensions of change and turbulence that are not extensions of the past – hence they are discontinuous. However, from the knowledge available they are predictable, and known in advance of their occurrence. An emerging technology that is known to industry members is one example. A change in legislation that affects the terms of public service marketing is another example. Level 5 is the level where the changes occur that have no ties with the past. They are discontinuous and unpredictable.

Levels of turbulence will determine the type of response an organization will need to make in order to successfully change and survive. For example, at relatively low levels of turbulence (Levels 1 and 2), a periodic or annual business planning approach may be adequate. Here, opportunities and threats can be anticipated in advance. When the planning cycle begins, the public sector unit's response can be built into unit and marketing plans. However, when turbulence levels increase (Levels 3 and 4), strategic issues that may affect the unit's ability to achieve its objectives may emerge at more frequent intervals, and between planning cycles.

Environmental turbulence measures could arguably greatly assist senior decision-makers to gain insights to conditions of their operating environment. For example, as an introduction to a board–management meeting that has been called to discuss the present position and future direction of the organization, individual members could indicate their scores for each of the variables selected for review. Differences in perceptions of environmental turbulence could be debated and particular areas discussed in depth. It can be a useful exercise to observe perceptions of turbulence for different times. This will indicate whether individuals perceive the rate of turbulence to be increasing or decreasing.

Environmental turbulence has been seen to involve monitoring three dimensions of each key environmental variable, namely the level of changeability, level of predictability and the degree of complexity (Ansoff and McDonnell, 1990). It would be useful for public services management and board members to discuss perceptions of environmental turbulence, as this would enable a meeting of minds regarding the scope and frequency of strategic discussions and planning sessions. Alternatively, if the senior management team compared their aggregate environmental turbulence score with that of the board, dialogue could follow to discuss reasons for any variance. During the process of turbulence assessment, particular issues and trends would be tabled and come to the notice of board and senior management. Gaps in knowledge would trigger action for further research and investigation. A rise in perceived turbulence levels could also trigger a review to existing practices of board–management communications and liaison. The end result should be a more informed and responsive board and management.

Figure 3.2 sets out the sequence of events that could be perceived as necessary for a public sector organization operating in high levels of environmental turbulence. Here, both internal and external forces are impacting upon the organization. At a high level, these forces manifest themselves by way of strategic issues that the organization needs to consider in terms of urgency and potential impact (situation A, Figure 3.2). The next phase in the sequence involves a considered and planned response for those issues that are classified as relatively high in impact

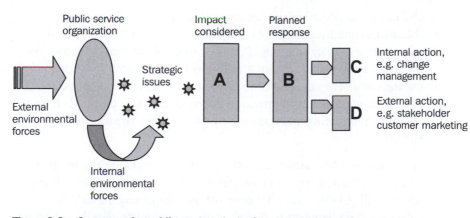

Figure 3.2 *Sequence for public sector strategic management action*

and urgency, and are capable of being processed with the available resources at a point in time (situation B, Figure 3.2). Implementation of planned response can then be streamed into two modes of action. Situation C (Figure 3.2) involves internal action such as organizational change, while situation D (Figure 3.2) will involve external action such as marketing or communications to public service consumers and/or stakeholders.

Strategic management

For public sector organizations to meet their new challenges, they may need to look to the private sector for guidance. For example, strategic management is seen as a potentially useful discipline as it creates the basis for allocating resources, evaluating performance, resolving conflicts, recruiting support, justifying decisions to legislators, explaining the organization to the public and performing a wide variety of other management chores (Behn, 1980). It has been seen as having the potential for introducing a rational technical perspective into the otherwise highly politicized processes of government (Wechsler, 1989).

Strategic management has been described as an integral part of the public sector change management process (Joyce, 2000), and broadens the traditional notions of strategic planning to include strategic thinking, strategy formulation and implementation. It merges short- and long-term planning by seeking immediate actions that simultaneously address issues in a dynamic, evolving environment (Nutt and Backoff, 1987). Strategic management provides organizations with a framework for developing abilities for anticipating and coping with changing environments (Montanari and Bracker, 1986). Poister and Streib (1999) argue that organizations of any size would find it impossible to manage results for the long or short term without a well-developed capacity for strategic management. They define this process as the integration of all other management processes to provide a coherent approach to establishing, attaining, monitoring and updating a public service agency's strategic agenda.

An important cornerstone of strategic management is the alignment of strategy and capability with conditions of the environment (Ansoff and McDonnell, 1990). Figure 3.3 demonstrates the manager's task in achieving this alignment so that strategic or capability gaps do not occur. Over time, an organization needs to manage a balance between conditions of the environment, its strategies to develop opportunities and overcome threats, and its capability to implement such strategies. If strategies are not in line with conditions of the environment, strategic gaps impede the ability to achieve growth and profit objectives. An example of a strategic gap would be a public sector organization offering a service that is no longer preferred or demanded in its current form.

Strategic management has become a central requirement of public management (Parkin, 1994; Bovaird and Russell, 2007). In essence, this involves each public service unit maintaining a balance between

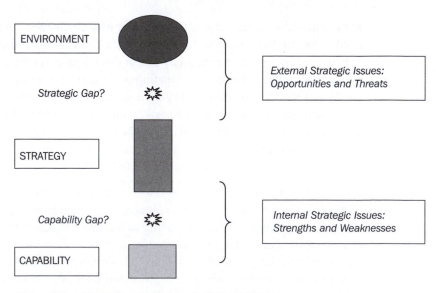

Figure 3.3 *Strategic management alignment task*

conditions of the environment (summarized as threats and opportunities) and formulating effective strategies and building the capability to implement these strategies (summarized as strengths and weaknesses). It has been said that, in turn, strategic behaviour shapes both the capability of the organization and its environment (Ansoff, 1987:513).

Uncertain operating conditions in a public organization may impose the need to employ both a conventional periodic planning system and a more dynamic strategic issue management system (SIMS) (Camillus and Datta, 1991). Using this dual approach, core strategies that are not expected to be impacted by changing conditions in the short term may be planned within the regular planning cycle. A SIMS would provide the capability to offer a more sensitive and immediate response to environmental changes that are less predictable.

Strategic issue management

An important element of the successful operation of a public sector organization over time will be its ability to process and manage emerging issues effectively. Strategic issues have been defined as potentially important developments that in the minds of decision-makers are likely to affect the organization's ability to achieve its objectives (Ansoff, 1980). Although the formation and focusing of attention is seen as a first step in the process by which issues are transformed into organizational action (Dutton *et al.*, 1983), it is the link between issue recognition and subsequent action that makes the understanding of SIMS important (Dutton, 1988). SIMS consists of routines and procedures that are designed to identify, track and resolve strategic issues. Strategic issues have been seen to play a critical role in initiating the process of strategic change in organizations (Dutton and Duncan, 1987). The major product of strategic issue management has been described as the dynamic strategic change agenda that serves to keep an organization in balance with its ever-changing environment (Eadie, 1989), and the process is seen to pass through a series of events or phases (Dutton and Duncan, 1987). These include:

- *activation of diagnosis*: recognition and isolation of issues for further attention;
- *assessment*: attempts to identify the degree of urgency of the issue;
- *feasibility*: making judgements about the feasibility of effort and commitment for action to resolve the issue.

Strategic issue processing techniques present the opportunity for managers to identify issues and plan appropriate actions that address high priorities (Palese and Crane, 2002). Stages in this process include issue capture, review of implications, assessment of importance, priority-setting and action-planning. Table 3.1 shows how these various phases, tasks and action steps blend to represent a strategic issue sequence appropriate for use by public sector managers.

During times of relatively high turbulence, an organization may relegate formal corporate plans to the background. Here a strategic framework in the form of an outline plan will set out the key parameters that are fundamental to the public sector unit's operation and are less likely to change over time. Decision-makers will then focus on strategic issue management by scanning the relevant sections of the environment, sorting and prioritizing issues as they emerge, and concentrating resources on projects that address critical issues. Just as radar and satellite surveillance management processes need to be upgraded in times of impending attack by enemy forces, issue scanning and processing capability in a public sector unit needs to be upgraded as environmental disturbance increases.

Table 3.1 *Integrated issue processing matrix*

Issue phase	Public management task	Action step
Activation of diagnosis	Issue recognition and capture	Scanning and collecting issues: ● *low turbulence* (e.g. level 1–2) ● *broad and periodic scanning* ● *moderate turbulence* (e.g. level 2–3) ● *selective and regular scanning* ● *high turbulence* (e.g. level 3–5) ● *focused and in-depth scanning*
Issue assessment	Assess issue urgency and impact	Use strategic issue priority matrix in a workshop to determine high-priority issues (immediate response issues). Refer to Figure 3.4.
Feasibility to process issue	Making judgement regarding the feasibility of resolving the issue	(A) *For stakeholder issues*, use stakeholder/lobby group action matrix in a workshop to decide action strategy. Refer to Figure 3.5. (B) *For customer issues*, use customer action matrix in a workshop to decide action strategy.

A public sector issue management team can meet for the purpose of conducting a strategic issue's workshop. Here, members list the issues that are relevant to the business unit's operation; they may be listed under the separate headings of *External Issues* (Opportunities and Threats) and *Internal Issues* (Strengths and Weaknesses). Working together, team members can place each issue in terms of its perceived level of urgency and potential impact on the business unit or organization on a *strategic issue priority matrix* as shown in Figure 3.4. The way a unit needs to respond to an issue will be determined by the perceived nature and size of the issue's impact on the unit's operation, and the level of urgency needed in dealing with the issue (Ansoff, 1980).

When plotted on the strategic issue positioning matrix, issues can be seen in terms of their relative importance. For example, issues that have high levels of both potential impact and urgency will fall in the bottom right-hand sector of the matrix. Because they are seen to be the most important issues faced by the unit at that point in time, action plans need to be formulated with some priority and the necessary resources required to address the issue identified.

POTENTIAL IMPACT of ISSUE

	Low	Moderate	High
Low	Drop from the List	Periodic Review	Monitor Continuously
Significant	Drop or Periodic Review	Periodic Review or Ongoing Monitoring	Plan Delayed Response
High	Monitor and Review	Monitor Continuously	Immediate Response * Detailed Planning and Implementation

URGENCY of ISSUE

Priority Issues (Top Ten)

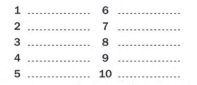

1 --------------- 6 ---------------
2 --------------- 7 ---------------
3 --------------- 8 ---------------
4 --------------- 9 ---------------
5 --------------- 10 ---------------

Figure 3.4 *Strategic issue priority matrix*

Using this approach it may be possible to eliminate or minimize strategic or capability gaps that could do serious damage to the standing and value of a public service unit or organization. During times of relatively high turbulence, it is likely that both board and senior management would be involved in the strategic issue management process.

Frameworks, workshops and processes that facilitate communication and awareness on critical issues and their potential impact on the organization will help prevent conflict and dissonance from occurring at a time when governors and managers feel the pressure of threat to the well-being of the organization. This change in emphasis does not suggest that strategic planning is not important. It merely suggests that in times of uncertainty and unpredictable change, board and management need to concentrate on priority issues that could threaten a unit's viability or offer it timely opportunities. It also means that highly detailed strategic plans may be subject to such frequent change that they become irrelevant and useless in a practical sense as a tool for directing and planning future direction.

Bovaird and Russell (2007) have highlighted the importance of external groups when determining the strategic direction of public service organizations – hence the need to consider the potential impact of strategic issues on key stakeholders. Public sector strategists must therefore take into account all parties that either affect or are affected by the organization's strategies (Nutt and Backoff, 1987). Some see a progressive shift away from an internal preoccupation with a public agency's own activities to the development of business practices that will prepare them for true market-driven competition (Towles, 2003).

There are likely to be a number of stakeholders and lobby groups of general interest to a public sector organization at a particular point in time. Stakeholder groups are wide-ranging in terms of their interest in a public sector organization and need to be considered separately and discretely. Managers must be able to classify stakeholders according to meaningful criteria in order to guide the amount of time and resources devoted to them. Savage *et al.* (1991) suggest that the literature often fails to classify stakeholders and delineate strategies for action. Stakeholder significance is seen to depend upon the particular issue being considered by management. Both stakeholder opinion or attitude and public sector manager action may vary according to the circumstances of the issue under consideration. For example, a public sector organization may contemplate changing the range of services it offers because of changes to its operating budget. Here, stakeholders such as trade unions, suppliers and other public sector organizations may express a particular opinion and may want to exert power to influence final outcomes. By contrast, if a priority issue was related to concerns of the organization's activities in the environment, then stakeholders or lobby groups such as residents, local councils and environmental protection groups may take more interest.

Managers must therefore continuously assess stakeholder significance in the light of each priority issue. To this end, an appropriate framework would guide decision-making and prevent *ad hoc* and hurried actions being made on a day-to-day basis. Although there may be a range of criteria that will be of interest to organizations managing stakeholder concerns, two will be of vital concern (Perrott, 1996). First is the level of interest stakeholder groups have in an issue at a particular point in time. The second is the power or influence they may bring to bear on the public sector organization and its strategy in dealing with the issue.

The *level of interest* a stakeholder or lobby group has in an issue will indicate whether an organization needs to consider strategies such as in-depth research and custom-developed communications. The *degree of power* a stakeholder group may exert over an organization in relation to an issue will also be of concern (Mintzberg, 1983). These variables could be important considerations in deciding priorities for action, the amount of resources allocated to dealing with the stakeholder or lobby group, and the type of interactive strategy adopted. A two-dimensional matrix developed around the level of interest and the degree of power provides a normative framework to assist public sector managers in developing appropriate action strategies for each group. Stakeholder or lobby group zones shown in Figure 3.5 can guide the formulation of effective strategies in dealing with the particular issue. A strategic management group (SMG) can be established that will be responsible for managing the monitoring of strategic issues, assessing their significance and deciding on appropriate action. This will provide the real-time approach to issue management that is seen to be critical during times of relatively high environmental turbulence (Ansoff and McDonnell, 1990). At a particular point in time the SMG can identify specific stakeholder groups relating to any particular issue. Each stakeholder group can then be plotted on the matrix according to its perceived level of interest in the issue, and its power to influence decisions or actions relating to the issue.

The SMG can embrace the responsibility of using the stakeholder group action matrix shown in Figure 3.5 to guide discussion and decision-making on how particular groups should be dealt with throughout the active term of an issue. General guidelines for possible action are as follows:

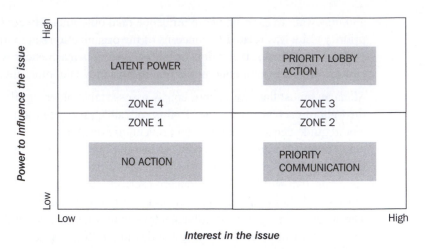

Figure 3.5   *Stakeholder/lobby group action matrix*

No Action (Zone 1): Groups in this zone have a low priority for attention because of the combination of their relatively low perceived power to influence either the organization or the issue. Accordingly, they also have a low level of interest in the issue. As the issue evolves over time, however, circumstances may change. Hence, ongoing monitoring of stakeholder interest levels and power bases is advisable, as a particular group's positioning may change as the issue moves along its evolutionary cycle.

Priority Communication (Zone 2): Here high interest groups are perceived to have relatively low power bases from which to influence the issue or the organization. Because of their potential to influence others, the nature of their interest needs to be accurately assessed and monitored through research. For example, a group in this zone may link up with a group in Zone 4, thus providing the power base that was not previously available to Zone 2 groups.

A cost-effective communication strategy needs to be formulated for each major stakeholder group in Zone 2. The strategy should include the organization's position and future actions proposed in dealing with the issue. Interests and concerns specific to each key group must be identified. Details need to be included of how the organization plans to address them. Even though the power to influence the issue is relatively low at this time, an early and effective communication strategy may prevent any tendency to escalate the level of power to influence the issue in the future.

Priority Lobby Action (Zone 3): Here the high level of interest and high power combination identifies groups for priority action. Qualitative research should identify concerns and interests specific to each group. Opinion leaders and factional interests within each group should be identified if effective strategies are to be developed and implemented. Comprehensive action plans should be formulated for each group, setting out how the issue is to be dealt with. The plans may include objectives to be achieved, strategies and the detailed tactics when final action priorities are decided. Strategies may include further research, meetings, a joint task force, consultative committees, strategic alliances, etc.

Latent Power (Zone 4): A combination of high power and low interest stakeholder groups should be handled with respect as they have the potential to become supporters or adversaries on particular issues if their interest level changes. Levels of interest and particular concerns should be monitored to detect any changes over time.

More comprehensive and tailored communication programmes in the form of integrated public relations strategies should be developed for important groups in this sector. Communications should convey how the public sector organization plans to deal with the issue in question and the particular aspects of potential interest to these groups.

This process should also track associations and alliances with other stakeholder and lobby groups, especially those from Zone 2 (Priority Communication), as these groups have high interest levels but lack the power base of groups located in Zone 4 (Latent Power). Strong alliances surrounding a particular issue between groups from these two different zones may present forces that equate with those located in Zone 3 (Priority Lobby action). Between them they possess high levels of interest and power that potentially impact on how the public sector organization may deal with the issue.

Although giving attention to all stakeholders' needs is a desirable state of affairs for public sector organizations, performance will ultimately be judged on an organization's primary function, which is to provide a range of services to customer groups in line with its legislative charter and ministerial guidelines (Alford, 2002). The language of customer service is seen as central to NPM, with parallels being drawn with what the public sector provides compared to the standards offered by comparable private sector organizations (Denhardt and Denhardt, 2007). Indeed, some see the increase in customer satisfaction and the improvement in service quality as being among the major causes and objectives of public sector reforms in both developed and developing countries (Hague, 2001) – hence public managers' increasing focus on efficiencies and effectiveness in service management.

Many public sector organizations have broadened the range of services offered as community interests have broadened to focus on services related to such matters as individual welfare and preservation of the environment. Some of these problems and issues are seen to include environmental pollution, recycling, traffic congestion, drug use, community safety, homelessness, social exclusion issues, unemployment, discrimination and well-being of the elderly (Joyce, 2000). Hence, there have been increasing pressures on public resources and priority management regarding the scope and depth of public services offered. Notwithstanding pressures to increase the range of public services on offer, there is also a strong drive to improve customer service quality in government. One comprehensive list of quality issues in local government demonstrates the scope of service quality measures of concern (Denhardt and Denhardt, 2007:61):

- *convenience*: the degree to which services are easily accessible and available;
- *security*: the degree to which services are provided in a way that makes citizens feel safe;
- *reliability*: the degree to which services are provided correctly and on time;
- *personal attention*: how employees provide information and work with citizens to help meet their needs;
- *problem-solving*: how employees provide information and services to solve problems;
- *fairness*: the degree to which government services are provided in a way that is equitable to all;
- *fiscal responsibility*: the degree to which citizens believe services are provided with financial responsibility;
- *citizen influence*: the degree to which citizens feel they can influence the quality of service they receive.

Conclusions

It can be argued that strategic management in the public sector has become a permanent fixture. It provides the frameworks for developing strategies and capabilities for anticipating and coping with changing operating environments. In the opinion of some, public sector organizations would find it impossible to manage results for the long or short term without well-developed capacity for strategic management (Poister and Streib, 1999). However, strategic management is a generic term that embraces all activities and processes that involve how an organization formulates, formalizes and implements strategy.

Important components of strategic management will be strategic planning and strategic issue management. Both of these functions are, arguably, essential instruments when it comes to managing organizational change, and fundamental to public sector managers in meeting the terms of their legislative charter and ministerial commitments. What should be the balance of emphasis between these two important functions? The balance of emphasis will largely depend upon the level of anticipated turbulence a public sector organization faces at a point in time. For example, in relatively stable environments, the strategic plan may be adequate to navigate the future as strategies and resources can be planned against a predictable environment.

However, near the other end of the spectrum, where turbulence levels are relatively high, more effort will need to focus on strategic issues as they arise from a less predictable environment. Under these circumstances, the strategic plan would cover core strategies that are unlikely to be changed by issues emerging in the planning period ahead. This may take the form of an outline strategic plan. In this operating environment the public sector organization would be advised to develop capability for effective strategic issue management process along the lines suggested in this chapter. Here strategic issues can be identified and processed, taking into consideration their importance and potential impact on key stakeholders. With such an approach, public sector managers will be taking advice from the research findings of private sector organizations operating in turbulent environments by providing greater adaptability and responsiveness to frequent change (Grant, 2003). Not only should public managers develop the capability to process strategic issues as and when they arise, but it has been suggested that they must anticipate the emergence of issues by thinking ahead (Leigh, 2003).

4 The ideological use of New Public Management concepts during organizational change initiatives

Thomas Diefenbach

- Introduction
- The concept of NPM-based change initiatives in public sector organizations
- Portrayal and interpretation of the business environment
- Managers' prerogatives, responsibilities and positions
- Managers' individual and group interests
- Organizational politics and power
- Conclusions

Introduction

There has been a plethora of research into the introduction of New Public Management (NPM) to public sector organizations since the early 1980s. Most of the research found mainly negative impacts and consequences, outbalancing the positive results by far (e.g. Deem and Brehony, 2005; Kirkpatrick *et al.*, 2005; Deem, 2001, 2004; Shattock, 2003; Spencer-Matthews, 2001; Hood, 1991; Pollitt, 1990). Some revealed even quite cynical motives behind many strategic change initiatives (e.g. Diefenbach, 2007; Clegg and Walsh, 2004; Clarke and Clegg, 1999). However, NPM is often justified and criticized as a *rational* concept, its consequences seen primarily in a strategically and organizationally *functional* sense. Against this backcloth I shall investigate how NPM is being used as an *ideology* for the justification and implementation of strategic change initiatives within public sector organizations. More importantly, as with any ideology, NPM is put forward by certain groups of proponents who benefit from it hugely. This chapter, hence, will particularly concentrate on how senior managers of public sector organizations use NPM – largely for their own benefit.

In the following, the concept of NPM-based change initiatives will be briefly described and its major ideological functions will be identified. The next section then reveals how the introduction of new change initiatives is justified largely by portraying the business environment in certain ways. The following three sections will further analyse the ideological use of NPM by referring to managers' prerogatives, responsibilities and positions, managers' individual and group interests, and organizational politics and power. Some conclusions will summarize the findings and insights gained from the analysis.

The ideological use of NPM will be investigated from a Critical Management Studies (e.g. Walsh and Weber, 2002; Alvesson and Willmott, 1992) and organizational politics perspective (e.g. Pettigrew, 1992; Burns, 1961) – particularly organizational politics during major organizational change initiatives (e.g. Buchanan *et al.*, 1999; Miller *et al.*, 1996; Beer *et al.*, 1990; Pettigrew, 1973). In doing so, the chapter contributes to Critical Management Studies which reveal that there is something seriously wrong with management as it is usually portrayed – and that it must be changed (Fournier and Grey, 2000).

The concept of NPM-based change initiatives in public sector organizations

Since the early 1980s, managerialistic change initiatives in the public sector have mainly been based on the ideas of NPM. Elsewhere, I have described NPM as an '(inconsistent) set of assumptions and conclusions about how public sector-organisations should be organised, run and function in a quasi-business manner. It might be defined as a strategic initiative . . . to make public sector organisations – and the people working in them – "market-oriented" and "business-like", i.e. performance-, cost-, efficiency- and audit-oriented' (Diefenbach, 2007:126–127). NPM change initiatives are often based on the 'standard model' of organizational change: planned, linear, top-down, and management driven (Burnes, 2004a). Accordingly, organizations are portrayed as functional, neutral and rational systems created and designed to convert measurable inputs into measurable outputs in the most efficient way (Shrivastava, 1986). NPM-based change hence allegedly concentrates on the rational aspects and managerial problems of organizations.

However, NPM is much more. It is a set of explicit and implicit assumptions about organizations, people and society. It is a set of beliefs about how these *should* be organized and function. Change initiatives based on NPM aim at changing an organization's main objectives, structures and processes, as well as the organizational culture and, most importantly, people's minds and attitudes. It is about changing how people do business, what they value, believe in and aim for, even how they think and act (e.g. Newton, 2003; Ylijoki, 2003; Spencer-Matthews, 2001; Martin *et al.*, 2001). In a word, NPM is an *ideology*. According to Hamilton (1987:38), an ideology is a 'system of collectively held normative and reputedly factual ideas and beliefs and attitudes advocating a particular pattern of social relationships and arrangements, and/or aimed at justifying a particular pattern of conduct, which its proponents seek to promote, realise, pursue or maintain'. In this sense, NPM's core ideological functions might be described as follows:

- First, NPM *explains*. It creates 'regimes of truth' (Foucault, 1980), 'beliefs about the causes and processes of events and their contiguity, the relationships people perceive among events [. . .] and the explanations they furnish to explain these relationships' (Hartley, 1983:23). An ideology is keen to explain why some things exist and others do not, what is good and what is bad, what is possible and what is not possible (Zammuto *et al.*, 2000; Therborn, 1980). NPM tries to explain why public sector organizations can only exist (in future) if they are business-like and function in accordance to criteria of efficiency and 'value for money', and it tries to explain the ways to achieve these criteria – at least in the eyes of its advocates and the people who buy into it.
- Second, it provides *meaning*. Ideologies provide human beings with a sense of identity and purpose (Griffin, 2006), with explanatory frameworks as to why things are the way they are and why human beings' actions are normal if they follow these natural patterns and laws. In this sense, NPM provides the new meaning for what organizations in today's world are to be. The allegedly outdated sense-giving systems of professional affiliation, public sector ethos or other cultural and ethical values are being superseded by the new agenda of NPM, its narrow performance and efficiency orientations, technocratic understandings of work processes, and measurable outcomes. People now have standards, league tables, performance measures and managerial feedback instead of a work ethos.
- Third, it *legitimizes*. NPM legitimizes not only the strategic objectives of increased efficiency and performance orientation, but the whole universe of social relations – first and foremost the prerogatives of management and managers, which are managing and control, and the

duties of staff, which are to function and to be controlled. With NPM's references to a much more challenging and changing business environment and the claimed necessity of fitting into this new order, literally everything can be legitimized provided it somehow looks like a management concept and is somehow of instrumental use for managers.

- Fourth, it *justifies*. NPM attempts to justify why public sector organizations *should*, even *must*, be changed into 'business-like' enterprises (Chiapello and Fairclough, 2002), as well as attempting to provide moral justification for behaviour (Hartley, 1983). For this, it often refers to higher values such as efficiency, rationality, market economy, choice, customer orientation, best practice, performance, and the like. In addition, justifying and legitimizing myths are created; for example, that a public sector based on market principles, management concepts and measurement systems provides the best and most efficient range of services.

- Finally, it tries to *convince*. By explaining the present and the need for change, by providing new frameworks of meaning, legitimacy and justifying myths, the proponents of NPM are trying to convince others of the necessity for as well as the superiority of NPM. Proponents of an ideology are generally quite concerned with 'declaring the legitimacy, justice, rationality, admirability, worthiness, validity, meaningfulness, rightness, morality, and so on, of a way of life, pattern of conduct, or programme of action' (Hamilton, 1987:36), since ideologies, as such, are usually anything but convincing. Hence so many 'vision' and 'mission statements', 'strategy papers', 'scenario planning', 'SWOT analyses', 'market reports' and 'unit plans'. Hence so many managers and committees trying to convince themselves and others of the importance of yet another managerial change initiative.

Identifying NPM as just another managerial ideology is one thing. In the next sections we will analyse how this ideology is being used by its proponents primarily to pursue their own interests.

Portrayal and interpretation of the business environment

Organizations face increased pressure and competition because of a much more challenging and changing business environment, according to the advocates of NPM (Newton, 2003; Ellis, 1998). Referring to the idea of 'isomorphism' – the attempts of systems to conform with, even internalize, the principles and forces of their environment – it is claimed that organizations must fit in with their business environment (Staw and Epstein, 2000; Meyer and Rowan, 1977). This means that organizations must change in order to fit into and to be successful in an ever-changing environment (Karp, 2005); change for the sake of change.

For this, NPM is introduced and justified in quite a determined and uncompromising way. Changes in the environment are portrayed as part of larger, epochal developments (i.e. globalization and neo-liberalism) and their rationale as 'the new spirit of capitalism' (Chiapello and Fairclough, 2002:186). Such framing suggests the 'historical inevitability' of NPM. It tries to identify natural forces at work as well as a natural order of things (Jacques, 1996). Whether someone likes it or not, what (allegedly) is going on in the environment is portrayed as inevitable, irresistible and irreversible (Steger, 2005); *it cannot be otherwise.* According to the proponents of managerial change initiatives, one simply cannot try to escape the consequences or deny 'the facts' and try to come up with alternative interpretations and solutions. Such an uncompromising view recalls Margaret Thatcher's once-famous 'TINA principle' – 'There is no alternative!' Public sector organizations can *only* change in the way NPM and its advocates suggest; they *must* change in that way. Obviously, such a portrayal of events or situations as 'inevitable' and of a possible response to these as an 'alternative-less necessity' is a typical characteristic of ideology.

If the 'inevitability' is not convincing enough, particularly for the people at the receiving end of change initiatives, the proponents of change have a broad repertoire of additional tactics at hand. One of the most widely used is to portray the environment as frighteningly as possible. To scare and frighten people is a psychological tactic widely used by any type of power-oriented leader who wants to be more persuasive. Just think about the former British prime minister Tony Blair's famous 'weapons of mass destruction' and '45 minutes' argument when he tried to convince the British Parliament and the public that British troops should join US troops in attacking Iraq. It is widely known among leaders that an 'enemy outside' is of great use when major changes are at the doorstep. It is almost irrelevant whether this enemy really exists or is really as powerful and dangerous as described. When it is about major organizational changes, too, the 'theme of danger occurs again and again' (Starr, 2004:390). Very typically for ideologies such as NPM, their proponents will use and address the whole range of negative psychological states people can be put in – such as uncertainties, anxieties and fear – in order to 'convince' them. To repeatedly portray the environment as alien and threatening helps upper echelons immensely in getting their change agenda through (Van Loon, 2001; Whittington, 1992; Bartunek, 1984).

At the same time, an ideology such as NPM aims to address potentially positive psychological conditions of people such as interests, needs, wants, desires and hopes (Burnham, 1941). Ruling ideologies 'must engage significantly with the wants and desires that people already have, catching up genuine hopes and needs, reinflecting them in their own peculiar idiom and feeding them back to their subjects in ways which render these ideologies plausible and attractive' (Eagleton, 1991, cited in Brookfield, 2005:78). Management fads and fashions seem to provide them with straightforward solutions. They deliver ideas, models, explanations and frameworks that provide order in a confusing world (Kieser, 1997). In the face of a changing and confusing environment, NPM represents 'a moment of certainty in an uncertain world' (McAuley *et al.*, 2000:96). It will put the organization into a position where it can successfully ride the wind of change – and all people on board (that is, the ones who weren't sacked, and stayed) will be on the winner's side, too.

All in all, it is a cunning mix of tactics which are at the same time frightening and reassuring, scaring and promising, in the face of an alleged inevitability that makes ideologies often so plausible and convincing. NPM is no exception, and aspirational managers know this.

Managers' prerogatives, responsibilities and positions

Major change initiatives within hierarchical organizations are usually initiated by senior managers – and particularly by the more ambitious and career-oriented ones. Senior managers see it as their primary responsibility to formulate and decide an organization's strategic objectives and strategy, its official vision and mission, the prevailing values and norms, the rationale and design of performance management and measurement systems, as well as the blueprint for the major structures and processes within the organization. Strategy is 'possibly the most managerialist of the management specialties' (Levy *et al.*, 2001:3), and the participation in strategic decisions is the sole responsibility, if not to say prerogative of senior management (e.g. Shrivastava, 1986). Accordingly, the design, development, formulation and implementation of strategic decisions are managerial, top-down and paternalistic in the old-fashioned way. It is this very nature of change initiatives such as NPM that makes them so attractive to ambitious senior managers. Radical change and restructuring programmes provide top management with excellent opportunities to underline their importance to the organization. Put slightly differently, discourses about strategic change underline managers' *social positions* (Biddle, 1979) within the organization. These positions are fitted with 'statutory capital' (Diefenbach, 2008:412) – that is, power, status and influence as well as rights and duties. Since the position of senior and upper middle managers within an organization usually encompasses – rightly or wrongly – high status and authority, great influence and power, but at the same time factual or perceived threats, senior managers are quite sensitive about their position and statutory capital. For them, most issues and activities are essentially about gaining, keeping or increasing power and control – that is, strengthening their position within a social structure (and weakening and undermining others' positions). Particularly before and during major changes, it becomes very important who sets the agenda and who decides on the crucial criteria against which everything else is finally judged and valued. The more one is identified, or can identify oneself, with the prevailing objectives and values of a social system, the stronger and safer one's position is. In this sense, strategic change initiatives can be used as yet another tool for strengthening one's position within and beyond the organization. Some senior managers therefore prefer strategic objectives and vision and mission statements, as well as change management initiatives, in which they can see their functional and positional interests being reflected most fully and by which they can gain, secure or increase influence and power, or increase their influence and power (Finkelstein, 1992).

Claims for the importance of management and the prerogative of managers are usually based on a rational and functional basis. Managers are portrayed as the experts who bring rational analysis and solutions to organizational problems. It is about the experience, skills and knowledge, the expert power of managers (Braynion, 2004; Finkelstein, 1992). It is the 'irreplaceable knowledge' of their organizations, even the monopolization of knowledge concerning managerial issues (Whitley, 1989), that, among other aspects, provides managers with such powerful positions. However, strategic issues require more than managerial skills. Management knowledge is accessible and can be learned by almost anyone (through teaching provided by business schools, training institutes, and other institutions, management concepts provided by academics, consultancies and management gurus, or business ideas disseminated through media such as television, books and journals). But *strategic* management and *strategic* change necessitate something much more important: they require *leadership*. There is a constant flow of so-called empirical evidence that key to every successful change is 'first and foremost leadership' (Gill, 2003:309), that leadership and 'the "package" of competencies possessed by leaders' (Stewart and Kringas, 2003:676) are crucial. To be clear on this, it is '*hierarchical* leadership' (Kerr and Jermier, 1978:375) that the advocates really mean and want. The introduction of a strategic change initiative is also a claim for leadership put forward by senior managers (Kieser, 1997). To embark on a strategic change initiative is an excellent opportunity for senior managers to join the bandwagon leading to the promised land of great leaders and leadership (Gill, 2003). Leadership arguably is a set of skills that cannot be captured by terminology or concepts. Hence, from a certain level upwards, management and leadership possess an increasing aura of mystique. It is 'a higher order of brain work which requires an elevation from mundane functions' (Parker, 2002:6). Moreover, it is only the 'select few' and 'insiders' who are able to grasp what management and leadership are really about. It is only the senior managers who belong to the small circle of those who (allegedly) know and who are, or can become, the true masters of business and change management. Fournier and Grey (2000:12) gave an excellent description:

> Thus, while the 'bureaucratic administrator' has been demonized, the manager has been depicted as a mythical figure requiring a rare blend of charismatic flair which cannot be routinized and codified in rules transferred through scientific training. This aura of mystification and glory with which managers (of the right kind) have been sanctified by the popular literature has served to increase the potential power and status of management.

It is this special knowledge, these skills of management and leadership, that distinguish between senior and upper middle managers on the one hand, and lower management and non-managers ('staff') on the other hand, between those who are involved in important decisions and those who are not. Bolchover (2005:8) is one of the few who does not buy into the leader-mania of change management:

> The fashionable, but misguided, philosophy of 'leadership' allows those at the top of organizations to ignore the chronic level of de-motivation and sluggishness beneath them, and instead to prance around exuding authority, making 'keynote' presentations, transmitting an example, developing their 'leadership style' and acting as a symbol of the 'culture' that doesn't even exist.

In this sense, NPM – like all the other orthodox change management concepts – contributes immensely to the further strengthening of the traditional understanding of leader and leadership. NPM strategies are therefore highly welcomed by the new breed of managerialistic managers in public sector organizations. For them, the content of NPM-based initiatives and their impact at the operational level is of secondary importance. What is important is that *NPM is a managerial concept stressing the importance of management and managers, and hence securing or even increasing managers' positions, responsibilities and prerogatives.*

Managers' individual and group interests

The analysis in the previous section has revealed that managers – like many other groups within an organization or society – are proponents of cosmologies who are keen to get their interests through as the social system's primary strategic objectives. Hence, strategic objectives can be viewed as 'reflections of the values and cognitive bases of powerful actors in the organization' (Hambrick and Mason, 1984:193). It is about whose agenda and interpretations will define organizational reality (Cohen *et al.*, 1999). In this sense, managers have vested interests in common simply because they have the same socially defined role and status, that of 'the manager'. Despite all internal clashes and in-fights for promotion (see the next section), to uphold the status and influence of 'the manager' is their common interest as a group. The 'group of managers' can be understood as 'a collection of individuals who perceive themselves to be members of the same category, share some emotional involvement in this common definition of themselves and achieve some degree of social consensus about their group' (Hartley, 1983:16, referring to Tajfel and Turner's (1979) definition of a social group).

The primary interest of managers as a group is 'the primacy of management in organisations and . . . the importance of management for management's sake' (Deem and Brehony, 2005:222). It is, as Grey (1999:567) put it so poignantly, '*the equation of management with managers*'. To keep their position and influence, it is important for senior managers that the tasks, roles and positions of managers are not only widely accepted as societal institutions but regarded as important, if not as *the* most important, aspects of business and of society as a whole. This is exactly why managers are so much in favour of a managerial concept like NPM: it supports and reproduces *their* ideas and understandings of management; it reproduces the status of managers and provides managers with an ideological basis for their claims (Deem and Brehony, 2005).

NPM is an ideology linked to 'the sectional interests of dominant groups in society who use ideas and knowledge to maintain their hegemonic control and perpetuate domination' (Shrivastava, 1986:364); public sector organizations shall and must be managed by managers. But what looks like a functional analysis is, in fact, pure ideology that serves and advances the sectional interests of a specific group (Burnham, 1941). Senior managers will therefore decide in favour of strategies that not only fit the latest fads and fashions and managerial ideologies but also, like NPM, underline the dominance and importance of management and managers as such.

But NPM does not only justify sectional interests. It portrays them as universal ones. It is yet another tool for the advancement of 'sectional interests in the name of a universal interest' (Alvesson and Willmott, 1992:6), even the '*universalisation of sectional interests*' (Shrivastava, 1986:366). Management, and managers' roles and responsibilities, objectives and interests, are portrayed as the objectives and interests of the organization, even the whole society. *This is the cynical as well as cunning strategy of those belonging to the dominant and ruling group. They do not merely claim that their partial interests are good for the whole. They claim that it is the interest of the whole which they 'serve'.* In this sense, managers are no different from other ruling groups or classes. It is in the very interest of managers that their actions are regarded as *not* (self-) interest driven.

> The privileged yet dependent positioning of managers within the industrial structure induces them to represent their work – to other employees and owners – as impartial and uncompromised by self-interest or class-interest, motivated only by the seemingly universal virtues of efficiency and effectiveness.
>
> (Willmott, 1996:326)

Interest-oriented managers claim they support the introduction of NPM not because it strengthens their own positions, but because it strengthens the organization's position. At the same time, however, they can demonstrate their professionalism by using managerial fads and fashions such as NPM. The use and application of the latest concept is seen as yet another sign of their managerial, if not to say their entrepreneurial, skills. According to Staw and Epstein (2000:528),

> Jumping on the bandwagon, even at the later stages of a management fad, may be perceived as a form of innovation when it is contrasted with the more passive act of ignoring industry trends or the more active stance of rejecting them altogether.

Furthermore, their environment expects them to utilize the latest management concepts and techniques (Suddaby and Greenwood, 2005; Carson *et al.*, 1999; Abrahamson, 1996; DiMaggio and Powell, 1983). Many senior managers simply follow and meet societal expectations, behaving like everyone else. In doing so, they can manage the introduction of 'innovative' business models and the whole process of change without taking too much of a risk and without really having to take full responsibility or face the consequences if it goes wrong. It can be argued that change for the sake of change is exactly what is expected from them and what they are paid for. They simply do what is expected.

The true reasons behind many strategic change initiatives, however, are arguably very different. Many managers are strongly driven by personal interests, if not to say very selfish and egoistic motives. They see management, their role and influence primarily *as a chance to advance their personal goals*. For example, Staw and Epstein (2000) provide thorough empirical evidence that the compensation of senior managers has increased dramatically, particularly in the past two decades – *without* close linkage to the actual performance of the organizations they work for. The remuneration of senior managers has reached a level in absolute as well as relative terms that is simply without any possible justification. Furthermore, senior managers have put a lot of effort into reaching their current position and, provided they have not already reached the very end of their business life and/or have ended up as complete cynics, are usually quite concerned about their present situation, the security of their job and career prospects. As with many other employees, their first allegiance is to their careers, private lives and their profession (Willmott, 1997) – not to their organization. Managers are, perhaps even more than other employees, dependent on their income since they have reached a standard of living that they would not like to lose. They therefore become very job- and status-sensitive and have learned to avoid taking personal risks, learned how to play the game to stay on the safe side (Zaleznik, 1989) and to focus on their career. Hierarchical positions, realms of influence, advantages and privileges that come with senior positions in orthodox organizations become means for very personal – primarily psychological, social and financial – ends. Vickers and Kouzmin (2001) argue that managers are corporate careerists, and most of them would not have reached their positions if they had not put their personal and career interests before those of the organizations they work for. They therefore usually have a very strong interest in keeping, if not increasing, what they have achieved so far (Thompson, 1961). Hence, when an organization faces strategic changes, senior managers will take into account their very personal interests such as financial aspects, work preferences, career aspirations and private issues. They will opt for strategies and change initiatives that will help them increase their market value, strengthen their position within the organization and offer the best 'package' for them and their personal, job-related as well as private interests. For many managers in public sector organizations, NPM provides the perfect opportunity to pursue their personal interests and make career steps they could not have done otherwise.

Organizational politics and power

Senior managers are very aware of the fact that discourses about strategy, issues of strategic importance, major change initiatives and claims for the prerogatives of management and leadership are not 'mere rhetoric' but (may) affect their interests. Strategic decisions are likely to change existing patterns and prerogatives of resource responsibilities (Pettigrew, 1973). It is about which and whose belief system reigns and how allegedly objective organizational structures and processes institutionalize imbalances of power (Pettigrew, 1992; Willmott, 1984). It is about gaining, keeping and/or increasing power and control (Diefenbach, 2005), influence over resources, social structures, processes and systematically asymmetrical relationships (Humphrey, 2005). Hence, strategic decisions can produce quite far-reaching changes for senior managers, particularly for *their* areas of responsibilities and influence (Coopey and Burgoyne, 2000). Many managers wish to keep and secure access to resources they are already responsible for, to gain access to more resources and to gain a comparatively larger share of what is overall available (Swedberg, 2005; Hales, 1999). In particular, strategic change initiatives provide many managers with even greater opportunities to pursue their own interests, to increase their power base and influence (Clegg and Walsh, 2004). From a manager's perspective, strategic change initiatives such as NPM are therefore primarily not a *functional* but a *political* issue. In this sense, strategic decisions and change management initiatives are all part of *organizational politics*, often even the product of internal politics of organizations (Burns, 1961). Organizations, especially at upper echelon level, can be seen as a 'political arena' (Mintzberg, 1985) providing the ground for clashes between competing paradigms and cosmologies, different perceptions, understandings and interests of powerful players (Burns, 1961). Organizational politics happen on a daily basis but they intensify and become more obvious when far-reaching decisions are on the agenda (e.g. strategy, mission, vision, budget, or major changes in structures or processes). The introduction of NPM is for many public sector managers an excellent opportunity to use discourses around its agenda for the pursuit of their own interests. Under the smokescreen of talks about market orientation, increased efficiency and value for money, power-oriented senior managers play *their* game to protect, or even enlarge, their realms of influence and resources while at the same time trying to reduce the influence and power bases of other managers, or other groups of possible influence (e.g. professionals, worker representatives).

For example, one tool for keeping or even increasing power and realms of influence in hierarchical organizations is *centralization* (Courpasson, 2000) – particularly the strengthening of central control concerning 'strategic' matters, such as policy and allocation of resources. At the same time, the realms of others can be reduced and weakened under the notion of decentralization. This is probably the main reason why we have witnessed, during many NPM-driven change initiatives, attempts to increase centralized control over strategic and policy matters of an organization, accompanied by the creation of operationally decentralized units (Hoggett, 1996). Hellawell and Hancock (2001:192) draw quite a telling picture of the idea of centralization:

> The spider at the centre of the web of a power culture [. . .] is often keen not to 'micro-manage' so that the subordinates are allowed to have considerable degrees of autonomy. But the spider retains central control of the key threads (usually financial), which link the outer and inner circles of the web.

Centralization increases rifts and clashes between the 'centre' and the 'periphery' because of its different implications for roles and responsibilities of managers (Newton, 2003:428). This explains why managers at different levels of the organizational hierarchy often see strategies and change initiatives quite differently. Senior managers, for example, may regard the introduction of NPM as a chance to strengthen (some of) their roles as 'decider' and 'controller', whereas middle managers will primarily see additional tasks (e.g. regular provision of more information) and a decline in their status (i.e. tighter control and less entrepreneurial elbow-room); 'the calculated hypocrisy of managerialism becomes very clear: all risk and all costs down the line to allow for guaranteed rent-seeking opportunities and outcomes up the hierarchical line' (Vickers and Kouzmin, 2001:111).

All in all, NPM is highly appreciated by, in particular, those senior managers whose main responsibilities are of an administrative nature and who are quite power- and control-oriented. It makes a convincing case for the centralization of power (thus strengthening their position) and the decentralization of operational tasks (keeping others busy and holding them responsible for the outcomes of the strategy). NPM as well as discourses and decisions concerning its implementation can be seen as yet another tool by which power-conscious managers can gain, keep or enhance their internal positions and influence. In fact, the whole concept is an ideology about power and control, the dominance and supremacy of management and 'the manager'. It is 'the modernist project which has as its heart the transcendence of professional management as a means of achieving control in organizations' (McAuley *et al.*, 2000:87).

Conclusions

The discussion in this chapter has revealed that NPM is much more than a mere functional concept. NPM is a *managerial* concept. Managerialism 'legitimates the interests of management in how organizations are managed, stressing the role and accountability of individual managers and their positions as managers' (Lawler and Hearn, 1995:8). Managerial concepts justify the economic privileges and social power of managers (Abercrombie *et al.*, 1980). Much more, they give managers, and only them, the right to manage (McAuley *et al.*, 2000). As such a managerial concept, NPM can be used by senior managers for the pursuit of their personal and group interests. Senior managers will decide in favour of *any* managerial strategy that provides them with tactical advantages in the internal competition with other managers or with other influential and/or aspirational groups. In this sense, NPM is ideological, and is used ideologically, since it covers up the pursuit of egoistic personal and group interests – the interests of many senior and upper middle managers who care much more about their own careers, market values and egos than about the organizations they work for or the people for whom they are responsible.

In this sense, NPM *is at the same time* about change and no change: as part of the managerial ideology, NPM promises and even delivers many changes – changes in the strategic direction of public sector organizations, in their mission and vision statements, their strategy and unit plans, changes in the organizations' structures and processes, performance management and measurement systems, and, of course, for all the people working there. However, NPM is more about *not* changing things. It leaves basic theoretical assumptions and factual social relations untouched. The nature of any NPM-based change initiative is that it does *not* change principal prerogatives. It reaffirms established relations between the top and lower levels and underlines, even further strengthens, the role and importance of management and managers. That is why many senior and (upper) middle managers are in favour of managerial change programmes: at the strategic level, and concerning the most important aspects of social systems, they do not really change anything (Bolchover, 2005).

The question is: what can be done? When the focus is on strategic change initiatives, it becomes clear that the operational, technical, functional and rhetorical aspects of change are only, so to speak, second-order problems. However, ideologies such as NPM do not come out of the blue. The worldviews and ideologies, convictions and interests, of individuals and groups behind such claims are far more relevant. Ideologies are formulated, supported and put into action by real people, by certain individuals and groups. If one begins to ask who formulates and supports which ideology, one very soon comes to the problem of interests. According to Hindess (1986:116), 'interests appear to provide an explanatory link between action and social structure. On the one hand they provide actors with reasons for action and on the other hand they are derived from features of social structure.' Interests draw attention to how concepts are being used for different purposes. Such a critical and reflective approach may help to produce answers to questions such as: What are or could be the interests behind X? Whose interests are served by X? Who are the people behind concepts? Can we name them? What do they really want and think? How do they operate? (Brookfield 2005:169, referring to Newman, 1994). By asking first-order questions, organization studies sheds light on why individuals or groups of people have vested interests in producing or justifying certain ideologies. It asks where epochal ideologies come from, what and where their sources, producers, contributors and main beneficiaries are. It is

> the commitment to critically explore taken-for-granted assumptions
> and ideologies that freeze the contemporary social order. What seems
> to be natural then becomes the target of 'de-naturalization'; that is, the
> questioning and opening up of what has become seen as given,
> unproblematic and natural.
>
> (Alvesson and Willmott, 1992:13)

It is therefore important for management research and organization studies to investigate more thoroughly the reasons and drivers behind (managerial) discourses. For example: What do certain individuals and groups of people regard as the purpose(s) of, reasons for and objectives of organizations? What are the rights and responsibilities of different members of the organization? How are their values and interests appreciated and the corresponding allocation of resources managed? What are the power relationships and what could and should be done about them (e.g. Jacques, 1996; Whittington, 1992; Argyris, 1977)? Unfortunately, despite some welcome exceptions such as Clegg *et al.*'s (2006) *Power and Organizations*, in the past two decades the issues of power and organizational politics have received less and less attention in organizational studies, strategy and change management, management research and organizational learning (Ferdinand, 2004; Coopey and Burgoyne, 2000). We need to intensify interest- , power- and ideology-oriented analysis of management and organizations (Diefenbach, 2009).

In addition to more critical analysis, we need further formulation of positive alternatives. NPM will not be the last managerial ideology to be used by powerful actors within and outside organizations to pursue their own interests. The damage done to our public sector organizations, as well as to many people working in them, is well known. What we need is not yet another managerial change initiative but alternatives that really care about the very idea of public goods and services, alternatives that appreciate the public service ethos and the people working in the public sector. For example, By (2007) has developed a model of *conscious versus unconscious change management* as one possible way of facilitating successful change in organizations while at the same time avoiding some of the major downsides NPM creates. Extending this model, strategic change within organizations is about 'the best alignment and discursive co-ordination of individual, group, organizational, sector and societal interests on the basis of procedural justice (democratic decision-making) and distributive justice (equal rights and equality)' (By *et al.*, 2008:28). What we need are true alternatives to managerial change initiatives as well as to managerial organizations – that is, highly participative and democratic decision-making processes within organizations as well as democratic governance structures for both public and private organizations.

5 Change from the middle? Exploring middle manager strategic and sensemaking agency in public services

Raymond Caldwell

- Introduction
- Conduits and creators
- Sensemaking and sensegiving
- Discussion
- Conclusions

Introduction

What roles do managers, and especially middle managers, play in processes of innovation and organizational change? Are they agents of change or simply its targets? These questions have often been answered negatively. As the intermediary 'linking pins' at the operational core of organizational hierarchies, middle managers are in a position to block change, both from above and from below (Likert, 1961). There is an extensive literature that has documented how middle managers can obstruct information flows, impede decision-making, over-manage subordinates and create unnecessary duplication of tasks and specialist functions (Argyris, 1990). Moreover, their role as guardians of administrative efficiency and functional expertise in large bureaucratic organizations puts them in a position to defend hierarchy and status, and ensure that procedures and processes are transformed from means into dysfunctional ends (Merton, 1968). It is no surprise, then, that middle managers have been condemned by a combination of their positional power and 'over-conformity' as a powerful constituency to resist change: the notorious 'change-resistant lump in the middle'.

With the onset of large-scale organizational restructuring over the past two decades, however, the villains now appear to have become the victims (Newell and Dopson, 1996; Redman *et al.*, 1997; Thomas and Dunkerley, 1999). Downsizing has reduced the numbers of middle managers, while delayering has compressed the levels in organizations, creating a vice squeezing out unnecessary variable costs and eliminating duplication in the name of 'flexibility'. Middle managers have been caught in the middle of this process, as well as the imperatives of process redesign and outsourcing. Process redesign in its various forms (e.g. re-engineering, shared services) has streamlined information flows and integrated work processes, reducing the need for supervision, while outsourcing has broken the boundaries of organizations, creating the spectre of work substitution by external providers, including consultants and interim managers. These processes have in turn led to the emergence of intensified work regimes and the erosion of traditional career paths in flatter and boundaryless organizations, creating a new double negative image of middle managers. They are now overworked, highly stressed, demoralized survivors and the victims of 'change fatigue', 'concertive control' and the ever-powerful exhortations of corporate ideology (Turnbull, 2001; Barker, 1999; Musson and Duberley, 2007). Moreover, as responsibility for managing is increasingly devolved to the local level and becomes a ubiquitous requirement of all employees – *everyone is a manager* – the unique function, role and identity of middle managers have been called into question. Some have even predicted the death of middle management and the rise of organizations without managers (Semler, 1989; Grey, 1999).

If the question 'what is happening to middle managers?' has produced a generally gloomy prognosis, the alternative question 'what influence do middle managers have in managing innovation and change?' has produced more encouraging perspectives (Huy, 2001a, 2002; Rouleau, 2005). From the onset of restructuring in the 1980s there were those who suggested that managers could be 'innovators', or at least 'adapters', in change implementation (Kanter, 1982a, 1986; Burglemann, 1983). The extraordinary ascendancy of human resource management (HRM) on the back of workplace restructuring also indicated that middle-level line managers were assuming an expanded, more generalist and increasingly strategic role within devolved forms of management control that emphasized the virtues of employee involvement and commitment (Walton, 1985). Evidence also began to emerge that middle managers could be agents for improving self-renewal processes in organizations. Nonaka (1988) argued that middle managers' contributions were being underestimated in resolving the gaps between strategic vision and the details of implementation, and he proposed the notion of 'middle-up-down management' with middle managers playing a crucial role in 'information creation' and the generation of new ideas (Nonaka,

1988; Nonaka and Takeuchi, 1995; Nonaka *et al.*, 2000). Building on this work, Floyd and Wooldridge (1992, 1997, 2000) argued that middle managers played more than an operational role in implementing 'deliberate strategy'; these authors also highlighted middle managers' more proactive roles in synthesizing information, facilitating adaptability and championing innovative ideas. More recently, Balogun (2003, 2006) has also characterized middle managers as 'change intermediates' who can play four interrelated roles during change implementation: they can be effective in two key 'sensemaking' roles of 'undertaking personal change' and 'helping others through change', and these two roles complement the other, more conventional roles of 'implementing necessary changes' and 'keeping the business going'. There is now a growing literature which suggests that middle managers can exercise both *strategic* and *sensemaking* agency during organizational change, and that the old dichotomies between innovator and maintainer roles, leading and managing, line and staff functions, and strategy and implementation must be reformulated to accommodate new organizational forms and the changing nature of managerial work in both private and public sector organizations (Caldwell, 2006).

This chapter offers a critical examination of the changing roles of public services middle managers in processes of organizational innovation and change by comparing and contrasting *strategic* and *sensemaking* agency perspectives. While these perspectives have emerged mainly from research on private sector organizations, they also highlight broader generic issues that have major implications for the changing roles of middle managers in public service organizations (Currie and Procter, 2005; see Boxes 5.1 and 5.2). The research work of Floyd and Wooldridge (1992, 1994, 1997, 2000) and Balogun (2003, 2006) is taken as broadly illustrative of the contrasting positions and their theoretical assumptions. It will be argued that strategic agency analysis provides new insights into the enhanced role of middle managers in the 'strategy process', while sensemaking interpretations provide a greater understanding of their role in the construction of meaning and self-identity during organizational change processes. However, the theoretical limitations of both strategic agency and sensemaking agency perspectives undermine attempts to build broader models of agency and change in organizations (Caldwell, 2006). Strategic agency perspectives within the 'strategy process' tradition still remain tied to role-centred and instrumental discourses on deliberate strategy that seriously underplay the possibilities and limitations of actor *autonomy* and *reflexivity* during processes of organizational change. In contrast, sensemaking perspectives partly abandon rationalist models of strategy and managerial agency without critically theorizing the nature of agency or organizational change. It is concluded that strategic agency perspectives need to be reconceptualized to accommodate new forms of dispersed leadership and distributed knowledge creation in organizations that redefine the scope of managerial agency, while sensemaking perspectives need to be extended by developing a more systematic and critical concept of 'sensemaking agency' that encompasses a synthetic understanding of both agency and change in organizations. Finally, without broader bridge-building exercises and the associated search for mediated theories and categories, strategic and sensemaking agency perspectives may increasingly become fragmented managerial research methodologies that lack epistemological coherence and practical efficacy.

Conduits and creators

The idea that middle managers are primarily strategy implementers derives from a particular view of how 'strategy' is conceived in large hierarchical organizations and public service bureaucracies. If strategy formulation is a rational policy planning process operationalized as sub-strategies for successful implementation, then middle managers play a crucial role in implementation. The underlying assumptions of this perspective are fourfold. First, strategy is a centralized planning function that can be controlled and coordinated from the top of organizations; it is leaders or policy-makers who create strategies, not managers. Second, there is a clear distinction between strategy formulation and implementation, or between planning and execution – and, by implication, leadership and management. Third, strategic change and innovation is an incremental process of diffusion and technology transfer (Clark, 2003). Fourth, strategy implementation is a cascade of sub-projects and means–ends decision processes that can be subject to supervision and monitoring. Overall, middle managers are positioned as intermediary links in this hierarchical process, both positively and negatively. They execute decisions, but if anything goes wrong, they can be partly blamed for implementation failures.

There is, however, a well-developed 'strategy process' literature in the strategic management field that has consistently questioned one or more of these assumptions (Bower and Gilbert, 2005). Bower (1970) gave middle managers a role as influential judges of resource allocation decisions, while Burglemann (1983) emphasized their role as organizational champions of new initiatives emerging at the operational level. With the growing loss of faith in top-down strategic planning processes during the 1980s, the re-evaluation of middle management roles entered a new phase. There was an intensified assault on strategy as a 'deliberate' process with a clear distinction between formulation and implementation. This was reinforced by broader attacks on organizations as goal-oriented systems and management as a set of prescriptive functions that defined managerial behaviour. Instead, the contextual focus was on 'what managers do' in all its bewildering complexity (Hales, 1999). In particular, managerial work was characterized by its intrinsically hectic pace, fragmented nature, brevity and variety, iterative decision-making processes, and extensive dependence on verbal communication and informal networks (Mintzberg, 1975).

This led to a re-evaluation of the multiple activities of both senior and middle management roles. Middle managers were no longer categorized as the *functional* intermediaries of coordination and direct supervision; they could also act as figureheads, influence management decisions, allocate resources, negotiate with various stakeholders, handle conflict and 'initiate strategic change' (Mintzberg, 1979:29–30). With this combined re-evaluation of the nature of planning and managerial work, it became clear that for strategy to be effective it had to be conceived as an *emergent process* of political compromises, consultations and bottom-up iniatives in which the implementers were directly involved in formulation (Mintzberg, 1994). This allowed middle managers a greatly enhanced role in strategic change processes. Rather than simply being conduits of senior management decisions, they were increasingly conceived as exercising *strategic agency* in creatively adapting or generating new processes, systems and ideas.

One of the most useful synthetic attempts to capture the new roles of middle managers as strategic actors has been outlined by Floyd and Wooldridge (1992, 1997, 2000). Using survey data on 259 middle managers in 25 organizations, they propose a fourfold typology of middle management roles during the strategy process that can potentially accommodate both deliberate and emergent strategies within specific organizational contexts (Figure 5.1). This is theorized in terms of a matrix of upward and downward influence patterns, and a cognitive continuum of strategy processes that range from integrated to divergent (Floyd and Wooldridge, 1992). Upward influences can be either divergent or integrated, allowing middle managers two strongly discretionary and potentially creative roles: *championing alternatives* and *synthesizing information*. The former role allows middle managers to decisively

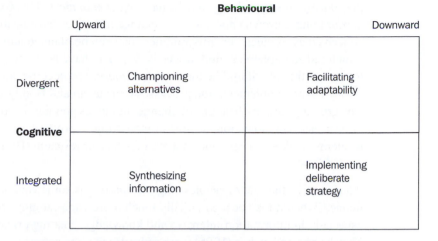
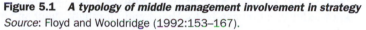

Figure 5.1 *A typology of middle management involvement in strategy*
Source: Floyd and Wooldridge (1992:153–167).

influence resource allocation decisions and the shape of strategic ideas
in a context where strategic ideas are divergent and senior management
are susceptible to upward influence. The latter role assumes that
middle managers are in a position to evaluate and integrate information
that is of strategic value to senior management. Alternatively,
traditional downward influences that can be either divergent or integrated
define two more conventional implementation roles: *facilitating
adaptability* and *implementing deliberate strategy*. The former role
allows some adjustment and refinements to corporate and operational
sub-strategies in a top-down strategy process, while the latter role is the
classical functional role of the middle managers in the execution of
strategy.

Floyd and Wooldridge's (1992) model has all the considerable strengths
of a synthetic typology: it simplifies and clarifies an enormously complex
empirical picture, and this has allowed it to be widely applied in both
private and public sector organizations (Currie and Procter, 2005). There
are, however, issues regarding the boundaries that define roles, the range
of roles encompassed in the typology, the internal complexity of roles,
and the potential for role conflict and ambiguity.

Floyd and Wooldridge (1992) use their survey evidence to confirm the
traditional role of 'implementing deliberate strategy', but the precise
scope and subdivisions of the role need more clarification. One
potentially missing sub-type is the implementation role middle managers

play during strategic change as *change project managers*. This role would appear to have grown enormously as change initiatives have been conceived as 'projects' or 'programmes' that can be planned and monitored as implementation proceeds. Yet there have been few attempts to explore the role of middle managers as *internal* project managers during change implementation processes (Buchanan and Boddy, 1992). The growing 'projectification' of change initiatives and the rise of project-based organizations within an increasingly 'project-driven economy' makes this an important area for further research (Bresnen *et al.*, 2004).

Alternatively, the role of *synthesizing information* is somewhat narrowly defined, when it may be a potentially much more wide-ranging role, especially in information-intensive and knowledge-creating organizations. Nonaka and Takeuchi's (1995) work indicates that the sources of knowledge creation can be localized and pluralistic, tacit and explicit, allowing middle managers a vital creative role as 'knowledge producers' – although they are less clear on what mechanisms and practices facilitate 'knowledge conversion' processes (Clark, 2003). More broadly, Nonaka *et al.* (2000) also argue that organizations constantly create new knowledge out of firm-specific capabilities: 'The organization is not merely an information processing machine, but an entity that creates knowledge through action and interaction' (2000:6).

Applying the Floyd and Wooldridge (1992) role model to public service organizations has also raised important issues regarding the scope of middle manager influence (see box). Currie (1999) has shown how middle managers are purveyors and recipients of strategic change in the National Health Service, and how they can modify the implementation of strategy. But Currie and Procter (2005) also illustrate how middle manager role conflict and ambiguity limit the more strategic roles envisaged for middle managers in public services organizations.

The changing roles of middle managers in public service organizations

Middle managers in public service organizations have often been conceived as neutral administrators or benign bureaucratic functionaries who occupy a formal and impersonal role defined by the execution of rule-bound policies that are applied equally to everyone and without regard to individual self-interest. In practice, the roles of middle managers have always been much more complex, and they appear to be becoming more diverse and problematic. Increasingly the roles of public service middle managers are being stretched far beyond the ideal of the neutral administrator inspired by a public sector ethos; such managers now encompass new roles as market-led service providers (Poole *et al.*, 2006). This has created new ideological tensions in the political–administrative relationship that underpins public service provision as well as deeper tensions between formal roles, social values and the identity and self-images of middle managers. These tensions are likely to intensify in response to:

- the erosion of the boundaries between public as against private sector provision and delivery models and the horizontal 'decontration' of the welfare state, including contracting out, outsourcing, internal markets, voluntary sector provision, shared services, process redesign, public–private partnerships, and private sector ownership and delivery of public services (Boyne, 2002);

- the growing redefinition of public services in terms of 'competition', 'customer service' and 'choice' (Le Grand, 2007);

- the increasing introduction of performance targets, outcomes and effectiveness measures into almost every area of public service provision;

- the relentless drive to cut costs and 'to do more with less' in more areas of the public services.

Some of the substantive gaps in Floyd and Wooldridge's (1992) role types may of course be partly resolved through more empirical research on the inner dynamics of strategic change (Mantere, 2007; Floyd *et al.*, 2008). But the real problem with the model is that despite its apparent emphasis on *emergent* strategy, it tends to read off roles as middle management functions in a *deliberate* strategy process (Floyd and Wooldridge, 1992). Floyd and Wooldridge's stated theoretical intent is to achieve a synthesis of action and cognition, but the model operates with an implicit distinction between strategy formulation and implementation; and this is reinforced by the absence of a reference within the model to emergent theories of organizational innovation and change that treat goals as problematic. In other words, the model is intrinsically static, and this limits the range of middle management roles that can be included in the strategy process. This also partly explains why issues of legitimacy, strategic intent and managerial power are treated as unproblematic, and why the multifarious issues of role conflict and identity confusion that have plagued middle management positions are rarely mentioned (Currie and Procter, 2005). In addition, questions of how middle managers interpret top management intentions and the implementation gaps between senior management plans and what actually happens cannot be fully examined (Balogun, 2003, 2006; Balogun and Johnson, 2005). As it is an essentially intentional model of strategy implementation underpinned by a functionalist reading of roles, all these perplexing issues tend to get written out of the scripts of the four roles. Paradoxically, a model conceived to underscore the *strategic agency* of middle managers tends to reinstate the autonomy of senior managers in exercising strategic choice, both in formulating strategy and directing its implementation.

Are there any ways of moderating this bias towards rationalism, deliberate strategy and strategic choice? Mantere (2007) has recently tried to both critique and extend Floyd and Wooldridge's (1992) typology of roles by highlighting how role expectations both enable and limit middle manager 'strategic agency'. This is certainly a valuable avenue for exploring the growing ambiguities of middle management roles in private and public service organizations. For Mantere (2007), middle managers have strategic agency within imposed role expectations that are 'structurally determined'. So, the question becomes 'How is "strategic agency" possible given the "disabling effects" of functionally prescribed role expectations?'

Mantere (2007:301) defines *strategic agency* as 'an individual's capacity to have a perceived effect upon the individual's own work on an issue the individual regards as beneficial to the interests of his or her organization'. Ostensibly, this Giddens-influenced definition treats 'agency' as *strategic* if middle managers affirm organizational interests as a motivation for their actions. It also allows Mantere (2007) to clearly uncover the limitations of functionalist role models by highlighting eight of the conditions that enable middle managers to exercise strategic agency: narration, contextualization, resource allocation, respect, trust, responsiveness, inclusion and refereeing.

Yet paradoxically, Mantere's (2007) overall definition of agency as 'knowledgeability' combined with interest and motivation seems to exclude the other critical requirements of intentional or strategic agency, namely *autonomy* and *reflexivity* (Caldwell, 2005; Llewellyn, 2007). When Giddens (1984, 1991) defines 'agency', he includes self-identity or how prescribed roles are reflexively redefined so that agents have the capability to act and the autonomy to 'act otherwise'. Mantere (2007) also tends to leave out the discursive or rhetorical formation of agency and how middle managers struggle for role clarity, meaning and self-identity in increasingly complex organizations, although there are undercurrents of these themes in his discussion of the eight enabling conditions. In practice, 'narration' may be not just an enabling condition of new roles, but an expression of discourses of 'flexibility' and 'change' that undermine the possibilities of middle managers' self-identity and their capability to act (Turnbull, 2001; Musson and Duberley, 2007). It is perhaps no surprise, then, that the enabling conditions of roles and agency are in conformity with both senior managers' expectations of middle manager roles and the functionally imposed forces of external market conditions. Ultimately, Mantere (2007) may have extended Floyd and Wooldbridge's (1992) model, but he cannot fully extricate 'agency' from the normative and functionalist determinism of role theory, even though he moves towards a broader theorization of the enabling and limiting forces of strategic agency.

Sensemaking and sensegiving

If strategic agency models partly redefine the role of middle managers in the strategy process, they still remain strongly indebted to concepts of deliberate strategy. In 'sensemaking agency' perspectives, however, the primary focus is on the emergent or interactional nature of strategy, and this appears to mark a much broader attack on rationalist ideas of management decision-making and strategic change. But can sensemaking as an implicit exploration of agency and change in organizations really replace or subsume the territory of strategic or intentional agency? Can it bring agency back into organizational change theory?

Sensemaking perspectives assume an enormous variety of forms, although their common epistemological origins are in pragmatism, symbolic interactionism and cognitive psychology (Garfinkel, 1967). Undoubtedly the most influential proponent of the sensemaking perspective in organizational theory is Karl Weick (1995, 2001). He defines sensemaking as a three-stage cognitive learning loop consisting of *enactment*, *selection* and *retention*. Enactment refers to processes of meaning creation through which individuals and groups interpret information from an uncertain environment to create interpretations of the organizational world they inhabit. This usually occurs in situations of equivocality rather than simply uncertainty, when there are too many meanings rather than too few (Weick *et al.*, 2005). The inductive cognitive processes of sensemaking are therefore by definition selective. Certain interpretations of the world are rejected in coping with equivocality while others are retained as a plausible 'empirical basis' for action, mainly because people need to make the unexpected and unpredictable 'manageable' by 'structuring the unknown' (Weick,

1995:127). In this respect, 'sensemaking is an attempt to produce micro stability amidst continuing change' (Weick, 2001:22).

If the cognitive theoretical underpinnings of sensemaking are deceptively simple, they also involve a series of related assumptions that are more complex and intriguing – and ultimately more confusing. These include the view that organizations are ongoing processes of enactment rather than systems, structures or functional entities with goals. In this respect, enactment occurs through narratives, symbols, talk and labels that create 'plausible stories' of events, actions and causes. For Weick (1995, 2001), 'plausibility' is always more important in sensemaking than accuracy or rationality. He also argues that managerial action is informed by self-fulfilling prophecies in which decisions become realized when they are treated as if they were true; or, alternatively, they are treated as rational when they are realized – strategy and strategic intent are self-confirming or post-rationalizing actions (Weick, 2001). Finally, it is assumed that human behaviour and identity are not prescribed by authority, rules or formal roles, but are constructed through the pragmatic self-efficacy of practice (see box).

Middle manager sensemaking in public service organizations

There have been few systematic attempts to apply sensemaking to the understanding of middle manager roles or 'identity construction' in public service organizations. The key assumptions of sensemaking may be useful because they partly debunk strategic models of managerial agency and challenge the idea that organizations have rational goals. The focus is on how managers attempt to selectively make sense of events and outcomes for themselves and others, especially during major disruptions of organizational routines (Weick, 1995, 2001). This is undoubtedly an important issue in many public service organizations. In particular, the blurring of the boundaries between private and public service provision and the increasing 'disconfirmation' of the traditional role and ethos of the public servant place new strains on the identity, professional values and autonomy of public service middle managers (Poole *et al.*, 2006).

Despite this micro construction of the macro, the decoupling of rationality from intent, and the disjunction between cause and effect, Weick's (2001) concept of sensemaking is not relativistic. Sensemaking may appear diffuse, confusing and arbitrary, but it is not meaningless. We can create stories and coherent narratives of the world and our actions through the retrospective 'induction generalizations' that we cognitively enact, select and retain. It is this epistemological faith in generalizations and narration that gives sensemaking a privileged scientific status, and this in turn allows Weick (2001) to keep at bay the more disconcerting anti-realist discourses of social constructionism that render scientific objectivity, narrative meaning, identity and agency deeply problematic (Gergin, 2001). Ultimately, for Weick (2001) sensemaking in all its varieties is a methodological defence against the corrosive possibilities of non-sensemaking.

There have been a wide range of case studies that have sought to understand how managers interpret events and make choices by applying 'sensemaking' and 'sensegiving' to processes of strategic change (Gioia and Chittipeddi, 1991; Maitlis and Lawrence, 2007). Gioia and Chittipeddi (1991:442) define sensemaking as 'the construction and reconstruction by involved parties as they attempt to develop a meaningful framework for understanding the nature of *intended strategic change*' (italics added). In contrast, they define the reciprocal process of sensegiving as the attempt to 'influence the sensemaking and meaning construction of others towards a preferred redefinition of organizational reality' (Gioia and Chittipeddi, 1991:442). Given that these two processes work in tandem and tend to be linear, Gioia and Chittipeddi (1991) group sensemaking and sensegiving into a four-stage change cycle: *envisioning* and *signalling* by top management, and *re-visioning* and *energizing* by key stakeholders, including middle managers.

Balogun (2003, 2006) and Balogun and Johnson (2005) have recently taken the study of sensemaking and sensegiving concepts a stage further by applying them to the interpretation of middle managers' roles during the implementation of strategic change. Using a case study of a UK privatized utility, with data collected through participant diaries, interviews and focus groups, Balogun (2003:70) classifies middle managers into four interrelated 'change intermediary' roles: 'undertaking personal change, helping others through change, implementing necessary changes in their departments and keeping the business going'. The typology (Figure 5.2) is designed to extend and deepen Floyd and Wooldridge's (1992) four implementation roles by questioning the nature of these roles in 'more detail'. Effectively this means moving away from the *strategic agency* and strategy process focus of Floyd and Wooldridge (1994, 1997) by giving priority to the emergent roles of middle managers as interpreters of change events who undertake personal change and help others through change. These are essentially personal 'sensemaking' and collective 'sensegiving' roles enacted through self-reflection, lateral communication and dialogue. Balogun (2003:79) therefore gives central

Nature of activity

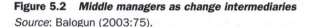

	Sensemaking	Coordination
Peer/self	Undertaking personal change	Keeping the business going
Team	Helping others through change	Implementing changes to departments

Organization (row label between the two rows, on the left axis)

Figure 5.2 *Middle managers as change intermediaries*
Source: Balogun (2003:75).

importance to the interpretative-therapeutic role rather than the instrumentalism of planned implementation: 'Undertaking personal change is in fact the key task for middle managers, since it informs all the other roles.' And because 'roles' are enactments of sensemaking and sensegiving interpretations, this appears to open up the possibility of an alternative explanation of what Floyd and Wooldridge (1994) term 'the implementation gaps between senior-manager intent and what actually happens' (Balogun 2003:79). For Balogun (2006) and Balogun and Johnson (2005), the intended and unintended outcomes of strategic change occur in the discontinuities between sensemaking and sensegiving.

While Balogun's (2003) overall image of middle managers as 'change intermediaries' is subtler and more context-rich than conventional strategic action perspectives on managers as implementers of change, it also generates other problems. The image is richer but it sometimes appears curiously passive and reactive: the roles of middle managers as change champions, adapters or information synthesizers that one finds in strategic agency models recedes from view. This shift in emphasis may be partly attributable to a different evidence base (e.g. qualitative case study findings versus quantitative survey data), but the counterpoint also appears intrinsic to the epistemological assumptions of the sensemaking approach. The idea of middle managers as strategic agents during the strategy process is replaced by the primacy of their sensemaking roles as creators and communicators of meaning, and these more reactive roles are invariably circumscribed by managerial changes imposed from above that have both intended and unintended consequences.

Of course, other, more proactive interpretations of middle manager change agent roles are possible. For example, Huy (2001a) outlines a fourfold classification of middle manager roles that overlaps with Balogun's (2003): *entrepreneur*, *communicator*, *therapist* and *maintainer*. The key difference is that Huy (2001a) tends to treat all four roles as proactive and adaptive forms of change agency that enhance middle managers' crucial stabilizing roles, especially during radical organizational change.

These differences in focus raise the awkward question of how 'roles' are conceptualized in sensemaking perspectives. It would appear that the key task of 'interpreting' personal change proposed by Balogun (2003, 2006) is not a prescribed role with pre-given functional or organizational attributes and a self-development remit; instead, it appears as essentially an *identity construct* enacted within the sensemaking process. But unfortunately, there is no clear definition of how 'roles' or 'identity' relate in the sensemaking process, and this raises additional questions. Do organizations as hierarchical entities with recursive socialization processes or systems of rules produce and reproduce 'roles', or does the search for 'identity' construction enact organizing? One can only assume that Balogun (2003, 2006), like other sensemaking theorists, tends to drift towards the latter view when she suggests, following Weick (2001), that 'sensemaking is *grounded* in identity construction' (italics added) (Balogun, 2003:79).

The lack of clarification of the concepts of 'role' and 'identity' is a persistent problem in sensemaking perspectives, as well as task-focused theories of managerial behaviour (Hales, 1999; Mantere, 2007; Simpson, 2008). Traditional role theories with their functional connotations suggest that roles are learned and prescriptively *acted out*. So, they are, in principle, independent of the person who performs them – the classic justification for the 'neutral' logic of bureaucratic rationalism in public service organizations (Kallinikos, 2004). In contrast, sensemaking suggests that roles are creatively *made up*: they are a retrospective interpretative construct *within* identity that can be changed. However, most sensemaking perspectives do not resolve the conceptual tensions between how roles are structured and constructed, preferring instead to weave in and out of 'role systems' and 'role sets' by treating them as underlying performative prescriptions for pragmatic action that are open to redefinition, reinterpretation and individual choice (Weick, 2001).

This problem is not a new one, of course. In symbolic interactionist theories, roles are the ongoing reworking, redefinition and renegotiation of meaning in processes of human interaction (Garfinkel, 1967). But sensemaking theories do not really take the legacy of interactionist analysis much further. Instead, Weick (2001) appears to blur role identity construction as sensemaking, essentially replacing *interaction* with *enactment* while making the process more subjective and ephemeral: individual cognition takes priority over social interaction. Moreover, unlike symbolic interactionism, which sought, in principle, to restore the actor's creative intentionality, enactment appears to pacify agency, partly because Weick (2001:96, 401) is strongly opposed to the more instrumental implications of rationalist decision models: 'sensemaking is accepting and coming to terms, rather than control and manipulation'.

More broadly, Weick's (2001) more passive image of agency *as* sensemaking and identity construction also has implications for the understanding of 'structure'. Sensemaking as a process construct tends to conflate agency with structure, conceiving both as cognitive modes of 'enactment', with the result that one is never sure when 'organizing' as ongoing micro-processes of action becomes relatively fixed and enduring. Nor is it clear where or when organizing as a change process begins and ends, or how actors effect change.

Again these are not new problems. Like the traditions of symbolic interactionism, sensemaking has enormous difficulties in theorizing systemic linkages between episodic streams of meaning and action, mainly because the concept of 'enactment' treats individual processes of learning and meaning creation as momentary, circular and self-referential (Contu and Wilmott, 2004). Organizations are therefore not treated as macro entities with recursive properties of production and reproduction that precede or define the individual, and that can be analysed, redesigned or *changed as a whole* (Weick *et al.*, 2005). Rather, organizations are 'a stream of problems, solutions and people tied together by choices', and this creates the possibilities for *incremental change* (Weick, 2001:28).

This optimistic destructuring of organizations and the identification of agency and change with choice also has major implications for the theorization of power. By conflating agency and structure as sensemaking, Weick (2001) does not seek to identify the points at which *organizing* as a process of sensemaking becomes identical with *organizations* as systems of power and control. This partly explains why power in organizations is rarely examined in sensemaking approaches, except in an *ad hoc* manner or as an incidental afterthought (Contu and Wilmott

2004; Weick *et al.*, 2005). Even 'sensegiving' as the more explicit attempt by leaders or managers to exercise power over others by defining 'reality' is rarely subjected to interrogation as a form of manipulation and potential managerial control. Without an analysis of power and, by definition, 'structure/structuring', the self and self-identity as constructions of sensemaking and sensegiving can potentially float free of power and the always intimate complicity between knowledge and power (Foucault, 2000).

Discussion

Strategic agency models of middle managerial roles in the strategy process mark an important shift from a purely intermediary implementation role for middle managers to a greater emphasis on their proactive involvement in strategic change (Floyd and Wooldridge, 1992, 1994, 1997, 2000). Yet despite this shift of emphasis, these models tend implicitly to operate with either a 'deliberate' concept of the strategy process or a broadly hierarchical concept of organizations that limits upward–downward influence to processes of implementation, delegation and authority-sharing.

A potentially more promising formulation of the changing nature of middle manager roles is possible if the influence process is situated within the *context* of 'knowledge creation' activities mediated through a panoply of information-sharing networks, cross-functional teams and collaborative projects. In this distributed model, middle managers are potentially key knowledge producers and creators. For example, Nonaka and Takeuchi's (1995) innovative focus on the process of middle-up-down management clearly opens up this possibility. Nonaka *et al.* (2000:22) conceive middle managers as strategic intermediates between top management and other organizational stakeholders: 'they are at the intersection of the vertical and horizontal information flows in the company'. In this role they can create knowledge from below as well as strategy from the middle, mainly because they can leverage their tacit knowledge and understanding of organization systems, processes and procedures.

But even this apparently more proactive, decentred and distributed model of knowledge creation and leadership tends to overemphasize the logical linkages between organizational vision and strategy processes. Nonaka *et al.* (2000) also underplay the chaotic and often disjointed nature of innovation and strategic change processes in organizations – as well as their unintended outcomes: 'To create knowledge dynamically and continuously, an organisation needs a vision that *synchronises the entire organisation*. . . . Therefore, it is important for top management to articulate a knowledge vision that transcends the boundaries of existing products, divisions, organisations and markets' (Nonaka *et al.*, 2000:23, italics added). This formulation of knowledge creation and strategy formulation shares uncomfortable affinities with earlier versions of post-industrialism and the 'knowledge economy' in which organizations were integrated systems or structures with strategies that could be pre-programmed through the technocratic interventions of experts and leaders.

The new political economy of network forms of organizing suggests, however, not only that organizational boundaries are blurred and hierarchies of control are undermined, but that markets and workplaces are fragmented, creating spatially diffuse and new virtual forms of organizing that are localized, heterogeneous and inherently risk based (Castells, 2000). Nonaka and Takeuchi (1995) partly recognize localness, issues of risk and the diversity of agents within networks, in their 'hypertext' concept of organizational layers, but they seriously underplay the tensions between the relatively autonomous role of middle managers as knowledge creators who can engender innovation and change and how this process is then managed or transferred through the strategic agency of leaders. Paradoxically, they still appear to be enthralled by overarching concepts of 'strategic intent' and centred leadership in what are essentially decentred network organizations and work systems in which agency, knowledge and power are increasingly more widely distributed (Gronn, 2002; Buchanan *et al.*, 2007).

If strategic agency models overly rely on the increasingly problematic notions of rationality, strategic intent and leadership in managing organizational innovation and change, sensemaking perspectives address these limitations, although not without engendering their own theoretical deficits. Sensemaking perspectives largely abandon the idea of strategy as a linear-adaptive process founded on a formulation–implementation dichotomy: 'execution *is* analysis and implementation *is* formulation' (Weick, 2001:353). Or in Weick's (2001) more cryptic formulation: doing is knowing. From this cognition-as-practice viewpoint, strategic change and organizational redesign are 'shaped more by action than plans, and more by interpretation than by decisions' (Weick, 2001:72). Moreover, the reference point of strategy is not rational managerial actors or leaders operating within integrated organizational systems defined by goals;

rather, organizations are conceived as 'loosely coupled systems' of self-organization in which improvisation and experimentation are central to the incremental processes of organizing, changing and strategizing (Weick, 2001:301).

This critique of strategy, strategic change and, by extension, change leadership also has broader implications for sensemaking as a potentially 'middle-range theory' that operates somewhere 'in between' organizational change and agency. In Weick's (2001) loosely coupled systems, organizational change is emergent and continuous while agency appears diffuse, iterative and distributed. Continuous change engenders improvisation as a normal response to organizational uncertainty; and it is through small-scale actions and the micro-practices of enactment that innovation and change occur: 'small-scale micro behavioural commitments can have macro consequences' (Weick, 2001:15). It is, however, 'micro changes' that predominate over their potentially larger effects (Weick, 2001). Weick therefore conceives loosely coupled systems as 'the ultimate neutralizers of managerial hubris' and rationalist models of strategic agency: 'Actors in a loosely coupled system rely on trust and presumption, persist, are often isolated, find social comparison difficult, have no one to borrow from, seldom imitate, suffer pluralistic ignorance, maintain discretion, improvise, and have less hubris' (2001:401).

While these ideas are intrinsically receptive to explorations of innovation and change in less hierarchical, complex systems, especially in information-intensive and knowledge-creating organizations, they also raise broader questions regarding the nature of agency and change (Caldwell, 2006). Because sensemaking cannot specify strategic ends, it is always in danger of becoming its opposite: self-validating actions or self-fulfilling prophecies that simply reproduce *more of the same*. Weick appears to reinforce this view when he suggests that self-belief, optimism, enthusiasm and behavioural commitment are more important in realizing goals than are plans, predicted outcomes, collective beliefs or expert inferences as to the causality of events:

> Whether people are called fanatics, true believers, or the currently popular phrase *idea champions*, they all embody what looks like strategy in their persistent behaviour. Their persistence carries the strategy; the persistence is the strategy. True believers impose their view on the world and fulfil their own prophecies.
>
> (2001:349–350)

Are Weick's (2001) apparently contradictory views on the limitations of management hubris and the possibility of self-fulfilling prophecies somehow compatible? Yes. Paradoxically, the passive self-image of sensemaking as a counter-force to the hubris of strategic agency has a Janus face: the voluntaristic self-affirmation of individual action and choice by those who act as sensegivers.

Some of the most persuasive attempts to reinstate the strategic agency of middle managers in processes of innovation and strategic change are based on attacks on concepts of deliberate strategy and top-down models of managerial action. Yet these new approaches to strategic change, organizational innovation and knowledge creation *from the middle* invariably faltered because they have been unable to fully explore the distribution or dispersal of strategic agency in organizations. To do so would require a deeper and more sustained exploration of agency and change that can accommodate issues of knowledge creation, network organizing and new modes of coordination, control and power in organizations. Ultimately this may lead to a more critical concept of strategic agency that can articulate not only the enabling and limiting conditions of middle manager roles ('what I do'), but also the ability of middle managers to question the growing discourses of 'change', 'flexibility', and 'innovation' that simultaneously affirm and threaten their self-identity ('who I am', 'what I believe' and 'how should I act?'). All too often, managerial research on middle manager roles has positively affirmed their growing influence and capacity to effect change and innovation, while failing to explore the degree of autonomy they have in organizational change processes or their capacity to reflectively examine their conduct or actions (Thomas and Dunkerley, 1999; Turnbull, 2001). A concept of strategic agency must include not only intentional action and the exercise of influence, knowledge or expertise, but also the boundaries and limitations of middle manager autonomy and reflexivity (Caldwell, 2006).

Sensemaking perspectives also promised to restore the roles of middle managers in strategic change, by exposing the limitations of top-down strategic action. But this shift of focus created new blind spots. The limitations of sensemaking models of managerial agency derive from their inability to provide a convincing systematic concept or counter-concept of agency that goes beyond cognitive concepts of enactment, selection and retention. These are essentially information processing and communication models of organizing. Weick (2001) can therefore replace the modalities of managerial agency as intentional action and instrumental control with essentially cognitive and interpretative schemas for the understanding of intentionality that rely on conversation, narration or storytelling. This is in many respects a positive development; it appears to open up new possibilities for the exploration of agency and change that partly levels hierarchies of expertise, knowledge and power while challenging managerial hubris.

But, paradoxically, Weick's (2001) attempt to write control and manipulation out of the script of management also allows him to idealize the inductive self-creation of individual meaning and identity through sensemaking as an empirical mechanism for controlling and managing meaning. We are apparently free to construct our identity without succumbing to the intentional thrust and determinism of rational action, but this occurs within discourses and narratives that offer us control of uncertainty. In this sense, sensemaking offers a retrospective and choice-driven concept of management control rather than an instrumental one. However, Weick (2001) does not ask whether sensemaking can be subject to ideological interpretation or the political construction and manipulation of identity. If meaning is imposed and agency and self-identity are socially 'interpolated', then sensemaking and sensegiving may be effects of power, rather than the ongoing outcome of choice or inductive identity construction (Caldwell, 2007).

Weick's (2001) quasi-voluntarist elevation of choice also partly explains why there appear to be no stable means–ends linkages in organizational decision-making processes that can be subject to some degree of rationality, objectivity or expert knowledge. Instead, the self-confirming logic of sensemaking treats interpretation, narrative and storytelling as 'real' causes and rationality as post-rationalization, although paradoxically all interpretations are not equally valid. For Weick, the researcher as *sensegiver* appears to take precedence over other sensemaking actors who understand their actions only respectively, and this is disconcertingly similar to his concept of idea champions and change agents who realize their self-fulfilling vision by imposing their views on the world. If classical managerial discourses on organizations as systems with rational actors pursuing goals begin and end with the vagaries of purposeful action, strategic decision-making and prescriptive role models, sensemaking begins and ends with the equally problematic ideas of identity construction and agency as self-validating action and choice.

Where does all this leave public services middle managers and the possibilities of change from the middle, both as a theoretical project and as an exploration of practice? Attempts to build bridges between strategic and sensemaking models of middle manager roles and identity construction during processes of innovation and change are likely to continue. In this respect there may be greater scope for creating synthetic 'middle-range theories' with common, or at least more convergent, research agendas (Floyd *et al.*, 2008). Undoubtedly this will take various forms, but one central task must be the clarification of how roles and identity construction are conceived. Is self-identity an enduring cultural construct subsuming normalizing and temporal managerial roles, or do roles have a life of their own as powerful patterns of prescribed action and behaviour that are both fixed and transitory? Weick *et al.* (2005) suggest that identity construction differentiates sensemaking from both role theory and cognitive psychology, and that identity is a 'mutable continuity'. These ideas need to be unpacked and more closely examined (Simpson, 2008).

The more critical research task, however, will be to clarify concepts of 'agency' and 'change' that allow an exploration of the possibilities and limits of strategic and sensemaking perspectives. Currently the concept of middle manager 'strategic agency' is still too dependent on actor rationality, deliberate strategy and conventional role theory, with the result that both the limitations and the possibilities of change from the middle are understated. In contrast, sensemaking perspectives have until recently avoided an exploration of 'agency' as prospective action and intention, as well as its constructionist counter-images: agency that is widely distributed or *decentred* (Caldwell, 2006). This is understandable. Sensemaking is conceived as a retrospective process of meaning creation that is self-confirming: agency is therefore subsumed within sensemaking practices: 'The language of sensemaking captures the realities of agency, flow, equivocality, transience, re-accomplishment, unfolding, and emergence, realities that are often obscured by the language of variables, nouns, quantities, and structures' (Weick *et al.*, 2005:410). This is certainly true. But the underlying nominalism of Weick's (2001) epistemological formulation of agency inevitably pushes sensemaking towards voluntarism as a strategy for change through self-affirming action while also critically disabling it as a systematic basis for a structural or relational exploration of power and control in organizations. Ultimately, a concept of agency is unsustainable if it refuses to confront the realities of power and knowledge as power (Foucault, 2000).

Another potentially important bridge-building task in creating more coherent research agendas will be to draw the strategy process analysis of strategic agency and sensemaking organizational perspectives into emerging 'strategy-as-practice' research programmes (Jarzabkowski *et al.*, 2007). Practice perspectives on the strategy process focus mainly on the micro-actions of 'strategy-making' by practitioners as they are enacted through ongoing strategy routines, social interaction and everyday conversation, as well as the analytical tools used in the process (Whittington, 2006). Strategy is therefore something organizational actors *do* (i.e. 'strategizing') rather than something an organization has. This new focus promises a 'reinstatement of agency', including middle manager agency, in the sensemaking processes and practices of strategy formation (Jarzabkowski *et al.*, 2007:6, 12). There is a danger, however, that strategy-as-practice perspectives may abandon the conventional macro-level strategy process focus on 'strategic change' as well as concepts of 'change agency'. This would be a somewhat paradoxical outcome: the practices of strategy formation would be uncovered in all their bewildering complexity, but we may gain little insight into the 'how to' of practice or the challenges of 'managing' organizational change.

Conclusions

The prospect of conceiving 'middle-up-down management' as a new panacea for organizational innovation and strategic change from the middle must be treated with considerable caution. The realm of the middle in organizations can no longer be defined by the inward-looking structural-functionalist default of 'adaptation' through conformity. This left organization theory without a concept of agency (Giddens, 1984). Nor can the middle be located in top-down hierarchies of control that once multiplied the dysfunctions of bureaucracy (see Merton's classic analysis, 1968). We may not, of course, be moving inexorably towards 'post-bureaucratic' or even remotely 'post-hierarchical' organizations in a new post-modern landscape, but there is mounting evidence that the old patterns of 'command and control' are being replaced by new distributed patterns of network organizing, empowerment and 'concertive control' (Barker, 1999; Kallinikos, 2004). This shift undoubtedly suggests more positive roles for middle managers in change processes, although one suspects that middle managers may still be capable of activating the old patterns of conformity, self-interest and resistance that made them the authors of their own negative self-images. But this controversy over positive versus negative self-images and changing roles may simply miss the point. There are other, more disconcerting forces lurking within new organizational forms that may irrevocably turn the old villains into new victims. These forces are often ignored by research agendas that identify 'emergent' or 'processual change' as the only constants in managerial discourses about middle manager roles, for they often obscure how new managerial rhetorics of 'change', 'transformation' and 'flexibility' challenge and ultimately erode the organizational rationale of middle manager values, autonomy and self-identity. The harsh reality is that in the new political economy of information networks, horizontal coordination and concertive control, the middle layers in organizations may be further compressed and even eliminated. With this prospect, change from the middle may be the beginning of the end for middle managers.

6 A convergence analysis of strategic change: the National Trust Case

Colin Carnall

- Introduction
- The National Trust
- The Organization Review
- Change architecture
- A convergence model of strategic change
- Assessing the National Trust's Organization Review, 2000–2007
- Conclusions

Introduction

The purpose of this chapter is to present the findings of an analysis of recent organizational change within the National Trust utilizing Carnall's (2007) convergence model of strategic change, which focuses on an acknowledged situation where most organizations are involved, not in the implementation of a single change initiative, but rather in a multitude of change initiatives at any one time. From this model emerges the change capability framework (Carnall, 2007), which has been utilized in order to facilitate a better understanding of the interactions, linkages and interfaces between simultaneously ongoing change initiatives, and in assisting the assessment of the degree of convergence. The present analysis is based on the experience gained through the direct involvement in the early stages of the Organization Review – a National Trust change programme – and access to documents, reports and interviews with a number of the key people involved in this particular change process. The chapter seeks to understand the processes and problems associated with these changes and to develop new thinking of relevance to both academics and practitioners concerned with the successful and sustainable implementation of significant organizational change.

The chapter provides an introduction to the National Trust before looking at the Organization Review and its change architecture. This is then followed by the application of the convergence model of strategic change (Carnall, 2007) and the change capability framework (Carnall, 2007) to this specific organizational context.

The National Trust

The National Trust was established in 1895 as an organization with the legal powers necessary for holding property for permanent preservation. By 2003 it was caring for 248,000 hectares of countryside in England, Wales and Northern Ireland; 600 miles of coastline; more than 240 buildings of historical importance; and 130 great gardens. Most of these properties have statutory protection and the majority are open to visitors. The collections therein amount to the most extensive and valuable composite museum in the world.

The Trust has always been a charity and is supported by 40,000 volunteers and over 3 million members. Its endeavours are framed by various Acts of Parliament, including the National Trust Acts of 1907, 1937 and 1971. During the twentieth century the Trust evolved through various changes, growing in complexity in terms of the forms of property in its care and the scale of its activities. By 1967 it became clear that the organization needed remodelling and, subsequent to the publication of the report of an advisory committee (Benson Report, 1968), the Trust was restructured into a regional administrative system. This was followed by a period of unprecedented growth.

Governance is via a Council (some members of which are trustees of the charity). The Council comprises 52 members, half nominated by organizations associated with the Trust's aims and half by the members. The Council appoints a director-general, who acts as chief executive and directs the affairs of the Trust in pursuance of its strategic objectives and decides issues of principle and policy.

The management of the Trust is undertaken by the director-general working with a Management Board comprising the directors of functional directorates and director-level appointees responsible for properties. This chapter seeks to establish both how and why certain changes came to be decided and implemented in a change programme commencing in 2000, and to assess the impact of them on the Trust. Collectively, the change programme came to be labelled the Organization Review.

The Organization Review

Since the 1990s a number of reviews of the National Trust had been undertaken, including reviews of working practices, reporting relationships and of head office location. Out of the Working Practices Review had emerged the concept of applying the notion of general management at property level and the creation of an area management tier, which was still being implemented in 2000, some seven years later. However, many of the recommendations provided by these reviews remained stalled. There was a sense that change was either slow or just not being faced up to with sufficient leadership and determination. Moreover, there remained a view that a head office in central London, which was both expensive to run and of insufficient size to accommodate all central functions, was not acceptable either financially or organizationally. Although this issue had been clearly identified, it had not been acted on.

There were also a number of ideas focused on the future informing and influencing the thinking of senior-level executives at the time of the Organization Review. It was felt that the Trust was not 'punching its weight' at national level. As a major landowner and a large membership organization, the Trust felt it was lacking influence on the national stage on issues of relevance to its purpose. In a world increasingly characterized by collaborative working and connectedness with other stakeholders, the ability to reach out, to set agendas and to create influential contacts with central government and other national bodies increasingly appeared to be part of the National Trust's approach to achieving its objectives. A focus on the future, on learning and education and on setting the agenda for debate on issues related to conservation, the land, and so on appeared to be more and more relevant.

Commencing in October 2000, the Organization Review was to be coordinated as a project by a newly externally appointed Personnel Director. Acting as review leader, the Personnel Director established a Programme Board (initially called the Review Board) consisting of seven members drawn from the Management Board and an external adviser (the chapter author), and a Project Group comprising 12 members of staff and consultants from a London firm (part of a US-based HR/compensation planning consulting group selected through a competitive tendering process). There was extensive consultation with staff and, following an invitation to submit written evidence, ideas and views, over 2,000 submissions were received in the form of notes, letters, emails and longer reports. In addition, the consultants involved reviewed a wide range of internal documents, visited various National Trust offices and properties, and interviewed over 100 members of staff.

The Review Board met regularly to establish an appropriate level of project governance and to produce an agreed strategic view of the future direction of the organization. The Project Group and Programme Board exchanged work regularly, and both the Personnel Director and the consulting team leader were actively involved in both groups throughout the process in order to facilitate and ensure a high degree of connectedness and continuity.

Change architecture

In some key respects the change architecture was extensive and robust. Overall, the change proposals were ambitious. The Programme Board acted on behalf of the director-general and the Management Board, overseeing the change process while the Project Group undertook the detailed change diagnostic work. In doing so this group was supported by a team of consultants. Furthermore, nine activity groups were established to focus on key areas of National Trust activities such as properties, conservation, customer service and education. Each group had a 'reference group' of staff members with whom they could check ideas. In all, 350 staff were involved in these various groups.

Following completion of the Organization Review, and the subsequent presentation of its findings and recommendations to the Management Board, an implementation phase was established. Preparations for implementation included the development of change management training, the election of staff representatives, a Change Programme Office structure, job evaluation and job matching activities to enable the transfer of people from the old to the new structure. This was followed by a two-month consultation period with staff representatives. Following on to the some 2,000 submissions of evidence, ideas and views made by staff, a two-way process of director updates, staff briefings, newsletters, videos, the circulation of minutes of staff meetings with the Management Board, the publication of all change proposals, and email hotlines was established.

A convergence model of strategic change

The analytical approach adopted in this chapter is based on Carnall's (2007) convergence model of strategic change which argues that the single most important condition for the successful implementation of sustainable organizational change is convergence. Recognizing that modern organizations typically have a number of change initiatives going on at any given point in time, this model takes a particular point of divergence with earlier models of strategic change such as, for example, that of Kotter (1996). Previous models tend to look at the conditions necessary for the successful implementation of a specific strategic change initiative, which link to diverse strategic change programmes, some emerging from different parts of the organization and some from strategic initiatives established in the past but not yet completed. Thus, a model of strategic change that focuses on one particular strategy, even if that leads to multiple initiatives, as is likely, cannot be a sufficient basis for explaining, let alone predicting, success or failure. What is required in order to explain and predict the outcomes of organizational change is a better understanding of the interactions, linkages and interfaces between all change initiatives running simultaneously. A strategic change model emphasizing the existence of such multiplicity, assisting the assessment of the degree of convergence, would be highly useful to academics and practitioners alike.

Carnall's (2007) convergence model of strategic change is based on the assumption that the higher the level of ambition inherent in change programmes, the greater the need for a comprehensive architecture operated effectively. Furthermore, the model assumes that any given organizational change is in reality a set of multiple initiatives and must be viewed in the context of other change initiatives already present and under way. It is not unusual to find that there are hundreds of change initiatives, spanning the dimensions of change outlined in Chapter 1, under way at any point in time, each demanding attention and resources. Many of these initiatives are inconsistent in terms of either the objectives and purposes being served or the demands they put on scarce resources. What is required is an examination of any change programme, and its associated change-related processes, as part of a series of change activities that need to be integrated and managed alongside the requirements of 'business as usual'. However, it should be noted that this proposed approach is focused on organization-wide change. Incremental change initiated within individual departments is a very different challenge, and one that may not justify such an approach.

This notion is, however, not new. Beckhard and Harris (1987) examine the features of effective action plans, identifying parameters such as integration, chronology and relevance when considering action plans as 'road maps' to set out implementation actions over time. Yet their work does not address the multiplicity point directly, as they focus on the action steps required to implement a particular change. Bruch and Sattelberger (2001) discuss the need for coherence in a multiple initiative-based action plan established by Lufthansa some years ago, and Pettigrew (2003) certainly approaches this issue in his work on complementarities and the link to financial performance. Finally, Klarner *et al.* (2008) look at *change capacity* in public services through an analysis of strategic change at the World Health Organization. They recognize the reality of viewing organizations as involved in a series of change initiatives at any one time, and argue for the need to learn from experience over time. Furthermore, they note the importance of issues such as trust, transparency and change culture, but fall short of the notion that we need to examine the possibility of convergence.

The convergence model of strategic change (Carnall, 2007) defines the level of ambition in any given set of change proposals and links it to success – the more ambitious the change initiative is, the more likely it is to be successful when based on a robust change architecture. It is assumed that change initiatives lacking in ambition are doomed to fail before they even start because they will not be meeting the challenges faced by the organization. The model does accept that it is possible to propose changes that are overly ambitious and that fail as a consequence. However, the position taken in this chapter is that changes mostly fail as a result of senior managers not having willed the means to success. The model has been translated into a change capability framework (Figure 6.1; for further information and details, see Carnall, 2007:326–339) – a tool designed to measure the change capability needed to ensure the convergence required for successful change.

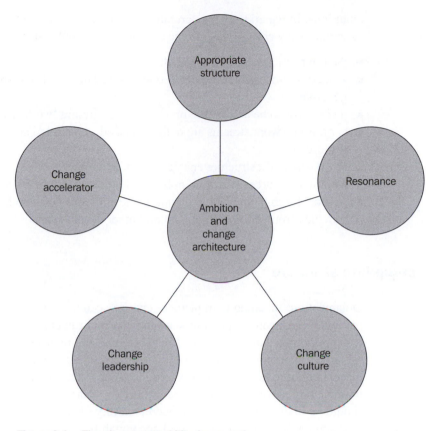

Figure 6.1 *The change capability framework*
Source: Carnall (2007: 328).

Change ambition and architecture

Carnall (2007) suggests that change ambitions can be recognized by the presence of creative destruction (i.e. change of structures), distinctive value (i.e. clearly identifiable growth in value or activity), distinctive operational efficiency (i.e. clear operational efficiencies), integration (i.e. integration of internal and external sources of knowledge) and simultaneous change (i.e. the identification of simultaneous change initiatives). It may be difficult to define the level of ambition in absolute terms as it must always be relative to the established 'needs' of the organization (i.e. increased revenues; modernization). However, it is important to establish whether the aims and objectives of any change plan are realistic and achievable, and linked to capability and past performance. It is also important to establish the ownership of these ambitions. In regard to change architecture the following components are essential to any change programme (Carnall, 2007:329–330):

- the top team needs to be engaged;
- a steering process must be devised to ensure effective leadership and governance;
- there needs to be an existing process for integrating 'work streams';
- appropriate work streams are defined, tasked, constituted and resourced;
- any needed infrastructure enablers must be in place;
- a human resources transition policy and process must be in place;
- support for implementation planning and activities needs to be provided from within operational and other departments.

Appropriate structure

Organizations planning to implement change need to ensure that particular management processes are in place and run effectively in order to support both 'business as usual' and ongoing and planned change initiatives. Not only should there be performance management systems in place, but, more importantly, they need to be operated as intended: to improve performance. Furthermore, robust governance arrangements should be in place to ensure clear accountability of any change programme. Established board-level accountability is necessary to ensure well-managed change processes and to avoid a culture of simply 'blaming' any failures on resistance to change. Organizations also need to make sure there is a structure in place to measure and mitigate any risk associated with change (e.g. unintended consequences; disruption; reputation).

Resonance

When a change initiative resonates, organizational stakeholders are of the impression that the change suggested is the right response or initiative at the time. Such resonance can be measured in the following terms (Carnall, 2007:332):

- felt need (i.e. does the change address a need felt by stakeholders?);
- convergence (i.e. do the different change initiatives reinforce each other?);

- adaptability (i.e. will the initiative allow for empowerment at a local level?);
- willingness to experiment (i.e. is the implementation process clear about the need for experimentation and gaining knowledge from this process?);
- customer primacy (i.e. will the initiative provide for developments required for customer service and delivery?).

Change culture

Carnall (2007:332–333) further suggests the following components to be investigated and fully addressed in order to establish or strengthen a healthy culture for organizational change:

- evidence-based leadership (i.e. are leaders prepared to learn from experience? Is the organization embracing the principles of a learning organization)?;
- informed choice (i.e. how credible is the decision for change?);
- problem orientation (i.e. will the management of the process focus on solutions and achievements rather than guilt and blame?);
- transparency (i.e. is the change process a transparent one or one full of secrecy and obscurity?);
- management of expectations (i.e. how will this impact on me/what is expected from me? Is this positive and achievable?).

Change leadership

Leaders, formal and informal, must be supported in their efforts as agents for change. Carnall (2007:334) suggests that successful change leaders should provide evidence of the following in order to implement and facilitate sustainable organizational change:

- credibility;
- visibility;
- learning orientation;
- sponsoring of early adopters;
- organizational slack;
- encouragement of learning through change.

Change accelerator

This final part of the framework considers the need for adopting programme and project management processes in the management of organizational change. Carnall (2007) argues the need for an understanding of how some of these are utilized to focus on the specific requirements of change initiatives:

- connectivity (i.e. does the suggested change initiative fit/connect to current organizational processes?);
- leverage (i.e. is the change initiative designed to follow a critical path – certain 'platforms' to be in place in order to enable further progress?);
- integration (i.e. does the management of all individual change initiatives take an integrated view of organizational aims and objectives?);
- critical mass (i.e. the result of high-level buy-in and engagement of key stakeholders, connectivity, leverage and integration).

Assessing the National Trust's Organization Review, 2000–2007

Perhaps the problem with organizational change is less about how to 'manage' change than about how to bring it to a conclusion (i.e. how to end change); how to sustain the effort of change management such that benefits are shown to have emerged; how to measure benefits so that they can be recognized; and how to create 'rites of ending' such that those involved recognize that progress has been achieved. Too often, organizations move from one initiative to the next without recognizing the progress made. Thus, it can be suggested that while those leading change can see real progress, others are much less clear. For the Trust, that would be compounded by the geography of the organization and by governance issues.

One issue with the Organization Review may have been the relative lack of resonance of the proposals and lack of benefits measurement and management. The focus was on inputs rather than outcomes, with the real exception to that being the 'New Ways of Working' effort. In so far as they existed, the change governance arrangements were disbanded long before the changes were complete. Through 2002 there was a major effort focused on job matching and appointments to the new structure. However, after 2002 there was less explicit change architecture in place around the Organization Review, although other changes were indeed implemented.

Initially the change architecture was robust. However, as the proposals lacked resonance to some extent, the change architecture was disbanded too early and insufficient focus was placed on benefits management, the management effort focused on job matching, appointments and buildings rather than on realizing the benefits of the Organization Review. In any event, these benefits were ill-defined and problematic, not least in terms of financial objectives. The means for accelerating change to drive benefits realization were not thought through and one significant consequence was that many staff did not recognize what had been achieved.

Conversely, all staff appeared to recognize that the completion of a new, 'iconic' headquarters building in Swindon represented a major step forward. There was an evident pride and satisfaction in this achievement, and the Organization Review was certainly part of this development. Similarly, the changed circumstances through which the Trust moved, subsequent to the review planning period and while the changes were being implemented, led the Trust to plan further financial changes. There is some justification for the argument that the experience of the review and its implementation had been leveraged in the achievement of these financial changes. Indeed, it may well be that the 'resonance' associated with the changes going into place was deepened by four factors: first, the new building and the recognition of that as an opportunity to build anew and for the future; second, the director-general's role in leading the culture change; third, the director-general and the top team's readiness to learn from experience and modify the new structure where it was not working; and finally, the explicit pursuit of financial improvements that many thought were a necessary and inherent part of the original plan. To some extent our analysis has now gone beyond the Organization Review and its implementation. But it could be contended that it would be artificial for it not to have done so. As previously argued, identifying particular changes and analysing them separately is precisely what is wrong with much that is written about change management. It can be suggested that the main error in planning the Organization Review was the constant restatement of the notion that it was meant to be financially neutral, which many actors just did not believe.

Looking at the National Trust in terms of change and change leadership over the period 2000–2007 reveals a mixed picture. Real progress has been made, but the organization has not fully captured the learning from this process. Conversely, change leadership overall was strong. Change culture and leadership are difficult to build up during the preparations for any given change initiative if they are second-order factors. Change resonance and the change accelerator can be worked on with immediate effect as part of a change planning process. If successful, this will build change leadership and culture in the medium term. Thus, it can be concluded that successful change requires resonant and convergent change decisions and choices alongside a high degree of integration (of change initiatives), leverage (both between initiatives and between existing systems, of reward, performance management and people development, and initiatives) and the engagement of key stakeholders. However, the latter needs to provide for post-implementation activity looking at how to tailor change to local conditions, particularly in such a geographically dispersed organization as the National Trust.

In practice, resonant and convergent designs are most important. You must seek to achieve change within the culture you have and with the leaders in place (except perhaps in the case of a business turnaround). Efforts focused on achieving behavioural change among the leadership cadre or to the corporate culture independently of a focus on ensuring taking the right change choices (resonance) and implementation decisions (the accelerator) are likely to be less effective. The evidence here is of pretty effective changes that are too little understood throughout the organization. However, in the past the Trust had not managed the 'ending' of the change process well, as it had allowed cascades of initiatives without having an effective 'grip' on whether or not the intended objectives and purposes were being achieved. Ensuring such a 'grip' in the future was acknowledged as essential in order to inform further change initiatives. Some would argue this to be a key part of the change management challenge: if you cannot connect your future to your past, how can you move the corporate culture forward? Showing how the Trust has achieved progress on a set of objectives and purposes that have endured through a period of both internal and external upheaval must be an important means of capturing understanding of the journey since 2000, and of how the Trust continually seeks to make itself fit for purpose for the challenges ahead.

Conclusions

Overall, the National Trust experience of change in the period 2000–2007 has been a positive one. After a period in which change was often mooted but little was achieved, a series of important change initiatives were successfully implemented. We can make sense of these various changes only if we 'connect' them; it makes no sense to seek to evaluate the impact of the Organization Review in isolation. It may be true that its impact was mixed in the sense that some of the specific changes recommended were later changed or still remain problematic. It may also be true that subsequent financial pressures have given new impetus to the need for further change. Nevertheless, viewed as part of a series of both internal and external developments, the Organization Review was clearly an important process playing a constructive role in preparing the Trust for changes. With a history of organizational and head office reviews that had led to nothing, and people talking about a culture of 'optionality', those leading the Review were determined that this time it would be different.

It is worth noting that the Organization Review was embarked upon partly using changes going on in the finance function that sought to improve its role and effectiveness and partly out of recognition that the Trust was a major landowner but lacked the influence that this implied. The appointment of a new director-general was seen as likely to lead to changes in that regard, and the review was seen as a means of creating a Trust viewed as modern, well organized and 'fit for purpose'. Initially the change architecture was robust, connected and comprehensive. Conversely, the change proposals emerging from it were of mixed 'resonance'. The decision to move the head office out of London was widely expected. Other organizational changes were controversial and the mantra of financial neutrality a source of doubt to many.

The job-matching process was lengthy and demanding of the efforts of senior managers in the Programme Board and Project Group. Once it was complete, the Programme Board and Project Group were dismantled. This was at least partially a mistake because there was still much work to do in implementing the changes. Not least here the newly configured Historical Houses Directorate, created out of the merger of various technical, conservation and other disciplines, represented a serious change management challenge. However, four points are worth noting. First, the director-general's role in leading the New Culture working group was important in providing a means of making sense of the new jobs, roles, etc. Second, the financial pressures gave renewed impetus to the need for change, and many felt that the experience gained from the Organization Review now helped in the implementation of these subsequent changes. Third, the move into the new headquarters building provided a target, process and a symbol of the Trust as an organization emerging from a period of change. Fourth, the executive team's willingness to learn from experience and quickly modify changes was a sign that real progress was being sought.

Overall, this series of changes begins to make sense. Change resonance eventually was high. Early on in the process a robust, connected and comprehensive change architecture, with the capacity to accelerate change throughout the organization, was more important, enabling the Trust to establish the need for change and to structure changes on a sustainable and irreversible basis. Once this was established, perhaps the single most important part of the change management process was the way the top team were open to learning from experience. They demonstrated both the willingness and the capacity to adapt to changed circumstances. Ultimately, change resonance created a sense of common purpose, providing the basis for longer-term changes to be implemented.

7 Organizational change in the public sector: the case for planned change

Bernard Burnes

- Introduction
- New Public Management
- The implications for change
- Approaches to change
- Lewin's planned approach to change
- User involvement in the NHS: the suitability of the planned approach
- Conclusions

Introduction

Most people in the developed world would find it difficult to envisage life without the provision of public services. Indeed, over the past 60 years the rise of the welfare state in Western Europe and 'big government' in the United States has seen a tremendous expansion of publicly funded, if not always directly provided, services (Burnes, 2004b; Flynn, 2002). However, as is noted in the introductory chapter to this volume, throughout the 1960s, and especially in the 1970s, the cost and efficiency of public services became a burning issue across the developed world (Clarke and Trebilcock, 1997; Common, 1998; Osborne and Gaebler, 1992). By the 1980s there was a rising clamour of voices calling for the rolling back of the welfare state (Doherty and Horne, 2002). However, though many state-owned industries and utilities were privatized over the next two decades, in the United Kingdom and most other countries the core of the welfare state and the level of public expenditure have survived astonishingly well (Flynn, 2002). Public services have often been criticized for being over-bureaucratic, resistant to change and poorly managed, yet over the past 25 years they have proved to be remarkably innovative and able to change in quite radical ways (Ferlie *et al.*, 1996).

As discussed in earlier chapters, the term New Public Management (NPM) has been given to the reinvention of public services across the globe (Hood and Peters, 2004; McLaughlin *et al.*, 2002; Sarker, 2006). Though NPM seeks to address traditional concerns such as efficiency and value for money, at its core are two radically different concepts for the public sector: competition and the empowered consumer (Cope *et al.*, 1997; Myers and MacDonald, 1996). Proponents of NPM have argued that only by opening up services to private sector competition and giving consumers the sort of influence and leverage they enjoy when purchasing goods and services from the private sector can the public sector survive (Gray and Jenkins, 1994; Osborne and Gaebler, 1992).

Not only has NPM led to a radically different approach to managing and providing public services, but, through the concept of the empowered consumer, it has also led to a radically different approach to running services. Rather than service users being the passive recipients of what service providers deem is necessary, NPM calls for them to have an equal role in developing and changing services (DETR, 1998; Harrison and Mort, 1998; Horton, 2006; Nash, 1996; NHS Executive, 1996; Pilgrim and Waldron, 1998; South, 2007). In the United Kingdom, running parallel with greater user involvement in changes to public services there have also been steps to ensure that managers operate in a more ethical, open and inclusive fashion (Committee on Standards in Public Life, 1995; Department of Health, 2002). However, if service users are to be effective partners in the change process, and if managers are to behave in an ethical and open manner, they need an approach to change that is underpinned by these principles and that can put them into practice. Though the public sector does not fall short of advice on how to manage change, it appears to lack an approach based on these values. In order to address this, this chapter reviews NPM and its implications for change. It then examines the main approaches to managing change and how they fit in with the principles of NPM and ethical management. The chapter concludes by arguing that Kurt Lewin's *planned* approach to change, with its democratic philosophy, is the most appropriate method for achieving participative change in the public sector.

New Public Management

NPM is a term that is used to describe the rise of a new and radical approach to running public services that has been taken up across the globe by governments of very different political complexions over the past 25 years (Hood and Peters, 2004; McLaughlin *et al.*, 2002; Sarker, 2006). The anti-public sector–pro-private sector conservatism of the Thatcher government in the United Kingdom in the 1980s is often cited as the driving force behind NPM (Ferlie *et al.*, 1996; Flynn, 1993). However, as Common (1998) points out, though the Thatcher government appeared to pursue NPM with the greatest zeal, the Swedish social democrats, Spanish and French socialists, and Labour governments in New Zealand and Australia were not far behind. Therefore, NPM should not necessarily be seen as a neo-liberal assault on the public sector per se, but rather as a reaction to the perceived weaknesses and shortcomings of public services.

The rationale for NPM was twofold. The first reason was the perceived inefficiency and high cost of the public sector. In the United Kingdom, claims of bureaucratic inefficiency and waste in public services were rife in the 1960s and 1970s, and even occasioned a number of official inquiries (Chapman, 1978; Fulton, 1968; Plowden, 1961). However, it was only with the downturn in public finances in the United Kingdom and across the Western world in the 1970s that the cost of the public sector became a major political issue (Clarke and Trebilcock, 1997; Hutton, 1995). This led to the election of the first Thatcher government in 1979, which made the reforming of 'bloated, wasteful, over-bureaucratic, and underperforming' public services the central target of government policy (Ferlie *et al.*, 1996:11). The second part of the rationale for NPM was the belief that the private sector, motivated as it is by competition, could provide better and less costly services than the public sector (OECD, 1993; Talbot, 2001).

Consequently, from 1979 onwards successive Conservative governments attempted to deliver better value for money in public services through measures such as privatization, outsourcing and compulsory competitive tendering (Flynn, 1993; Horton, 2006). In essence, the Thatcher government took central responsibility for deciding what should be delivered and how, but delegated actual delivery to a plethora of private, public and hybrid organizations (Doherty and Horne, 2002). Indeed, the notion of competition, or 'marketization' as it is sometimes labelled, whether provided through privatization or outsourcing public service to the private sector or through promoting competition within the public sector, appears to have become the defining principle of NPM (Cope *et al.*, 1997; Gray and Jenkins, 1994; Osborne and Gaebler, 1992). As Cope *et al.* (1997:449) assert, NPM 'reflects the view that greater competition between the public and private sectors and within the public sector promotes greater efficiency by making public sector agencies more consumer-responsive'.

According to Myers and MacDonald (1996:86–87), one of the objectives of NPM is to change the role of service recipients:

> Instead of users and carers being subordinate to the wishes of service providers, the roles will be progressively adjusted. In this way users and carers will be enabled to exercise the same power as consumers of other services. . . . In addition to enabling users to be empowered consumers it is suggested that this degree of involvement: discourages dependence, facilitates greater commitment – on the part of the user and the carer – in realising objectives, and gives users and carers a sense of having some control over what is happening.

In the United Kingdom, a key initiative in this respect was the *Citizen's Charter*, launched by the Conservatives in 1991 and revamped as *Service First – The New Charter Programme* by the Labour government in 1998 (Flynn, 2002). A central component of both was that public services should be open and accountable, and involve users in service development in order to give them greater choice over the type of service they received and when, where and how services should be delivered (Vidler and Clarke, 2005).

Therefore, not only does NPM seek to change the balance between the public and private provision of services, but also it seeks to change the balance of power between service providers (whoever they may be) and service users. In the United Kingdom this concept of the 'empowered consumer' now appears central to the provision of most public services, from obvious services, such as the National Health Service (NHS), through to less obvious services, such as parts of the criminal justice system (Horton, 2006; Nash, 1996; South, 2007; Vidler and Clarke, 2005).

The implications for change

If a cornerstone of NPM is to equalize the balance of power between service providers and service users, this presents a major challenge to what their critics often refer to as self-serving public bureaucracies (Ferlie *et al.*, 1996; Osborne and Gaebler, 1992). In the United Kingdom the public sector organization that faces perhaps the biggest challenge in this area is the NHS. This is partly because of its size – it employs more than 1.3 million people – but also because it has a low level of user involvement compared to other organizations (Department of Health, 2000). In the NHS Plan in 2000 the government stated that 'the NHS will shape its services around the needs and preferences of individual patients, their families and their carers . . . [and that] . . . patients and citizens will have a greater say in the NHS' (Department of Health, 2000:4). In order to achieve this, the NHS Plan Implementation Programme (Department of Health, 2001) outlines how patient views will be given greater prominence in shaping NHS services. All parts of the NHS, as well as care homes, must monitor patient and carer experience and satisfaction and publish the views received and action taken in a Patient Prospectus; all NHS trusts and primary care trusts must have a Patient Advocacy and Liaison Service and Patient Forums, and all health authorities must establish Independent Local Advisory Forums. The NHS Plan and its Implementation Programme open the door for greater public involvement in the control and management of the NHS. These objectives were made legally binding when the Health and Social Care Act 2001 was passed by Parliament.

Though a clear commitment to participation (especially when enshrined in law) is a necessary step to greater user involvement in and control over the services users receive, by itself it is not sufficient. As Poulton (1999) noted, there have been many attempts to involve users in designing and running health services in the United Kingdom, but they have not met with success. Work by Walshe and Higgins (2002) gives a strong indication of why this is so. They examined a series of major inquiries into failings in the NHS between 1969 and 2001, which ranged from the ill-treatment and abuse of long-stay patients through to the case of the mass murderer Dr Harold Shipman. These inquiries exposed a worrying culture of secrecy and user exclusion by those who manage health services. Walshe and Higgins (2002:895) observed that '[m]any inquiry reports highlight similar sorts of failures, suggesting that lessons are not always learnt. Often these failures are organisational and cultural, and the necessary changes are not likely to happen simply because they are prescribed in a report.'

The failure to implement effectively the recommendations of major inquiries, and the tendency for similar mistakes to occur time after time, led the NHS to introduce a *Code of Conduct for NHS Managers* (Department of Health, 2002). Not only did the Code represent a sea change in how managers in the NHS should behave, but also it chimed with the NPM call for greater user involvement in services. The code (Department of Health, 2002:3) states that managers will observe the following principles:

- make the care and safety of patients my first concern and act to protect them from risk;
- respect the public, patients, relatives, carers, NHS staff and partners in other agencies;

- be honest and act with integrity;
- accept responsibility for my own work and the proper performance of the people I manage;
- show my commitment to working as a team member by working with all my colleagues in the NHS and the wider community;
- take responsibility for my own learning and development.

The code (Department of Health, 2002:4) goes on to state that managers will also seek to ensure that:

- the public are properly informed and are able to influence services;
- patients are involved in and informed about their own care, their experience is valued, and they are involved in decisions;
- relatives and carers are, with the informed consent of patients, involved in the care of patients;
- partners in other agencies are invited to make their contribution to improving health and health services.

The then chief executive of the NHS stated that the purpose of the code was:

- to guide NHS managers and employing health bodies in the work they do and the decisions and choices they have to make;
- to reassure the public that these important decisions are being made against a background of professional standards and accountability.

(Crisp, 2002:1)

Though the code applies only to NHS managers, other parts of the public sector have also adopted similar arrangements in order to bring themselves into line with the Nolan Principles on Conduct in Public Life (Committee on Standards in Public Life, 1995) which, among other injunctions, stresses that holders of public office are accountable for their decisions and actions to the public.

Taken together, the NPM and the Code of Conduct lay out a philosophy of managing change that is radically different from what went before. Instead of being excluded from the process of change, the recipients of services become a central component of the process. Instead of change being decided upon by a few, it becomes the prerogative of the many. Instead of being powerless, users and recipients become powerful. Or, at least, this is the intention. However, in order to enact this intention, the public sector needs a model of change that embodies these democratic and ethical principles.

The public sector is not short of advice on how to manage change. For example, the Office of the Deputy Prime Minister (2005) produced

*An Organisational Development Resource Document for Local
Government.* This document is dotted with references to the need for
employee involvement in change but only once does it speak of 'greater
user choice and involvement' (Office of the Deputy Prime Minister,
2005:5). Nor does it give guidance on the process of involving users or
the underlying principles that should guide such involvement. Indeed, the
overall impression is that change is value-free. A similar approach can be
seen from advice on change issued by the NHS. In *Managing Change in
the NHS: Organisational Change* (Iles and Sutherland, 2001), there is
reference to employee and partner involvement but not to patient or carer
involvement. The document lists a number of change tools and techniques
but there is no indication as to their underlying principles. For example,
Lewin's force field model (Cartwright, 1952) is described but there is no
mention of the ethical and democratic principles that underlie it. Nor is
there any recognition that Lewin developed the model as an integral part
of his *planned* approach to change rather than something that could be
used on its own (Burnes, 2004a).

Similarly, Waterman *et al.*'s (1980) 7S Model is advocated and described,
but once again the underlying principles are not mentioned. The 7S
Model is an instrument developed by Tom Peters and colleagues at the
management consultants McKinsey & Company to allow senior managers
to gain an overview of their business in order to identify what needs
changing. It was developed at a time in the late 1970s when most Western
companies were in trouble, and 7S provided them with an instrument for
rapid and coercive change. Involvement was not a part of the vocabulary:
vicious downsizing was (Peters and Waterman, 1982).

Therefore, while the public sector may not be short of advice or tools and
techniques, it does not appear to possess (or perhaps even understand the
need to possess) an approach to change that is based on democratic and
ethical principles and that includes and gives equal weight to both service
users and service providers. However, this does not mean that such an
approach does not exist.

Approaches to change

As Dunphy and Stace observe (1993), there are a wide variety of
approaches to change, which range from small scale to large scale and
from participative to directive. However, there is general agreement that
the two main approaches are the *planned* approach to change and the
emergent approach (Beer and Nohria, 2000a; Burnes, 2004b; By, 2005).

For proponents of the *emergent* approach, change is a continuous, dynamic and contested process that emerges in an unpredictable and unplanned fashion. As Weick (2000:237) states,

> Emergent change consists of ongoing accommodations, adaptations, and alterations that produce fundamental change without a priori intentions to do so. Emergent change occurs when people reaccomplish routines and when they deal with contingencies, breakdowns, and opportunities in everyday work. Much of this change goes unnoticed, because small alterations are lumped together as noise in otherwise uneventful inertia.

The rationale for the *emergent* approach stems, according to Hayes (2002:37), from the belief that 'the key decisions about matching the organisation's resources with opportunities, constraints and demands in the environment evolve over time and are the outcome of cultural and political processes in organisations'.

In particular, advocates of *emergent* change claim that the process of change is a complex and untidy cocktail of rational decision-making processes, individual perceptions, political struggles and coalition-building (Huczynski and Buchanan, 2001). Though there is much support for the *emergent* approach (Beer and Nohria, 2000a), there are two main drawbacks from the viewpoint of NPM. First, if fundamental change is achieved through an ongoing process of small and unnoticed change, the scope for the empowered service consumer to participate and exert influence is significantly diminished. Second, not only does it stress the political and power issues involved in change, but it advocates the use of power and politics to accomplish change; in essence, change is seen as a battle of opposing forces (Burnes, 2004b). This is a criticism levelled by a number of writers (Collins, 1998; Pugh, 1993) and is best summarized by Hendry (1996:621), who argues that '[t]he management of change has become . . . overfocused on the political aspects of change'.

This does not mean that power and politics are not important issues in change. However, in terms of the public sector, an approach to change that offers advice on winning the battle for your side is much less desirable than one that seeks to openly confront and resolve conflict. Indeed, according to Pascale (1990), openly confronting and resolving conflict, as opposed to ignoring it or one group seeking victory over another, is the secret of how successful companies stay ahead of the competition.

In terms of an approach to change that is consciously embarked on and that stresses conflict resolution, the *planned* approach has much to recommend it. As Schein (1988:239) commented, 'There is little question that the intellectual father of contemporary theories of applied behavioural science, action research and planned change is Kurt Lewin.' Lewin's seminal work on leadership styles and the experiments on *planned* change that took place in the 1930s and 1940s created the basis on which the study and practice of organizational change rested for the next 40 years (Burnes, 2007). However, Lewin's primary interest was not in organizational change per se, but in resolving social conflict through behavioural change, whether this be within organizations or in the wider society.

Underpinning Lewin's work was a strong moral and ethical belief in the importance of democratic institutions and democratic values in society. Lewin believed that only by strengthening democratic participation in all aspects of life and being able to resolve social conflicts could the scourge of despotism, authoritarianism and racism be effectively countered. Since his death in 1947, Lewin's wider social agenda has been mainly pursued under the umbrella of action research (Dickens and Watkins, 1999). This is also the area where Lewin's *planned* approach has been most closely followed. For example, Bargal and Bar (1992) described how, over a number of years, they used Lewin's approach to address the conflict between Arab-Palestinian and Jewish youths in Israel through the development of intergroup workshops.

In terms of change within organizations, after his death in 1947 Lewin's *planned* approach was taken up and advanced by the Organization Development (OD) movement in the United States, which continued to promote an ethical-participative approach (Cummings and Worley, 1997; French and Bell, 1995). As French and Bell (1973) have shown, the values that OD practitioners espouse include the following:

- they believe that the needs and aspirations of human beings provide the prime reasons for the existence of organizations within society;
- change agents believe that organizational prioritization is a legitimate part of organizational culture;
- change agents are committed to increased organizational effectiveness;
- OD places a high value on the democratization of organizations through power equalization.

Therefore, in meeting the public sector's need for a tried and tested approach to change which embraces both users and providers in an ethical, democratic and participative manner, *planned* change has much to offer. In addition, it also has a great deal to offer as a rigorous and effective approach to managing change, as the next section will show.

Lewin's planned approach to change

Lewin believed that the key to resolving social conflict was to facilitate learning and so enable individuals to understand and restructure their perceptions of the world around them. A unifying theme of much of his work is the view that 'the group to which an individual belongs is the ground for his perceptions, his feelings and his actions' (Allport, 1948:vii). His *planned* approach to change comprises four elements: Field Theory, Group Dynamics, Action Research and the Three-step model of change. Though these are often treated as separate themes of his work, Lewin saw them as a unified whole, with each element supporting and reinforcing the others and all of them necessary to understand and bring about *planned* change, whether it be at the level of the individual, group, organization or even society (Bargal and Bar, 1992; Kippenberger, 1998a, b; Smith, 2001). As Allport (1948:ix) states, 'All of his concepts, whatever root-metaphor they employ, comprise a single well integrated system.' This can be seen from examining these four aspects of his work in turn.

Field Theory

Field Theory is an approach to understanding group behaviour by trying to map out the totality and complexity of the field in which the behaviour takes place (Back, 1992). Lewin maintained that to understand any situation it was necessary that '[o]ne should view the present situation – the *status quo* – as being maintained by certain conditions or forces' (1943:172). Lewin (1947a) postulated that group behaviour is an intricate set of symbolic interactions and forces that not only affect group structures, but also modify individual behaviour. Therefore, individual behaviour is a function of the group environment, or 'field' as he termed it. Consequently, any changes in behaviour stem from changes, be they small or large, in the forces within the field (Lewin, 1947b).

Lewin's view was that if one could identify, plot and establish the potency of these forces, then it would be possible not only to understand why individuals, groups and organizations behave as they do, but also to establish what forces would need to be diminished or strengthened in order to bring about change. In the main, Lewin saw behavioural change as a slow process; however, he did recognize that under certain circumstances, such as a personal, organizational or societal crises, the various forces in the field can shift quickly and radically. In such situations, established routines and behaviours break down and the status quo is no longer viable; new patterns of activity can rapidly emerge and a new equilibrium (or quasi-stationary equilibrium) is formed (Kippenberger, 1998a; Lewin, 1947b).

Field Theory, because of its potential to map the forces impinging on an individual, group or organization, underpins the other elements of Lewin's work.

Group Dynamics

Lewin was the first psychologist to write about 'group dynamics' and the importance of the group in shaping the behaviour of its members (Allport, 1948; Bargal *et al.*, 1992). Indeed, Lewin's (1939:165) definition of a 'group' is still generally accepted: 'it is not the similarity or dissimilarity of individuals that constitutes a group, but interdependence of fate'. In organizational terms, groups are usually conceived of as collections of staff who have the responsibility for undertaking particular tasks or discharging particular responsibilities. However, Lewin's concept of 'interdependence of fate' can also be seen to include service users as well as service providers, at least in the public sector. For example, if the NHS staff responsible for providing an orthopaedic service in a hospital do not meet the needs of people with arthritis, there will be two interlinked consequences. The first is that patients will suffer needlessly. The second is that the service will be seen to be failing and may be shut down as patients, and the general practitioners who refer them, seek a better provider, which might or might not be another part of the NHS. If the NHS as a whole failed, then it could be broken up and privatized, with patients paying directly for the service they require. When it comes to publicly funded services, the fate of service users and the fate of service providers are interdependent.

To come back to Group Dynamics: as Kippenberger (1998a) notes, Lewin was addressing two questions: what is it about the nature and characteristics of a particular group that causes it to respond (behave) as it does to the forces that impinge on it, and how can these forces be changed in order to elicit a more desirable form of behaviour? It was to address these questions that Lewin began to develop the concept of Group Dynamics.

Group Dynamics stresses that group behaviour, rather than that of individuals, should be the main focus of change (Bernstein, 1968; Dent and Goldberg, 1999). Lewin (1947a) maintained that it is fruitless to concentrate on changing the behaviour of individuals because the individual in isolation is constrained by group pressures to conform. Consequently, the focus of change must be at the group level and should concentrate on factors such as group norms, roles, interactions and socialization processes to create 'disequilibrium' and change (Schein, 1988).

However, understanding the internal dynamics of a group is not sufficient by itself to bring about change. Lewin also recognized the need to provide a process whereby the members could be engaged in and committed to changing their behaviour. This led Lewin to develop Action Research and the Three-step model of change.

Action Research

The term 'Action Research' was coined by Lewin (1946) in an article entitled 'Action research and minority problems'. Lewin (1946:201) stated in the article:

> In the last year and a half I have had occasion to have contact with a great variety of organizations, institutions, and individuals who came for help in the field of group relations. . . . [However, though these people exhibited] a great amount of good-will, of readiness to face the problem squarely and really do something about it . . . [t]hese eager people feel themselves to be in a fog. They feel in a fog on three counts: 1. What is the present situation? 2. What are the dangers? 3. And most importantly of all, what shall we do?

Lewin conceived of Action Research as a two-pronged process that would allow groups to address these three questions. First, it emphasizes that change requires action, and is directed at achieving this. Second, it recognizes that successful action is based on analysing the situation correctly, identifying all the possible alternative solutions and choosing the one most appropriate to the situation at hand (Bennett, 1983). To be successful, though, there also has to be a 'felt need'. Felt need is an individual's inner realization that change is necessary. If felt need is low in the group or organization, introducing change becomes problematic. The theoretical foundations of Action Research lie in Gestalt psychology, which stresses that change can successfully be achieved only by helping individuals to reflect on and gain new insights into the totality of their situation. Lewin (1946:206) stated that Action Research 'proceeds in a spiral of steps each of which is composed of a circle of planning, action, and fact-finding about the results of the action'. It is an iterative process whereby research leads to action and action leads to evaluation and further research.

As Schein (1996:35) comments, it was Lewin's view that 'one cannot understand an organization without trying to change it'. Indeed, Lewin's view was very much that the understanding and learning that this process produces for the individuals and groups concerned, which then feed into changed behaviour, are more important than any resulting change as such (Lewin, 1946). To this end, Action Research draws on Lewin's work on Field Theory to identify the forces that focus on the group to which the individual belongs. It also draws on Group Dynamics to understand why group members behave in the way they do when subjected to these forces. Lewin stressed that the routines and patterns of behaviour in a group are more than just the outcome of opposing forces in a forcefield. They have a value in themselves and have a positive role to play in enforcing group norms (Lewin, 1947b).

Action Research stresses that for change to be effective, it must take place at the group level, and must be a participative and collaborative process that involves all those concerned (Allport, 1948; Bargal et al., 1992; French and Bell, 1984; Lewin, 1947a).

Lewin's first Action Research project was to investigate and reduce violence between Catholic and Jewish teenage gangs. This was quickly followed by a project to integrate black and white sales staff in New York department stores (Marrow, 1969). However, Action Research was also adopted by the Tavistock Institute in Britain, and used to improve managerial competence and efficiency in the newly nationalized coal industry. Since then it has acquired strong adherents throughout the world (Dickens and Watkins, 1999; Eden and Huxham, 1996; Elden and Chisholm, 1993).

In organizational terms, the classic Action Research project usually comprises three distinct groups: the organization (in the form of one or more senior managers), the subject (people from the area where the change is to take place) and the change agent (a consultant who may or may not be a member of the organization). These three distinct entities form the learning community in and through which the research is carried out, and by which the organization's or group's problem is solved.

The three entities must all, both individually and collectively, agree to come together, as a group, under mutually acceptable and constructed terms of reference. This usually small face-to-face group constitutes the medium through which the problem situation may be changed, as well as providing a forum in which the interests and ethics of the various parties to this process may be investigated. It is a cyclical process whereby the group analyses and solves the problem through a succession of iterations. The change agent (consultant), through skills of coordination, links the different insights and activities within the group so as to form a coherent chain of ideas and hypotheses that leads to an agreed form of change (Heller, 1970).

However, Lewin (1947a:228) noted that implementing an appropriate and agreed form of change did not always guarantee success:

> A change towards a higher level of group performance is frequently short lived; after a 'shot in the arm,' group life soon returns to the previous level. This indicates that it does not suffice to define the objective of a planned change in group performance as the reaching of a different level. Permanency at the new level, or permanency for a desired period, should be included in the objective.

It was for this reason that he developed his Three-step model of change.

Three-step model

The Three-step model of change is often cited as Lewin's key contribution to organizational change. However, it needs to be recognized that when he developed his Three-step model, Lewin was not thinking only of organizational issues. Nor did he intend it to be seen separately from the other three elements (Field Theory, Group Dynamics and Action Research that comprise his *planned* approach to change). Rather, Lewin saw the four concepts as forming an integrated approach to analysing, understanding and bringing about change at the group, organizational and societal levels.

A successful change project, Lewin (1947b) argued, involved three steps:

Step 1: Unfreezing. Lewin believed that the stability of human behaviour was based on a quasi-stationary equilibrium supported by a complex field of driving and restraining forces. He argued that the equilibrium needs to be destabilized (unfrozen) before old behaviour can be discarded (unlearned) and new behaviour successfully adopted. Given the type of issues that Lewin was addressing, as one would expect, he did not believe that change would be easy or that the same approach could be applied in all situations:

The 'unfreezing' of the present level may involve quite different
problems in different cases. Allport . . . has described the 'catharsis'
which seems necessary before prejudice can be removed. To break
open the shell of complacency and self-righteousness it is sometimes
necessary to bring about an emotional stir up.

(Lewin, 1947b:229)

Enlarging on Lewin's ideas, Schein (1996:28) comments that the key to
unfreezing 'was to recognise that change, whether at the individual or
group level, was a profound psychological dynamic process'. Schein
identifies three processes necessary to achieve unfreezing:
disconfirmation of the validity of the status quo, the induction of guilt or
survival anxiety, and creating psychological safety. He argued that
'unless sufficient psychological safety is created, the disconfirming
information will be denied or in other ways defended against, no survival
anxiety will be felt. And consequently, no change will take place'
(1996:30). In other words, those concerned have to feel safe from loss and
humiliation before they can accept the new information and reject old
behaviours.

Step 2: Moving. As Schein (1996:32) notes, unfreezing is not an end in
itself; it 'creates motivation to learn but does not necessarily control or
predict the direction'. This echoes Lewin's view that any attempt to
predict or identify a specific outcome from *planned* change is very
difficult because of the complexity of the forces concerned. Instead, one
should seek to take into account all the forces at work and identify and
evaluate, on a trial and error basis, all the available options (Lewin,
1947b). This is, of course, the learning approach promoted by Action
Research. It is this iterative approach of research, action and more
research that enables groups and individuals to move from a less
acceptable to a more acceptable set of behaviours. However, as we have
seen, Lewin (1947b) recognized that without reinforcement, change could
be short-lived.

Step 3: Refreezing. This is the final step in the Three-step model.
Refreezing seeks to stabilize the group at a new quasi-stationary
equilibrium in order to ensure that the new behaviours are relatively safe
from regression. The main point about refreezing is that new behaviour
must be, to some degree, congruent with the rest of the behaviour,
personality and environment of the learner or it will simply lead to a new
round of disconfirmation (Schein, 1996). This is why Lewin saw
successful change as a group activity, because unless group norms and
routines are also transformed, changes to individual behaviour will not be

sustained. In organizational terms, refreezing often requires changes to organizational culture, norms, policies and practices (Cummings and Huse, 1989).

Like other aspects of Lewin's work, his Three-step model of change has become unfashionable in some quarters over the past 25 years (Dawson, 1994; Hatch, 1997; Kanter *et al.*, 1992). Nevertheless, such is its continuing influence that, as Hendry (1996:624) commented, 'Scratch any account of creating and managing change and the idea that change is a three-stage process which necessarily begins with a process of unfreezing will not be far below the surface.'

Since its creation by Lewin, *planned* change has been developed and elaborated on by the OD movement to the extent that it is supported by and comprises a whole host of tools and techniques for effective change (Cummings and Worley, 1997; French and Bell, 1995). However, the underlying philosophy and rationale remain the same: the promotion of democratic participation in order to enable individuals to understand and restructure their perceptions of the world around them and in so doing resolve conflict, whether that conflict be within society at large or organizations. Therefore, central to *planned* change in organizations is the emphasis placed on the collaborative nature of the change effort: the 'group' – managers, staff, service users, etc. – jointly diagnose the problem, and jointly plan and design the specific changes.

Therefore, to summarize, the key elements of Lewin's *planned* change are the following:

- It is a long-standing and robust approach to change. *Planned* change started in the 1940s and has been constantly developed since into a well-supported, flexible and successful approach to change.
- Power equalization and democratic participation are central elements. All the parties concerned agree to participate on an equal footing to achieve an appropriate and sustainable change.
- It stresses learning and support. It recognizes that not all the parties start from the same base in terms of their knowledge, skills and confidence, and that building these is a central element of successful change. Above all, it recognizes that learning is central to successful change. To achieve this, the participants are aided and guided by an experienced and neutral change agent.
- It is a coherent process aimed primarily at behavioural change. Its four core elements, Field Theory, Group Dynamics, Action Research and the Three-step model of change, are designed to analyse, understand and change the behaviour of those involved.

- It is a process that is designed to draw out and resolve the differing and conflicting agendas of the participants.

User involvement in the NHS: the suitability of the planned approach

Lewin's *planned* approach to change is well developed and participative, and has a long track record of effectiveness (Burnes, 2004b; Cummings and Worley, 1997). Further evidence of its appropriateness to the needs of the public sector can be seen by examining past attempts to involve users in change initiatives in the NHS.

As noted above, much has been written about the need for user involvement in the public sector in general and the NHS in particular. User involvement parades under a number of different labels and seems to be used in a broad and imprecise manner. For example, Hill *et al.* (2000) prefer the term 'public involvement' to describe the democratic involvement of patients and service users in the planning and delivery of health care. Such involvement can take a number of different forms, such as audit, appraisal, research and decision-making. They also point out that it requires a great deal of work on the part of managers and professionals to 'enable' the public to participate effectively. In addition, Hill *et al.* (2000) identify two major drawbacks to public involvement initiatives. First, they are of such a diverse nature that it is difficult to judge their impact in terms of improving patient care. Second, there is an imbalance of power between the public and the professionals: regardless of the merits of the views and judgements of users and carers, the final decision on any change to the service lies with NHS managers and professionals.

Harrison and Mort (1998) also drew attention to the issue of power imbalances in their study of user involvement in services for patients with mental health problems and physical disabilities. Though the managers and professionals charged with providing these services stressed their commitment to user involvement, there was no commitment to accepting the views of users. Indeed, some managers even spoke of 'playing the user card' – that is, using the views of users to support their own agendas. Conversely, where user views conflicted with their own wishes, NHS staff often labelled user groups as unrepresentative or extremist. Similarly, Pilgrim and Waldron (1998) found that whatever the strength of user views or the quality of users' arguments, without the support of the professionals and managers who run mental health services, their views tended to be ignored. A study by Rush (2004) came to the same conclusion. He found that there are many tensions and conflicts between users and professionals that, if left unresolved, prevent users from having a say in the services they receive. Rush (2004:317) argues that 'the key to resolving these conflicts is to make them explicit and then to engage in meaningful discussion about them'.

It is apparent from these studies of user involvement that, in most cases, involvement is at arm's length from decision-making. Users are asked either directly or indirectly for their views. Sometimes this takes the form of asking individuals or groups to fill in a questionnaire; in other cases they may be asked to be involved in a service review or audit either separately from or jointly with NHS staff. Nevertheless, regardless of the nature of their involvement in assessing the case for change, it stops short of actual participation in the decision-making process. Their views are put forward but it is the service professionals and managers who make the actual and final decision on any changes. In these instances, participation does not involve their having a vote and it does not meet the call for democratic participation in decision-making.

Poulton (1999) reviewed the various approaches to user involvement in the NHS. He identified a spectrum of involvement that ranged from providing users with information, included accessing their level of service satisfaction, to user empowerment.

> Empowerment is the ultimate form of participation as it signifies the development of the power of individuals, groups and communities. True power sharing between health service users and health care providers is invariably a vision rather than a reality in a system that remains professionally dominated.
>
> (Poulton, 1999:1291)

In a recent review of user involvement, Beresford (2007:311) points out that users are unlikely to be in a position to make an effective contribution unless they receive the support to make this possible, in particular:

- the acquisition of relevant skills and experience;
- confidence-building and the raising of self-esteem;
- the resourcing of people's involvement through payment and the meeting of costs incurred;
- the provision of opportunities to get together with each other.

The issue of support for users was also a key finding from the United Kingdom's largest survey of health researchers. In the survey, Barber *et al.* (2007:383) found that successful involvement requires that '[c]onsumers are offered training and personal support, to enable them to be involved in research'. However, the research also found that only a small proportion of NHS researchers were actively involving users.

Therefore, in looking at some key studies of user involvement in various aspects of the NHS over the past decade or so, a number of key findings emerge:

- There is no established or accepted approach to user involvement in the NHS.
- User involvement does not seem to have been particularly successful, and in some cases it seems to be used more to bolster the agenda of managers and professionals than to further the interests of patients. This power imbalance between users and NHS managers and professionals arises from users being excluded from the decision-making process.
- Users need training and support to participate effectively, but unless managers and professionals also change their attitudes and behaviour, the views of users may continue to be ignored.
- There is a lack of coherence in the many methods used to collect and analyse data and to bring about behavioural change.
- There are conflicts and tensions between users and professionals that need to be openly acknowledged and resolved.

If we now return to the summary of *planned* change at the end of the previous section, we find that the weaknesses of the NHS's current approach to user involvement are addressed by the main elements of the *planned* approach. This can be seen in Table 7.1, which compares the two.

Table 7.1 *NHS user Involvement versus planned change*

NHS approach to user involvement	Planned change
Lack of a robust approach	A tried and tested robust approach
Lack of power equalization	Power equalization is a central element
Need for learning and support for users and behavioural change by managers and professionals	Learning, support and addressing behavioural issues are central elements
Mishmash of tools and techniques that are insufficient to achieve behavioural change	A coherent system of data collection and analysis, and of behavioural change
Beset by conflicting aims and agendas	Designed to expose and resolve conflicts

Conclusions

The public sector across the world has been going through major changes over the past 25 years. Although there have been strong challenges to the legitimacy and cost of the public sector, public expenditure continues to account for a large percentage of GDP. In the United Kingdom, the public sector accounts for around 40 per cent of GDP and it still provides, either directly or through a third party, a wide range of services, from the criminal justice system to health care, and including education and social services (Flynn, 2002). Regardless of this, if public services are to survive and provide the level of service expected by an increasingly demanding body of users and taxpayers, they have to be able to change to accommodate technological, economic and social conditions. However, such change cannot be driven solely by technocrats from on high, nor can it be arrived at by a process of open or covert warfare between the parties involved. Instead, the process of change has to be one that has legitimacy for all the parties concerned.

As this chapter has sought to show, the need for such legitimacy has arisen from a combination of forces. On the one hand, there has been the emergence of the empowered consumer of public services promoted NPM (Common, 1998). On the other hand, certainly in the United Kingdom there has been the increasing stress on ethical behaviour by public sector managers, promoted by the government and often driven by scandals and failures in and by public services (Walshe and Higgins, 2002). These have combined to create a need for an approach to public sector change that promotes inclusiveness, power equalization and democratic participation. Such an approach recognizes that service users and service providers must work as equal partners in developing and improving services. Though there are many approaches to change (Burnes, 2004a), the main ones tend to be found under the umbrella of either *planned* or *emergent* change. From the *emergent* perspective, change is a battle from which there can only be one winner. From the *planned* perspective, change involves conflict that can only be resolved by the equal participation of all the parties concerned. It follows from this that *planned* change appears to be the most appropriate approach to the needs and aspirations of the public sector.

This does not mean that the *planned* approach is suitable for all situations, even in the public sector. As Stickland (1998:14) remarks, 'the problem with studying change is that it parades across many subject domains under numerous guises, such as transformation, development, metamorphosis, transmutation, evolution, regeneration, innovation, revolution and transition to name but a few'. Consequently, organizations are faced with a confusing array of change situations and change approaches. None of the many approaches to change is perfect or suited to all situations (Burnes, 1996). What organizations need to do is to choose the approach to change that is most appropriate to their circumstances (Burnes, 2004b). For the public sector, especially in the United Kingdom, there is a need for change to be inclusive, for users and providers to be equally involved and for ethical considerations to be paramount. Under such circumstances, the *planned* approach does seem the most appropriate.

Note

I am grateful to my colleagues Professor Ruth Boaden and Dr Claire Harris for their assistance with this chapter.

Part III
Implementing and evaluating public services change initiatives

8 Public sector compensation: the management of change

David Lewin

- Introduction
- Public sector pay practices: concepts and definitions
- At-risk compensation in the US public sector
- At-risk compensation perceptions and preferences
- The future of at-risk compensation in the US public sector
- Strategies of change in public sector compensation
- Conclusions

Introduction

The management of change in public services is receiving renewed global scholarly attention. This development is due to several factors, including movement towards more market-oriented economies in many nations, political regime changes in certain regions and nations, rising citizen dissatisfaction with publicly provided services, enhanced scrutiny of the quality and costs of public services, and increased recognition of the common problems faced by large organizations irrespective of their private, public or hybrid sectoral status. Hence, there is a new (or renewed) movement under way to conceptualize and debate public services and public management practices.

An important component of this 'new thought' involves the management of change, in particular the extent to which received models of organizational change apply to public services. Such models range from that initially developed by the psychologist Kurt Lewin (1939, 1943, 1946, 1947a, b, 1951) to those advanced some half-century or so later by Weick and Quinn (1999), Brown and Eisenhardt (1997) and Tushman and O'Reilly (1997), among others. Central to these models is the concept of an organization life cycle, which by its very terminology suggests that organizations are always in flux. While this is perhaps more true of private than of public organizations, given that the former can go out of business, it is nonetheless true of the latter as well.

A notable area in which the public sector is undergoing questioning, ferment and change is the management of human resources – in particular, employee compensation. The key question (or challenge) in this regard involves whether and to what extent public sector compensation practices can be changed to be more performance based. In broaching this question, it is important to recognize the fundamental changes that have occurred in private sector compensation practices during the past quarter-century or so. The thrust of this change can be summarized as a movement away from pay-for-time and towards pay at risk (Mitchell *et al.*, 1990). To illustrate, whereas in 1970 only about 5 per cent of US employees (excluding sales employees) on private sector payrolls had some pay at risk, by 2005 about 78 per cent of such employees had at least some pay at risk. During the same period, by contrast, the proportion of US public sector employees who had some pay at risk increased modestly, from less than 1 per cent to approximately 7 per cent. Moreover, the proportion of total compensation represented by pay at risk grew markedly for private sector employees during this same period, amounting to about 19 per cent at the end of the period, but grew much more modestly for public sector employees, amounting to about 6.5 per cent at the end of the period. Nevertheless, the fact that at-risk compensation has been introduced into and is practised in some parts of the US public sector gives rise to the question 'What are the prospects for greater use of at-risk compensation in the public sector?' A companion question is 'How can public sector organizations manage the change from pay-for-time to greater use of pay at risk?' This chapter addresses and attempts to answer these two interrelated questions.

Public sector pay practices: concepts and definitions

To begin, it will be helpful to define and clarify certain compensation concepts and practices. Pay-for-time, which is also known as pay-for-input or pay-for-showing-up (at work), is exemplified by such provisions as hourly wages, annual salaries and most fringe benefits (e.g. retirement, life insurance and medical care plans). Pay at risk, which is also known as variable pay, contingent pay or pay-for-output, encompasses a wide variety of pay practices that can be decomposed into incentive-type pay and share-type pay. Incentive pay takes such forms as commissions, piece rates and bonuses, whereas share pay takes such forms as gain-sharing, profit-sharing, stock purchase, stock grant and stock option plans (Lewin and Mitchell, 1995; Gerhart *et al.*, 1992). With the possible exception of gain-sharing, share-type pay practices are inapplicable to public sector employees because public sector organizations do not seek or make profits and are not publicly (or privately) traded. Therefore, the basic type of at-risk pay that applies conceptually and in practice to the public sector is incentive-type pay – in particular, bonuses.

Where does merit pay fit into this categorization of pay types in the public sector? For the most part, as practised in the US public sector, merit pay is a form of pay for time. This is because the performance appraisal system that predominates in this sector features the assessment by supervisors and managers of employee performance – an assessment that is typically conducted annually – on a variety of dimensions of employees' jobs using a rating scale for each dimension, ranging, for example, from 1 = low or unacceptable to 5 = high or outstanding. The pay increase that is 'merited' by an employee on the basis of his or her overall performance is added to the employee's existing base pay, thereby forming a new, higher pay rate than existed previously. From the point at which this new, higher pay rate becomes operative, however, the employee is once again being paid for time and will continue to be so until a subsequent performance appraisal is conducted and additional 'merit' pay is awarded. Hence, the only risk that attends this process and outcome is the risk that an employee will be rated so low that he or she will not receive a merit pay increase. In either case, however, the employee will continue to receive pay-for-time. Therefore, merit pay as currently practised in the vast bulk of the US public sector does not constitute pay at risk according to the definition of this term proffered above.

Where does collectively bargained pay fit into this categorization of pay types in the public sector? This is an especially important question given that the US public sector is approximately 36 per cent unionized (whereas the US private sector is approximately 7.5 per cent unionized). The basic answer to this question is 'pay-for-time'. This is because the main outcome of collective bargaining is a set of annual base pay rates for the jobs and the employee holders of those jobs that are included in the bargaining unit and represented in negotiations. Once a collective bargaining agreement is reached between a US public employer and a represented group of employees, the negotiated pay rates resulting therefrom are established for a multi-year period on a position-by-position basis. This means that holders of these positions will be paid the hourly wage rates or annual salaries specified in the collective bargaining agreement. These wage rates and annual salaries typically rise annually during the life of the agreement, and are either explicitly stated in the agreement (via an escalator clause) or subject to a cost-of-living adjustment (COLA) based on changes in the Consumer Price Index (CPI). Further, these wage rates and annual salaries are typically not subject to or dependent upon annual employee performance appraisals.

At-risk compensation in the US public sector

As noted above, there has been a modest rise in the use of at-risk compensation in the US public sector during the past 35 years or so, but just how extensive is this use? To answer this question, consider the data presented in Table 8.1. These data were derived from a survey conducted

Table 8.1 *Incentive compensation usage in state and local governments, by level of government and employee occupational group, 2006 (%)*

| Characteristic | Overall usage | Perf.-based pay | Merit pay | Incentive compensation usage by type of plan | | | | |
				Productivity-sharing	Gain-sharing	Skill-based pay	Pay-for-knowledge	Bonus pay
Level of govt								
State govts (*n* = 35)	97	82	88	18	29	41	12	12
Local govts (*n* = 368)	85	69	73	17	35	42	14	7
Total govts (*n* = 403)	86	70	74	17	35	42	14	8
Employee group								
Manager	69	54	56	9	15	16	8	11
Professional	82	64	67	13	19	39	26	8
Technical	79	63	64	15	17	51	21	12
Clerical	38	34	36	7	13	32	13	4
Operative	58	51	42	26	41	44	8	6
Manual	34	28	24	12	28	34	5	5
Other service	51	43	42	14	19	39	9	3

Source: 2006 Survey of US state and local governments.

in 2006 of all 50 US state governments and 500 local governments that, collectively, had more than 11 million employees (excluding education employees). In the survey, at-risk compensation was defined to include (1) performance-based pay, (2) merit pay, (3) productivity-sharing, (4) gain-sharing, (5) skill-based pay, (6) pay-for-knowledge, (7) bonus pay and (8) other. Brief definitions of each of these types of incentive compensation were provided in the survey.[1] Respondents were asked to indicate which of these types of at-risk compensation were used by their respective governments and to identify the major employee groups – managerial, professional, technical, clerical, operators, manual, and other service – for which they were used as well as the agencies or departments in which they were used.[2] Completed surveys providing fully usable data were received from 35, or 70 per cent, of the state governments and 368, or 73.6 per cent, of the local governments.

Regarding the breadth of incentive compensation usage, Table 8.1 shows that all but one of the state governments and 85 per cent of the local governments use some incentive compensation. Performance-based pay and merit pay are the most prevalent types of incentive compensation in these governments, followed by skill-based pay and gain-sharing, while bonus pay is least frequently used. Among major employee or occupational groups, Table 8.1 shows that incentive compensation is most prevalent among professional and technical employees and least prevalent among clerical and manual employees. There is also considerable variation by agency or department in the use of incentive compensation (not shown in Table 8.1), with such compensation being most widely used in taxation, finance (budget), welfare, health care, sanitation, highways and utilities (i.e. water and power), and least widely used in public works, motor vehicles, general services, criminal justice (excluding police) and protective services (including police). Concerning the duration of incentive compensation plans, a few of these state and local governments adopted one or another incentive compensation plan in the mid- to late 1970s, but the 'typical' government in this sample began to use incentive compensation in the early to mid-1990s. Also of note, some unionized employees in these governments tend to be covered by productivity-sharing and gain-sharing plans, while non-union employees are primarily covered by performance-based pay and merit-pay plans.

Concerning variation by employee/occupational group in US state and local governments' use of at-risk compensation, the data in Table 8.1 indicate that performance-based pay, merit pay and pay-for-knowledge plans predominate for professional and technical employees; productivity-sharing and gain-sharing plans predominate for operatives;

skill-based pay predominates for technical employees and operatives and, to a lesser extent, professional and other service employees; and bonus pay predominates for managerial and technical employees. The overall incidence of pay-for-knowledge and bonus plans in these governments, however, is far lower than the overall incidence of pay-for-performance, merit pay, skill-based pay, productivity-sharing and gain-sharing plans. To state this differently, an employee in any of these US state and local governments is far more likely – about five times as likely – to be covered by a pay-for-performance or merit-pay plan than by a pay-for-knowledge or bonus plan.

To examine the determinants of at-risk compensation usage in these governments, an at-risk compensation index was constructed from the survey data. The index incorporates (i.e. assigns points to) the types of incentive compensation plans used by each government, employee coverage of the plans in each government, and the agency or department coverage of the plans in each government.[3] This index was regressed onto several independent and control variables. The statistically significant findings from this analysis (not shown here) were that larger and older governments, governments with relatively high retail sales and income tax rates, governments with high ratios of white-collar to blue-collar employees and total public expenditures to total economic activity, governments with prevailing wage policies, governments in the Midwest and Southwest regions, and governments that recently used a compensation consultant were most likely to use at-risk compensation. Also, among local governments, those with a city manager form of government were significantly more likely to use at-risk compensation than governments with mayor, mayor–council, council only, or other forms of government. By contrast, employee unionization and the presence of a living wage statute or policy were not significantly associated with the use of at-risk compensation in state and local governments. These statistically insignificant findings are substantively significant, however, in that they suggest that governments' use of at-risk compensation is not affected (i.e. constrained) by the unionization of their employees or by their adoption of living wage statutes or policies.

Turning from the breadth to the depth of at-risk compensation usage in government, it may be asked, 'What proportion of total compensation paid to employees of state and local government is accounted for by at-risk compensation?' This is an important question, especially in light of the continuing debate over the (relative) amount of at-risk compensation that is required to motivate enhanced employee performance, whether in the public or the private sector (Ingraham, 1993; Milkovich and Newman, 1999). Data to answer this question were provided by the survey, which asked respondents to state or estimate total direct compensation (i.e. excluding benefits) paid to employees of their respective state and local governments during the most recent fiscal year, and then to state or estimate total incentive compensation paid to these same employees during the most recent fiscal year.[4] Additional questions elicited similar data for major employee or occupational groups and agencies or departments; the data are summarized in Table 8.2.

On the basis of these data, at-risk compensation accounted for slightly more than 6 per cent of base compensation (i.e. salaries and wages) paid to employees of state and local government in 2006. Among employee or occupational groups, at-risk compensation as a proportion of base compensation was highest for technical and professional employees and lowest for clerical and managerial employees. Among agencies or departments, at-risk compensation as a proportion of base compensation

Table 8.2 *Incentive compensation as a percentage of total direct compensation in state and local governments, by agency/department and employee group, fiscal 2006 (%)*

Employee group		Agency/department	
All employee groups	6.15	All agencies/departments	6.15
Professional	7.75	Taxation	8.10
Technical	7.60	Finance	7.55
Operative	6.45	Utilities	7.45
Other service	5.65	Sanitation	6.35
Manual	4.80*	Highways	6.10
Managerial	4.40*	Health care	5.75
Clerical	4.15*	Welfare	5.45
		General services	5.05
		Protective services	4.85
		Motor vehicles	4.15
		Public works	3.85
		Criminal justice	3.05**

Note: *(**) Significantly different from other employee groups at p = < 0.10 (0.05).
Source: 2006 Survey of state and local governments.

was highest in taxation, finance and utilities and lowest in criminal justice, public works and motor vehicles. On balance, then, the use of at-risk compensation appears widespread – that is, broad – in state and local government, but the amount of such compensation relative to base compensation is small – that is, not very deep, falling well short of the depth that most experts believe is required to enhance employee and government performance (Levine, 1997; Risher, 1999).

At-risk compensation perceptions and preferences

Now that we have considered patterns of actual at-risk compensation usage in US state and local governments, let us consider next the perceptions and preferences of key public sector 'actors' regarding such compensation; the main groups of actors include public officials, managers, employees and citizens. Of particular interest are (1) differences among these groups regarding perceived at-risk compensation usage in government, (2) differences between actual and perceived use of at-risk compensation, and (3) differences regarding preferences for at-risk compensation usage. For this purpose, the aforementioned study included surveys that were administered to samples of elected officials, managers, (non-management) employees, and residents of six state governments and 25 local governments (none of which was located in the six states). Sample selection yielded 110 elected officials, 132 managers, 220 employees and 440 residents to whom the survey was mailed.[5] This procedure, together with a follow-up mailing and telephone calls to 20 per cent of the total sample, resulted in an overall response rate of 62 per cent, composed of 57 per cent of elected officials, 64 per cent of managers, 59 per cent of employees and 65 per cent of residents.

As summarized in Table 8.3, large majorities of elected officials and managers believe that at-risk compensation is used by their respective governments, compared to only 41 per cent of employees and 26 per cent of residents. When asked about the percentage of government employees covered by at-risk compensation, the responses ranged from a high of 75 per cent among elected officials to a low of 15 per cent among residents. When asked to estimate the percentage of total direct employee compensation represented by at-risk compensation in their governments, the mean responses were 15 per cent among elected officials, 9 per cent among managers, 6 per cent among employees and 3 per cent among residents. Several of these inter-group differences were statistically significant.

Table 8.3 *Perceptions of and preferences for incentive compensation usage in six state and 25 local governments, by respondent group, 2006 (%)*

	Perceptions of:		
Respondent group	*Incentive comp. used by own government (% responded 'yes')*	*Percentage of employees covered by incentive comp. (response mean %)*	*Incentive comp. as percentage of total direct comp. (response mean %)*
All groups (*n* = 563)	51	49	8
Elected officials (*n* = 63)	71	75	15
Managers (*n* = 84)	66	64	9***
Employees (*n* = 130)	41*	44**	6***
Residents (*n* = 286)	26*	15**	3***
	Preferences for:		
Respondent group	*Incentive comp. use by own government (% favouring)*	*Type of incentive comp. plan (plan with highest % favouring)*	*Incentive comp. as percentage of total direct comp. (response mean %)*
All Groups (*n* = 563)	74	71 (skill-based pay) 69 (gain-sharing)	16
Elected officials (*n* = 63)	85	91 (pay-for-performance)	12***
Managers (*n* = 84)	78	84 (bonus pay)	20
Employees (*n* = 130)	61**	72 (skill-based pay) 64 (pay-for-knowledge)	14***
Residents (*n* = 286)	72	77 (productivity-sharing) 74 (gain-sharing)	11***

Note: *(**,***) Significantly different from elected officials, managers and/or residents at p = < 0.10 (0.05, 0.01).
Source: 2006 Survey of state and local governments.

Notably, employees were more accurate than elected officials, managers and residents in their estimates of the ratio of at-risk compensation to total direct compensation in these governments. Using data from this study's first survey, the mean ratio of at-risk compensation to total direct compensation in these governments was 6.80 in the most recent fiscal year, with a standard deviation of 1.65 per cent and a range from 3.50 to 8.10 per cent. Thus, employees' mean estimate of 6 per cent for this ratio was close to the actual ratio, whereas elected officials and managers substantially overestimated the actual ratio and residents substantially underestimated the actual ratio of at-risk compensation to total direct compensation in their respective governments (Table 8.3).

Survey respondents were also asked about their preferences for using at-risk compensation by government. As shown in Table 8.3, 85 per cent of officials, 78 per cent of managers, 61 per cent of employees and 72 per cent of residents favoured at-risk compensation. Across the four surveyed groups, the most common reason for favouring such use was 'to improve government performance'. Elected officials in particular cited 'increased agency accountability' in favouring the use of at-risk compensation by government, whereas managers most often cited 'increased employee motivation' and residents cited 'better-quality services' in this regard. Employees who favoured greater use of at-risk compensation by their governments cited 'increased compensation' as the main rationale for their position, while employees who opposed greater use of at-risk compensation by their governments cited 'management favouritism', 'pay inequity' and 'measurement problems' as the main reasons for their position.

Concerning the types of public sector at-risk compensation favoured by survey respondents, overall support was strongest for pay-for-performance and skill-based pay arrangements and weakest for bonus plans. Among the four surveyed groups, officials most strongly favoured performance-based pay, managers most strongly favoured bonus pay, employees most strongly favoured skill-based pay and pay-for-knowledge, and residents most strongly favoured productivity-sharing and gain-sharing-type incentive compensation plans (Table 8.3). In explaining their preferences, managers view bonus pay as recognition for achievement of agency or department-wide performance objectives and as a mechanism for bringing them 'up (or closer) to par' with their private sector counterparts. Notably, and by contrast, employees explained their aversion to performance-based pay and merit-pay plans by questioning management's competence to establish performance or merit criteria and to judge employee performance or merit. These employees regard skill-based pay and pay-for-knowledge plans as relatively unambiguous and, because such plans are viewed as enhancing their work-related competences, favour them over other at-risk compensation plans.

As to their preferences regarding the amount of total direct compensation that should be represented by at-risk compensation in their governments, the mean response was 16 per cent for the entire sample and 12 per cent among officials, 20 per cent among managers, 14 per cent among employees and 11 per cent among residents (Table 8.3). Thus, all of these groups favour a significantly larger ratio of at-risk compensation to total direct compensation than actually exists in these governments as a whole (i.e. 6.80 per cent) or in the single government with the highest ratio (i.e. 8.10 per cent). However, managers, employees and residents favour a larger ratio, while elected officials favour a lower ratio of at-risk compensation to total direct compensation than they respectively believe presently exists in these governments.

To summarize, analysis of data obtained from samples of elected officials, managers, employees and residents of six state and 25 local governments indicates that all these groups have strong, though varying, preferences for the use of at-risk compensation by their respective governments. Additionally, all four groups would prefer that such at-risk compensation be a larger proportion of total direct compensation than is actually the case in these governments. In other words, they prefer more pay at risk in public sector compensation systems. This study also found that perceptions of and preferences regarding governments' use of at-risk compensation are systematically related to certain demographic characteristics of survey respondents as well as to particular economic and organizational characteristics of the governments themselves.[6]

The future of at-risk compensation in the US public sector

On balance, the story told herein is one of broad but not deep use of at-risk compensation in the US public sector. Most jobs and employees in the governments studied here are covered by one or another type of at-risk compensation plan, but the amount of such compensation as a proportion of total direct compensation is relatively small compared to that in the private sector and to the (relative) amount of compensation that motivation and compensation theories suggest is required to bring about improved individual and organizational performance. Looking ahead, it may be asked, once again, 'What are the prospects for greater use of at-risk compensation in the US public sector?' To answer this question requires prognostication about compensation developments in both the public and the private sectors.

Among the factors that imply deeper future use of incentive compensation by government are the preferences of citizen-residents as well as employees, managers and elected officials. As shown earlier, each of these groups clearly prefers more use of incentive compensation by government, especially a higher ratio of incentive compensation to total direct compensation, than presently exists. It is one thing for scholars, practitioners and public sector experts to advocate greater use of pay for performance by government, but quite another, more compelling, thing for citizens, managers, employees and elected officials to advocate the same. If representative democracy works effectively, the preferences of these actors should influence future practice and thereby lead to deeper use of incentive compensation by government.

More extensive adoption by governments of prevailing wage policies and more aggressive implementation of such policies by governments that already have such policies in place should also lead to broader and deeper use of incentive compensation in the public sector. The available evidence shows that governments with prevailing wage policies are more likely to practise incentive compensation than governments without such policies. Furthermore, governments that implement their prevailing wage policies by conducting their own pay (compensation) surveys use incentive compensation more broadly and deeply than governments that have prevailing wage policies but do not conduct their own pay surveys. In this regard, the preference of elected officials for greater use of incentive compensation in the public sector is likely to lead more governments to adopt prevailing wage policies, especially if coupled with arguments advanced by those who favour the broader 're-invention' of government (Levine, 1997; Gaebler and Osborne, 1992). An additional pressure on governments with prevailing wage policies to conduct their own pay surveys is likely to emanate from unionized public employees, thereby also potentially leading to deeper use of incentive compensation by government. This view is consistent with the empirical finding that public employee unionization is not negatively associated with – does not serve as a barrier to – the use of incentive compensation by government.

As noted earlier, proponents of government re-invention typically contend that such re-invention will result in smaller, less hierarchical, more efficient and responsive government. But the movement to re-invent government may also be seen as a movement to preserve government and, in this regard, to limit the extent to which public services are subcontracted to industry or privatized altogether. From this perspective, achieving the relatively limited goals of government re-invention will most likely be aided by greater use of incentive compensation in the public sector, especially for executives and managers. Such incentives can include bonuses for department heads in municipal governments who manage their operations particularly efficiently over a multi-year period, meaning that their operational expenditures do not exceed or even fall below budgeted expenditures. In another example, citizen (external customer) satisfaction with government services, as determined through surveys of random samples of residents of local government jurisdictions, can serve as one criterion for determining bonus or performance-based payments to local, state and even federal government executives and managers. The more fundamental point, however, is that the government re-invention movement is likely to enhance rather than retard the use of incentive compensation by government.

Just as the economic recession of the early 1990s spurred additional use of incentive compensation by government, the economic recessions of the 2000s are likely to do the same. Though relatively mild by historical standards, the 2000s recessions, like others before them, resulted in shrinking governmental revenues and budgets, conversion in many governments of budget surpluses to budget deficits, and public sector workforce reductions. In order to preserve and deliver public services in such an economic environment, and also to ward off further erosion of their resources, governments will most likely go further and deeper in their use of incentive compensation – perhaps in the same way that firms that become overly mature make greater use of incentive compensation as a tool for renewing themselves (Milkovich and Stevens, 2000).

It may be argued that a focus on direct compensation, including incentive compensation, in the public sector overlooks employment stability and fringe benefits in this sector, both of which are often claimed to be significantly greater than in the private sector (Kellough and Selden, 1997; Risher et al., 1997). From this perspective, consideration of direct compensation, including incentive compensation, together with fringe benefits and employee turnover/retention, will show that, on balance, the private and public sectors are in rough equilibrium in so far as their compensation or reward practices and labour market positioning are concerned. Stated another way, the higher ratio of incentive compensation to total direct compensation in industry than in government can be explained – and is offset – by comparatively lower employment stability and fringe benefits in industry than in government. Following this reasoning, there is no rationale for increasing either the use of incentive compensation or the ratio of incentive compensation to total direct compensation in government.

While it is true that continuity of employment is relatively greater in government than in industry, this has been true for a long time, including when governments did not use incentive compensation.[7] Furthermore, there is now more volatility – less stability – in government employment than in prior eras. As to fringe benefits, government employers do expend a larger portion of a payroll dollar on fringe benefits than do private employers (US Department of Labor, 2005:96, table 6), but this was also the case when governments did not use incentive compensation. What has changed most in the past two decades is the rapid growth in the private sector of incentive compensation as a proportion of total direct compensation, which contrasts sharply with the modest growth of such compensation in the public sector. In the light of this widening difference or gap, arguments about the superior employment stability and fringe benefits in government compared to industry are unlikely to stem other, aforementioned pressures for expanded use of incentive compensation in the public sector.

Other factors, however, may mitigate expanded future use of incentive compensation in the public sector. As noted earlier, many governments have in place prevailing wage policies that require public sector pay to be set in consideration of private sector pay. While there are both market and equity rationales to support a prevailing wage policy, governments have been shown systematically to implement this policy by 'overpaying' employees at the lower end of the skill/occupation distribution and 'underpaying' employees at the upper end of the skill/occupation distribution (Fogel and Lewin, 1974; Lewin, 1974) so that governments to some extent ignore private market pay data (even when they collect it) and adopt more egalitarian pay structures than those in industry. Such egalitarianism is further reinforced by the widespread use of minimum wage statutes by state and local governments, statutes that typically provide for higher minimums than those required of private employers. Hence, equity considerations dominate market considerations in public sector pay-setting, resulting in significantly less steep occupational pay structures and much smaller executive-to-employee pay ratios than in the private sector. It is unlikely that these intersectoral pay policy and practice differences will change markedly in future. Indeed, to the extent that new incentive compensation initiatives threaten relatively egalitarian public sector pay structures, such initiatives are likely to be curtailed or abandoned.

Further evidence of government's dominant concern for pay equity rests in the recent adoption by numerous local governments of 'living wage' statutes and policies that go beyond minimum wage laws that apply only to governments' own employees. Fuelled in part by periods of rapid economic growth during the 1990s and 2000s and in part by perceived widening of economic inequality, elected officials in Los Angeles, Philadelphia, Chicago, Santa Monica, St Louis and numerous other US cities have enacted living wage statutes requiring contractors, subcontractors and consultants to the local governments to pay (at least) the specified living wage to their employees. Indeed, under these statutes a written commitment to paying this wage is required of contractors, subcontractors and consultants as a condition of their doing business and securing contracts with a municipal government. Typically, these living wage statutes specify two pay rates, one being lower if the employer provides fringe benefits to employees and the other being higher if the employer does not provide such fringe benefits. As an example, the City of Santa Monica's living wage statute calls for contractors, subcontractors and consultants to pay their employees $10.50 per hour if fringe benefits are provided and $13.25 per hour if fringe benefits are not provided. During economic recession the further spread of governmental living wage statutes is problematic and some of these statutes may be suspended or rescinded. Nevertheless, the existence of such statutes provides further evidence of government's dominant concern for equity over market considerations in the area of compensation – whether public sector or private sector compensation. Instructively, none of these governments' living wage statutes so much as mentions incentive compensation for private employees, implying that such compensation is also of relatively minor concern to these governments, per se.

On balance, and looking ahead to the next several years, one can expect incentive compensation to become somewhat more widely used by governments. This forecast gives substantial weight to the argument that in the case of many of the services it provides, government is no longer a monopolist; there are various private market alternatives or supplements to publicly provided services (Meehan, 1991). This forecast is also based in part on the evidence that elected officials, government managers, public employees and citizen-residents of government jurisdictions prefer deeper use of incentive compensation, and in part on the likely continued growth of incentive compensation in the private sector which, in turn, will widen the private–public sector gap in this regard. While governments at all levels will no doubt continue to include equity considerations in their compensation policies and practices, they will place relatively stronger emphasis on market and constituency considerations in changing these policies and practices – meaning more use of at-risk compensation.

Strategies of change in public sector compensation

Given this forecast, how can public sector organizations manage the change from pay for time to greater use of pay at risk? To answer this question, consider three strategies for change, namely (1) proceeding experimentally, (2) diffusing or spreading successful experiments, and (3) overcoming resistance to change.

Proceeding experimentally

As with any organizational change, a change from time-based to (relatively more) at-risk compensation in the public sector can proceed on an experimental rather than on an organization-wide basis. To illustrate, when pursuing a productivity-based gain-sharing pay practice for its employees, the City of New York focused on its sanitation service and negotiated a series of 'productivity-sharing' provisions into collective bargaining agreements with the Sanitation Workers Union (a Teamsters affiliate). These provisions provided for bonus pay to sanitation workers based upon regularly reported, quantitative measures of refuse picked up, processed and disposed of on a street-by-street and area-by-area basis. When volumes achieved in this regard exceeded 'standard' volumes on a department-wide basis over specified time periods – for example, one month – without changes in manning levels, a gain in the form of a cash payment was made to all sanitation workers. When volumes achieved were at standard or below standard, no such cash payment was forthcoming. This compensation arrangement was accompanied by technological changes, such as automated side-loading refuse container pick-up trucks, standardization of the size and configuration of refuse bins, computer-controlled compression of picked up waste in truck rear-end waste holders, and enhanced in-front cab, driver-operator electronic controls of refuse pick-up, compression and disposal functions. The longer-term results of this experiment included a substantially increased volume of refuse pick-up, processing and disposal, a shorter average time to complete a pick-up, processing and disposal work cycle, reduction of the average sanitation crew size from three to two employees per truck, substantially increased total compensation per sanitation worker, and a modest reduction in the ratio of total department-wide labour costs to total operating costs (Lewin, 1987).

Another experiment, also based in New York City, featured the introduction, reporting and monitoring of weekly crime statistics on a precinct-by-precinct basis in the city's Police Department. This department-wide computer-driven system, known as COMSTAT (i.e. command statistics), is accompanied by a weekly Monday morning meeting of senior Police Department officials and all precinct captains in which each precinct's crime statistics are reviewed on an overall and category-by-category basis (e.g. robbery, assaults and property destruction) and in which each precinct captain is asked to explain changes – especially increases – in criminal activity, arrests and clearance rates. This system, which has been emulated in other US police departments, is accompanied by bonus payments to precinct captains whose precincts show short-term as well as longer-term declines in criminal activity, especially violent-crime-type criminal activity, and is also used as one factor in determining which precinct captains will (and will not) be promoted to higher-level positions in the department.

Still another experiment – a series of experiments – in public sector at-risk compensation has been conducted in various US local school districts, specifically involving teachers. In some of these experiments, teachers are awarded annual bonus pay based on student evaluations or the percentage of students who successfully complete the school year and pass on to the next grade or the scores achieved by students on standardized knowledge tests. Similar experiments have been undertaken in British schools (Marsden and Belfield, 2007). In other, related experiments, school principals and assistant principals have been made eligible for bonus pay based on the percentage of students who graduate from their respective junior high (or middle) schools and high schools, and/or on the percentage of students who pass standardized knowledge tests. These experiments are controversial, primarily because student achievement is believed to be influenced by factors outside the control of school officials and teachers, but also because of the incentives provided in these pay arrangements for teachers to liberally pass students on to the next grade and for school principals to permit underachieving students to graduate. Nevertheless, such experiments underscore the strong interest among the tax-paying citizenry, elected officials, including school officials, and teachers in using at-risk compensation to further the strategic objectives of public schools.

Diffusing successful experiments

It is one thing for an experiment to be conducted successfully, but quite another to diffuse the results of such an experiment more broadly to other parts of an organization, let alone throughout an organization as a whole. This is reflected in the widespread attention given in the organization behaviour and strategy literatures to the diffusion of innovation (Tushman and O'Reilly, 1997). The same dictum applies to public sector compensation – that is, it is difficult to extend and replicate a successful experiment in at-risk compensation from one governmental department or agency to others, and even more so to the entire governmental entity. Why is this?

One major stumbling block or bar to the diffusion of at-risk compensation experiments in the public sector lies in the vertical organizational structure of governments in which each department is viewed and for the most part treated as a separate, distinct entity. While there is a long-standing rationale for this form of governmental organization based on concepts of functional specialization, distinct citizen-customer base, and in some cases separate funding sources, from a compensation perspective there is good reason to question the persistence and suitability of this organizational form. When it comes to the recruiting, selection and hiring of employees, a government typically uses standardized criteria that apply across departments and agencies. The same is typically true of a government's job classification, performance appraisal, training, promotion and discipline standards. And it is even more true when it comes to compensation, given that a government typically maintains one overall pay system or grid featuring specified job grades, pay per grade and pay steps per grade. This type of pay system, which has its antecedents and analogues in private sector pay systems, is grounded in principles of equity – that is, treating all employees of a government the same – and non-patronage – that is, basing employment and pay on standardized criteria rather than on political connections or fealty.

As the aforementioned experiments in public sector at-risk compensation suggest, however, the vertical organization structure and standardized human resource management practices of a typical government may be outdated when it comes to motivating employee performance and delivering services to the citizenry. This, in turn, means that government officials and managers should seek to modify such arrangements, either by top-down reforms or by a relatively more bottom-up approach in which successful experiments in at-risk compensation in one or more agencies and departments are extended to (or attempted in) others. Given the difficulty of achieving top-down-led organizational reform, a bottom-up approach is more likely to be successful when it comes to diffusing innovation at-risk compensation in the public sector.

Overcoming resistance to change

Rather than being 'abnormal' or unusual, resistance to change is typical in organizations whenever a new initiative is undertaken. Such resistance has been well documented and is fundamentally understandable when one considers that organizations are established to bring order, control and coordination to the activities that permit them to generate goods and/or services (Coch and French, 1948). Instructively, resistance to change is weakest during crisis conditions and therefore stronger when conditions fall short of crisis.

Applying these principles to public sector compensation, it is a rare government that will fall into the (private sector) company equivalent of bankruptcy; generally speaking, governments do not go out of business. But as with companies, governments do move through various stages of the organizational life cycle – that is, some are relatively young start-up types; others are in a growth stage; some others are mature, perhaps highly mature; and some are in various stages of decline. When it comes to compensation, therefore, a compelling case cannot be made that governments should adopt widespread at-risk compensation policies and practices because the very existence of these governments is in question.

Yet if going out of business, so to speak, was the only circumstance in which organizational change would be made, there would be very few changes to organizations irrespective of their public or private sector status. Hence, it is more useful to consider an evolutionary perspective when it comes to changing public sector compensation policies and practices. The evidence adduced in this chapter strongly suggests that there is widespread support for changing public sector compensation away from an emphasis on pay for time towards an emphasis on pay at risk. It is incumbent on public sector officials and managers to take cognizance of this support and to undertake new initiatives regarding at-risk compensation for the employees whom they are ostensibly managing (some of whom are among those supporting more use of at-risk compensation). They can do so and potentially make progress in this regard by following the well-established principles of unfreezing employee attitudes towards, and behaviour regarding, established compensation practices, introducing on an experimental basis or diffusing on a successful experiment basis new initiatives in at-risk compensation, and motivating support among employees for such new initiatives. For this three-step process to work well, public sector officials and managers must fundamentally believe in the principles and propriety of at-risk compensation – and they have a variety of successful experiments in this regard to justify such a belief.

Conclusions

The key theoretical and practical implications of the preceding discussion for change management in relation to public sector compensation are as follows. First, and following the precepts of contemporary models of change management, public management scholars should more explicitly and forcefully incorporate into their models of change management those exogenous factors – movement towards more market-oriented economies, political regime changes, rising citizen dissatisfaction with publicly provided services, enhanced scrutiny of the quality and costs of public services, and increased recognition of the common problems faced by large organizations irrespective of their private, public or hybrid sectoral status – that are driving the push for more at-risk public sector compensation. Second, these same scholars should incorporate into their models of change management key concepts of payment for time versus payment for output, and also take account of the considerable evidence showing the trend away from the former and towards the latter, not only in the private sector but in the public sector as well. Third, public management scholars should incorporate into their models of change evidence about citizen preferences for more at-risk public sector compensation, especially because it is the tax-paying citizenry that ultimately must provide the resources for and approval of new public sector at-risk compensation initiatives.

Regarding public management practitioners, especially high-level practitioners (i.e. elected officials and senior executives or managers), they should pay particular heed to examples of successful public sector at-risk compensation initiatives and carefully assess the extent to which the organizations they lead and manage are susceptible to the application of similar initiatives. They should also consider and undertake small-scale, experimental at-risk compensation initiatives in those agencies and departments that most lend themselves to such initiatives, and then extend the successful initiatives to other agencies and departments and even to their organizations as a whole. By doing so, these officials and executives can demonstrate that they can effectively lead organizational change rather than simply follow long-standing public sector compensation practices.

Notes

1 As examples, performance-based pay was defined as 'pay changes based on achievement of individual employee performance goals, such as those set through Management by Objectives (MBO)', and merit pay was defined as 'pay changes based on the results of a supervisor's appraisal of an employee's job performance'.

2 The survey was sent to the chief administrative officer of each of the state governments and the chief administrative officer, head personnel officer or, in some cases, city manager of the local governments. Of the 403 completed surveys, about 50 per cent were signed by a head personnel officer, 40 per cent by a chief administrative officer and 10 per cent by other officials or managers (e.g. city manager, head budget officer or head financial officer).

3 Values for this index ranged between 0 and 40, with a mean value of 17 and a standard deviation of 3.6. Another version of the index includes the length of time, in years, that each incentive plan has been in place. For this version, the incentive compensation index ranged between 0 and 50, the mean value was 20, and the standard deviation was 3.9. On average, incentive compensation plans in these governments had been in place for 7.2 years. Two local governments had had one or another type of incentive compensation plan in place for more than 50 years.

4 The survey did not ask respondents for data on or estimates of fringe benefits for employees, which are more difficult to value than direct compensation. More to the point, fringe benefits are generally not considered a form of incentive compensation, and benefit coverages typically do not vary by agency or department or employee group in state and local government (Risher *et al.*, 1997).

5 None of the residents was an elected official, manager or employee of the six state or 25 local governments. That is, the resident sample is entirely separate from the three other groups and is regarded as representing citizens of the respective government jurisdictions included in this portion of the study. A variety of sources were used to identify and select the four sample populations, including state and local government personnel listings, human resource/personnel directors, and zip code listings. Additional information about sample selection for the four surveyed groups as well as design and administration of the surveys is available from the author.

6 For a related study, see Lewin (2003).

7 For example, unemployment among 'government workers', as reported by the US Bureau of Labor Statistics, is typically much lower than among non-agricultural wage and salary workers in the US economy, and this continues to be true even as overall unemployment has declined sharply in recent years. Thus, in 2002, 2003 and 2004, unemployment rates were 5.0, 4.6 and 4.3 per cent respectively among non-agricultural wage and salary workers, compared with 2.6, 2.3 and 2.2 per cent respectively among government workers (US Department of Labor, 2005).

9 Delayed due to heavy turbulence: an analysis of power, political tactics and, ultimately, the abortion of a major organizational change initiative

Eric Lofquist and Rune Lines

- Introduction
- Organizational change and power
- The Avinor case: Take-Off 05
- Discussion
- Conclusions

Introduction

This chapter reports on a qualitative, in-depth case study of how power, and the use of power, determined the fate of a major organizational change initiative in Avinor, a Norwegian public service organization. Avinor, an abbreviation for Aviation Norway, is a state-owned limited company that owns and operates 46 airports (14 of these in association with the armed forces) and is responsible for air traffic control services and airport management.

The chapter focuses on three issues related to power in organizational change. First, it tries to identify the power bases used in the political play between proponents and opponents of the change initiative. Power is highly situational (Mizruchi, 1992) – that is, both the presence and the usefulness of particular forms of power vary from one situation to another. Therefore, it seems reasonable to try to increase knowledge of the types of power that allow for political action during the particular change initiative reported on. Second, the chapter sets out to gain more knowledge about the behaviours used in political games during organizational change. Much of what is known about power-plays and influence strategies utilized in organizations is based on research in non-change settings, and it can be argued that portfolios of behaviours during major change could be different from behaviours observed in more mundane day-to-day settings. Third, the chapter sets out to contribute to knowledge about who are the individuals and groups that become involved in political activity during change, as well as what their motives for this engagement are.

Organizational change and power

Because of their near-continuous changes in thinking, motivation, people, practices, and certain aspects of strategy and structure, it can be argued that most organizations are in a permanent state of change. This makes the distinction between periods of organizational change and stability blurred. The concept of 'organizational change' is perhaps best seen as fuzzy, with no sharp borders delineating it from other important organizational conditions. For the purpose of this chapter, the type of situation we have in mind is a clearly identified initiative taken by some actors, within or outside the focal organization, in order to change for the better the organization's systems, formal structure, strategy or work processes. Typically, the initiative is accompanied by a set of formal objectives for improvement in one, or several, areas of organizational performance.

Organizations are partly bounded rational systems striving towards a common set of goals, and partly 'polities' with interest groups, distributions of rights and duties, and governance systems (Cyert and March, 1963). Organizations have been conceptualized as 'contested terrains' where actors with different values struggle for control – a battle won by the most powerful. Although power issues are permanent parts of organizational life, there are several reasons why they emerge as an especially important factor in times of change. First, organizational change often involves changes in power patterns in organizations. Such changes in the distribution of power among actors, groups, organizational subunits and power positions, vis-à-vis external constituencies, may be intended, and may even be the primary motive behind a change initiative. More often, perhaps, changes in power patterns are a secondary and unintended consequence of changes to other aspects of the organizational structures and systems. For example, the introduction of a performance

measurement system, while primarily seen as an incentive system and a
decision-making tool, simultaneously increases the power of those with
access to the information and hence can lead to shifts in power
relationships within and between organizational units. Findings by
Tsamenyi *et al.* support the presence of such effects. On the basis of their
investigation of changes in accounting and financial information systems
in the Spanish electricity company Sevillana-Endesa, they reported that

> [s]ome of the employees also questioned the top management's claim
> that the main rationale for the unified accounting and financial
> information system (SIE-2000) was to reduce costs. Instead, these
> employees were of the view that the SIE-2000 was implemented
> mainly to facilitate head office control over the subsidiaries.
>
> (2006:422)

Second, organizational change seems to chronically activate latent power.
Latent power is always present in, and between, organizations because of
individuals' and groups' differential positions on relevant power
dimensions. However, prior to major change initiatives this power is not
used, and thus is largely an invisible organizational trait. Organizational
change generates short- and long-term benefits and hardships that are
unevenly distributed among individuals and groups. Buchanan and
Badham (1999:610) point out that '[s]ignificant reconfigurations
invariably trigger conflict and resistance, both overt and covert, motivated
by a blend of organizational concern and self-interest.'

Third, and finally, new forms of power are created during organizational
change as a response to individual and group attitudes towards the
pending change. Actors do not only use their existing power bases in
order to fight for or against organizational change. If important values are
perceived to be threatened by the change, they respond by building new
power bases, such as by means of information-gathering or the
establishment of coalitions composed of members from within and/or
outside the organization. Before introducing SIE-2000, the top
management of Sevillana-Endesa made changes to the key management
team and appointed powerful and influential project leaders in order to
accumulate enough power to implement the new financial information
system (Tsamenyi *et al.*, 2006). In times of relative stability, organizations
are characterized by political alignments – that is, coalitions made up of
individuals with similar values and interests (Bacharach and Lawler,
1998). Such alignments may be used during change for concerted action
in support of, or against, a proposed change. In addition, new alignments
may form based on a new set of common interests that are created by

specifics of the change which threaten or favour specific values or interests (Lines, 2006). For example, if the general level of work autonomy is threatened by a proposed organization-wide standardization of work processes, coalitions may form across subunits with little prior history of political alignment.

Together, such processes give power issues during organizational change a strong dynamic flavour that is not fully reflected in the traditional organizational literature on power, influence and politics. Much of the empirical literature on power in organizations tends to focus on more static issues of established power bases and their interrelationships with, and use of, limited sets of influence tactics. This does not imply that dynamic aspects are totally ignored in writings on power. On the contrary, writers such as Mizruchi (1992) stress that power is situational, and that the intra-organizational distribution of types and amounts of power varies from one situation to the next. For example, the legitimate power held by a given manager varies greatly from one decision area to another.

Power bases during organizational change

The amount of power held by an actor during change can be seen as some form of combination of the actor's position in a number of power bases. Hence, organizations can be seen as n-dimensional power spaces, where n equals the number of relevant bases of power. According to the situational view of power, n is likely to vary across time and so is the actual composition of power bases for a given n. A large number of power bases have been discussed in the literature, but little empirical research has attempted to clarify the exact bases that underlie political action during organizational change. One important power base in modern organizations is expertise. Actor A has expert power over actor B when he or she possesses knowledge that is important to the achievement of B's objectives. A's power increases to the extent that few alternative knowledge-holders are available to B. Expert power is highly situational because the content of relevant knowledge shifts from one situation to the other. For example, in the change situation at Sevillana-Endesa, IT experts became powerful because they had knowledge that was decisive for the smooth functioning of the change. Their power was partly caused by top management's decision to construe the change in exclusively technical terms, where the organizational implications of the change were actively downplayed in an attempt to control change recipients' reactions.

Political action during organizational change

A recurring theme in the political literature on organization is how latent power is activated through verbal and non-verbal behaviours in order to influence outcomes in organizations. A number of influence strategies, or power tactics, have been identified, and some of these behaviours have also been linked to specific power bases as behavioural tendencies of power holders. Generally, this research has supported a link between what seems to be a preference for specific behaviours held by actors with particular forms of power (e.g. Yukl and Falbe, 1990; Yukl and Tracey, 1992; Lines, 2007). Although latent power – that is, an actor's position in relevant power dimensions (bases) – may influence others' thinking, emotions, attitudes and behaviour in the absence of specific power-based behaviours, most writers seem to agree that the effects of power are heavily mediated by the power-holder's actual or potential behaviour. A direct influence may occur when a target person, or group, actively reflects on how a power-holder would react to their own thinking, emotions, attitudes or behaviours vis-à-vis an issue (i.e. change). Theories of social information processing (Salancik and Pfeffer, 1978) would imply that a direct influence, unmediated by behaviour, could be more often present than the mainstream power literature seems to presume. For example, when deciding whether to comply with, or resist, the consequences of a reorganization, organizational members may take into account what the reactions of peers, subordinates and superiors would be to their alternative reactive options. In their discussion of innovation as political processes, Frost and Egri (1991) list a number of political games that have been identified in prior research within and outside the area of innovation. These include acquisition or expansion of power through mentoring, sponsorship, upward influence and empire-building; maintenance of existing power bases via lording, rule-citing and appeals to higher authorities for support; manipulative communication by means of impression management, labelling, reasoning, assertiveness, manipulative persuasion, gatekeeping, covering up, and networking; and controlling resources and outcomes including budgeting, expertise, line versus staff, rival camps, making out, negotiation, bargaining, coalition-building, strategic candidates, building consensus and framing perspectives, management and resisting change by controlling decision premises and agendas, and selective use of decision criteria. At a deeper level, Deetz (1985) identifies four ways in which political actors may construe an issue (i.e. the change and a specific way in which to view its consequences) for their own benefit: naturalization, neutralization, legitimation and socialization. When change proponents and opponents play the *naturalization* game, the change, or status quo, is presented as the only reasonable way to work, organize, control, etc. The game can be played by referring to leaders in the industry or sector. *Neutralization* is a tactic by which actors in the power struggle actively downplay the distributive aspects of the proposed change (or status quo). Most organizational changes carry with them unintended distributive consequences and thereby create sub-groups of winners and losers. For example, the implementation of participative decision-making (PDM) is simultaneously a way to tap employee expertise and a change in middle management power and prestige (Cotton *et al.*, 1988). Proponents of PDM use the neutralization tactic when they focus exclusively on the organizational and employee benefits of this arrangement.

These vehicles of social construction of change remind us that power struggles are concerned not only with the distribution of material goods, but also about meaning. Actors engage in fights to influence dominant meanings, ideologies and discourses (Morrill *et al.*, 2003). Such fights are highly recursive, as arguments and counter-arguments, framing and reframing of issues, move back and forth between groups of stakeholders. The process seems remote from the model of one-way communication prevailing in many normative texts on change management.

Actors in the political game

There is little research that tries to identify who are the actors that become activated in political behaviour during change. Simon and Oakes (2006:113) define power as follows: 'A (a person or group) has power insofar as it recruits human agency in service of its agenda.' From this definition a distinction can be made between two sets of agents: the agents who take initiatives to support or resist a pending change, and the agents who are recruited (mobilized) to support or resist by this first group of agents. Theories of organizational members' reactions to organizational change (Lines, 2005, 2006) predict that actors in the political game would be those whose important values are threatened by change. Actors who think that their values are strengthened by the change are likely to engage actively through a variety of political behaviours in its support. Their roles would either be as initiative-takers or as recruited members of the *ad hoc* political coalition. Actors who believe that important values are threatened will engage in political behaviours in order to modify or terminate the change, or at least alleviate its most

noxious consequences. Actors who believe that the change has little
consequence for important values are indifferent to the change and will
most likely remain passive during the change process. In the case of
Sevillana-Endesa (cited earlier), employees became politically active
because a number of relevant values were challenged by the change. First,
the change implied some level of downsizing and relocation (both within
the organization and geographically). Both of these consequences are
directly related to the core work value 'job security'. Second, the changes
were perceived to negatively affect organizational autonomy vis-à-vis the
holding group and job content. Finally, a very low level of authentic
participation was experienced by the affected employees. Together, these
perceived negative consequences for important values led employees to
engage in a political struggle that was ultimately lost, but that delayed
change implementation.

The Avinor case: Take-Off 05

In this section we follow Avinor during a volatile three-year deliberate
strategic change process that ended abruptly with the sudden departure of
the director, removal of the chief executive officer and replacement of the
chairman of the board. This happened despite the fact that Take-Off 05,
a planned strategic change process, was 80 per cent complete, financial
targets were well ahead of plans, and no change in safety outcomes (the
company's highest stated priority) were reported by the top management
team. So what went wrong?

Background

On 1 January 2003, Luftfartsverket, the Norwegian civil aviation
management authority, was officially transformed into the government-
owned limited company Avinor. This company is responsible for the air
traffic control services, the management and security of 46 national and
regional airports, and all associated national civil aviation infrastructure
in Norway. The transformation was motivated by the international civil
aviation privatization initiative under the banner of corporatization. In the
civil aviation context, corporatization is a New Public Management
initiative with the specific goal of making national civil aviation activities
more competitive and cost-effective, while simultaneously maintaining
and/or improving upon ultra-safe levels of flight operations (ICAO, 2002).

The issue of transforming the government-administered civil aviation organization into a state-owned limited company was first debated by the Norwegian government in early 2000. However, no agreement was reached as to the best organizational form for restructuring at that time. With deteriorating economic conditions within the entire civil aviation industry during the subsequent years, the economic situation, with particular reference to 9/11 as a contributing factor for reduced revenues and future uncertainty for the industry, was eventually considered to be serious. Because of these developments, the Norwegian government's transport committee reopened the transformation discussion. During the subsequent discussions the majority of the political parties believed that the government-administered form in use at the time was the least effective option available, and also potentially problematic in a deteriorating civil aviation environment. Instead, the majority preferred, and recommended, that Luftfartsverket be converted into a limited, state-owned company. This would arguably provide many advantages for the new company that were not available in the current form. The decision to initiate this transformation was issued in a subsequent budget session. Luftfartsverket officially became Avinor, effective on 1 January 2003. This event was chosen as the starting point for a study following the company over a three-year period leading up to the eventual collapse of Take-Off 05 in December 2005.

Take-Off 05 was a results improvement project initiated by Avinor's top management team in early 2002 as a consequence of deteriorating economic results. Supported by government mandates issued with the new company structure, Take-Off 05 went ahead in March 2003 with the primary goal of reducing annual costs within the company by a minimum of 400 million NOK per year by 2006. This complex corporatization process included a new business model, a total reorganization of its management structure, significant downsizing in personnel in order to increase efficiency and reduce costs, adoption of a new safety management system and introduction of new technologies.

The stated goal of the Avinor top management team was for all the change activities to be accomplished without any reduction in customer service, closing of airports or reduction in air traffic safety. Moreover, although the change process was presented as a results improvement programme, the real focus was on cost reduction through downsizing of personnel, with a goal of cutting over 25 per cent of the workforce by 2006. These savings were to be achieved through organizational synergies created by a combination of new operating processes and the implementation of new air traffic control information transfer technologies.

But was the change a success? The company did succeed in changing the business model. In addition, the restructuring and the implementing of a new management system and headquarters structure, covering 80 per cent of the planned changes, were successful. However, in the final analysis the Take-Off 05 project failed to achieve many of the key goals specifically identified by the top management team. First, dramatic disruptions in customer services received near-daily national media focus in 2004/2005, including several periods in which all air traffic in southern Norway was grounded for several days. Of the original 725 employees identified to be cut, fewer than 100 actually left the company through downsizing, but many employees, including air traffic controllers forcibly moved during the restructuring of air traffic control centres in Norway, left the company unexpectedly. In addition, many of the planned changes in operational processes and implementation of new air traffic control technologies were not achieved before the collapse of the project. And finally, national concerns for air traffic safety were so great in 2004 that the government directed the Norwegian National Transportation Board to conduct a national study of air traffic safety in Norway. With the collapse of the Take-Off 05 project in December 2005, all downsizing actions were stopped. Plans to close down another air traffic control centre were put on hold, and eventually abandoned.

The Take-Off 05 project

Take-Off 05 was divided into three distinct phases: analysis, design and implementation. The stated objectives for these phases were to define potential savings, to design solutions and to implement decisions (Avinor, 2003). During the analysis phase, working groups formulated potential savings measures in eleven sub-categories within the company. These analyses were later incorporated into one integrated plan for implementation of the planned process. Participation in the project was described in the following terms:

> Avinor has a comprehensive cooperation model with both the employees and the employees' official representatives. These methods were also used in connection to the results improvement program. The program has also worked out its own communications plan both for the program in its entirety, but also for individual sub-projects. The employees and employee representatives were invited to submit ideas

and recommendations during the entire process, and the central
employee representatives will have regular meetings with the program
leadership and project groups underway. There has been a great deal
of engagement evident and a large number of improvement
suggestions from employees from the entire country.

(Avinor, 2003:4)

This was echoed by the board, which stated: 'The board sees the
importance of a good process with the employee representatives in
coordination with the mandates of the main agreement, and instructs the
administration to prioritize this in their further work.'

The eleven sub-groups were populated with a mixture of senior managers,
employees and external consultants. Although the Norwegian air traffic
controllers' union did not participate directly in the sub-project process,
individual air traffic controllers did participate in the analysis phase of the
project. They were satisfied with their contributions, and believed they
were making a real contribution to the change process. One employee
member of one of the sub-groups stated:

> We were very satisfied with our contribution. We worked hard during
> these brainstorming sessions to find as many potential cost savings as
> possible that would eventually be put into a comprehensive
> implementation plan that would go through an extensive quality
> control and risk analysis process.

The employee representatives believed that their inputs during what were
described as brainstorming sessions for potential savings would be
integrated into an eventual Take-Off 05 implementation plan that would be
both quality-assured by the members and analysed for risk before being
sent to the Avinor board of directors for approval. At the end of the design
phase there was general consensus within the organization regarding the
need for change, including a national model that would reduce the number
of air traffic control centres (ATCCs) in Norway from four to two.

However, when the final implementation plan for Take-Off 05 was
unveiled by the top management team in November 2003, many within
the organization, including the employee members of the various
sub-projects who were directly involved in the design phase of the project,
were stunned by the breadth and depth of the plan, and the pace at which
it was to be implemented. One member stated:

> I was shocked by the Take-Off 05 plan as it was presented to the
> board, as it did not truthfully reflect the expectations of the employee
> members that participated in the planning phase. The management

team simply took all of the potential savings ideas and combined them into one plan that was not integrated, as expected, and was not analysed for quality or potential risk to safety.

The member also added:

> In addition, we [employee members of working groups] were looked upon by our colleagues as being personally responsible for the contents of the plan, and this made life very difficult. I regret that I had anything to do with the Take-Off 05 process, and I will never volunteer for anything again within this organization.

When the plan was officially presented to the Avinor board of directors for approval in November 2003, the three employee representatives on the board expressed their doubts concerning the assumptions upon which the plan was based, and asked for a delay in approving the project so that the key elements upon which the plan was based could be further evaluated. This request was rejected by the board by a vote of 5 to 3, and the Take-Off 05 implementation plan was accepted.

The next shock came three months later when the decision was made to shut down the Trondheim ATCC and to consolidate its activity into the Bodø ATCC, located in northern Norway, over a compressed time-frame. The decision was made by the project management team without any input from the unions or union members, and documentation upon which the decision was based was not released. When it was presented to the board, the employee representatives once again asked for a delay to investigate the background documentation that supported this decision, but again were voted down 5 to 3. It was clear at this point that the participative process was over and that all future decisions would be purely top-down. The acceptance of this decision by the board marks the loss of both the content and the scope of consensus (Markóczy, 2001) concerning the strategic change initiative by the company's strongest subculture (air traffic controllers), and symbolized the first shot of an internal war that would continue until the departure of the CEO in December 2005.

The key players

The main internal actors in the following struggle included the Norwegian air traffic controllers' union, representing 20 per cent of the Avinor employee base, and the new Avinor management structure. The struggle also included numerous influential external stakeholders, including national and international regulatory agencies; the government, represented by the Norwegian Transport Ministry; and the national news media, representing the public interest.

As was mentioned earlier, at the time of the collapse of the Take-Off 05 project, 80 per cent of the planned change had been completed, which is representative of the employee base that presented little or no opposition to the change process. This was mostly because they were represented by various sub-groups that were not strong enough to oppose the change directly. A few of these unionized members later joined with the air traffic controllers' union to express a loss of confidence in the Avinor top management team in a formal letter to the board in the summer of 2004. This action was followed by a 5 to 3 vote of confidence from the board.

A direct result of the Take-Off 05 process was the early removal of many of the key middle managers who would be responsible for the change implementation process, to be replaced by others hand-picked by senior management. The management team described the changes as such:

> As a result of the changed organization, Avinor will employ many new managers at the 2nd and 3rd levels. Many of these new leaders will occupy leading positions in Avinor with significant responsibility and new tasks. It must be assumed that they will not, in the same way as leaders that have followed the entire process, have the same understanding of the process that the company will go through. There must, therefore, be given a certain weight on good organization of the transition phase, as well as, management training and learning for the affected managers. At the same time, it is clear that the candidates in the selection process understand that the positions carry a mandate for fulfilling the measures decided by the steering group for Take-off 05. This also places demands for a clear formulation of the individual projects mandate.
>
> (Avinor, 2003:22)

The new managers were, for the most part, experienced air traffic controllers with significant operative experience but with little or no formal management education, and even less management experience. The employees considered these new managers as 'yes-men' chosen specifically to carry out the plans of the top leaders without resistance.

Power bases

The Avinor top management team had legitimate power that was strongly supported by Avinor's owners, represented by the Norwegian Transport

Ministry. This support was very strong and active, particularly during the transition phase from a government management agency to becoming a state-owned limited company in 2003, and also during the early phases of the internal conflict. While the top leaders were credited with expert knowledge in the field of economics, they were strongly criticized for their total lack of expertise in the area considered most important by the air traffic controllers – specifically, safety considerations in civil aviation operations. Some of the leaders could even be characterized as charismatic, but their charisma seemed to be displayed only to followers located at the same level within the Avinor hierarchy, and did not extend to layers below.

However, as national media attention related to the developing conflict within Avinor became more and more public, the support being given to the top management team by Avinor's owners appeared to weaken gradually over time. At one point the negative media attention was so intense that the safety of the entire civil aviation industry was questioned, causing the government to initiate a national civil aviation safety investigation. The results of the investigation were not totally favourable to the Avinor management team, further affecting government support and fuelling the air traffic controllers' case. This trend continued until a sudden change in government led to a change of transport ministers. This marked the apparent loss of political support for both the Avinor management team and the change process. The CEO resigned two months later, followed shortly thereafter by the chairman of the board.

The Norwegian air traffic controllers' union, on the other hand, representing the largest and most influential individual sub-group within Avinor, had real positional and expert power. This power was supported by a long history of successful conflicts with management, particularly during change processes, the conflicts often leading to visible opposition in the form of organized actions. These conflicts were legendary within the Norwegian memory, kept alive by the news media, and even though there had not been any official union actions in Norway since the early 1990s, these memories were still fresh. This is mostly because air travel is a critical means of transport in Norway, and is totally dependent upon air traffic control. If air traffic controllers strike, Norway essentially stops functioning, and this vision conditions most Norwegians' opinions of air traffic controllers.

Political tactics

The loss of consensus for the change project led to a gradual loss of trust in the Avinor management by the Norwegian air traffic controllers' union. At this point, the union wanted to use its expertise to dispute the data used as the basis for the management's change decisions. The top management team simply resisted by reverting to a purely top-down implementation of the approved plan without deviation, and continued this approach until the collapse. This was possible during the early phases of the change implementation process; however, as the process continued, air traffic controller resistance increased gradually, though no coordinated actions were ever initiated.

This led to loss of efficiency in the form of an increase in the use of sick leave and the unexpected loss of many air traffic controllers who resigned in order to take up work for other employers. In addition, external stakeholders initiated incremental organizational changes that had unexpected significant negative impacts on Take-Off 05. The regulatory agencies, concerned with the deteriorating safety environment, limited the use of overtime, which had a significant impact on several key units within Avinor. Additionally, new requirements for annual certifications for air traffic controllers, together with mandatory refresher training periods and a reduction in the age limit for those working in operational services from 65 to 60, adversely affected the available operative workforce.

One tactic that both the Avinor leaders and the unions used extensively was exploitation of the news media in all forms. At the height of the internal turbulence, newspaper articles addressing the conflict were headline news several times a week. During some periods this increased to several articles per day, and often included national television coverage.

Discussion

Precipitating event

As we have seen, the Take-Off 05 project started out in a mood characterized by relative harmony among initiators and recipients. However, merely three months into the implementation process, this changed abruptly, and a situation of hostility emerged which lasted until the CEO and most of the top management team were replaced. How could this happen? The key precipitating event in this case seems to have been the shift from a participative change management style to a process mode where change recipients' opinions and expertise were no longer considered an important input to the process. This shift coincided with a dramatic change in recipients' attitude towards the Take-Off 05 process, in particular that of the air traffic controllers. From this point onwards the relationship between air traffic controllers and the top management team deteriorated rapidly, and grew into one characterized by suspicion, mistrust and opposition. Trust in leadership and management and behaviours during a period of change can be seen as reflecting a group's attitude towards change (Lines, 2005). A group's attitude towards change results from a process by which individuals consider selected aspects of a change process, and its likely outcome, and relate these aspects to important values (Rokeach, 1973). For example, much research has shown that consideration of fairness during change is strongly associated with the recipients' change-relevant attitudes (Tyler, 1994; Siegel *et al.*, 2005). In this context, the right to influence the change process through participation in decision-making can be considered an important value. The right to participate is simultaneously an instrumental and a terminal value. It is instrumental because research has shown that participation is associated with decision control – that is, the degree to which individuals and groups perceive that they have some influence on the decision outcome. When individuals and groups are invited to participate in decisions, they perceive themselves as having more influence on the decisions made than when they are merely consulted, or when the decision is made in an autocratic manner. The general finding that participation is positively related to job attitudes is partly accounted for by increased perceptions of decision control. The right to participate can also be considered a terminal value – that is, a state that is preferred over non-participation regardless of its influence on decision outcomes. In Norway there is a long tradition of participative leadership and decision-making, and the right to participate in decisions that affect one's work is regulated by law. Hence, in this setting there is a strong baseline expectation among those involved to be invited to participate in processes such as Take-Off 05. These expectations were most likely strengthened further as participants felt that they were playing an important part in the first phase of the process.

The right to participate was not, however, the only value that was challenged in this process. One important professional value among air traffic controllers is that of safety. Throughout their education, safety is stressed as the most important issue to be respected when performing their function. It is likely that members of this profession emphasize safety much more strongly than other important outcomes of their job, such as punctuality and economic efficiency. The focus on safety prevails when they enter organizations such as Avinor, although temporarily the focus may shift to economic efficiency, especially under scenarios of stagnating income and increasing costs such as the one that was depicted by the Take-Off 05 management team. Air traffic controllers might have reacted less strongly to cost-saving measures if they had felt that the organization's capacity to maintain safety in the air space was not being diminished.

When these important values were violated, reactions became strongly negative, and these reactions generalized into a strongly negative attitude towards the change generally. The development of an attitude towards change represents a pivotal event in most change trajectories. Research on attitudes towards other objects shows that information processing differs dramatically from pre-attitude to post-attitude formation phases. Before attitudes are formed, individuals tend to process information in an explorative, open manner in order to make sense of the change, how the process is structured, what the positive and negative consequences for the individual are, the relevant groups, and the organization at large. In this phase, change management can have considerable influence on how the change is perceived and evaluated. Once attitudes have hardened, this is much less likely to be the case. Attitudes, positive or negative, have been shown consistently to impact information processing in a systematic manner. People tend to actively search for and selectively pick up attitude-consistent information, they retrieve consistent information from memory and they interpret information actively so that it becomes consistent with prior attitudes. This can be thought of as cognitive resistance towards information that attempts to influence attitudes, as such attitude-defensive tendencies make it very hard to change attitudes once they are formed. In addition to the influences on information processing, attitudes influence behaviour. When given some behavioural discretion, people tend to behave in a manner that is consistent with their attitudes. Thus, in an organization where a group, such as the air traffic controllers in this case, has formed negative attitudes towards the change, those attitudes are likely to persist, and it is likely that behaviour directed at resisting the change initiative will be observed. In a similar vein, the supportive behaviours that are so important for successful implementation of change are not likely to be observed.

The first conclusion to be drawn from this case is that although power and power differences exist among relevant parties involved in a change process, they remain latent until important values of at least one of the parties become challenged. In this case, it was the right to participate that was challenged when the top management team chose to shift from a participative change management style to an authoritarian one. By challenging the right to participate, and partly control the process, the management ignited a highly political process where the focus of the participants shifted from common organizational goals and values to the relationships between the change and values at the group level. This new perspective on the change process persisted throughout the following phases until the top management team was ultimately replaced.

The players, their power bases and their political tactics

The main players in this political struggle were clearly composed of two groups: the top management team and their staff on the one hand, and the air traffic controllers and their union on the other. Normally, because of the top management team's high level of position power, one would expect it to be the main power base. Position power comes in several forms, including formal authority (legitimate power), control over information, control over resources and rewards, control over punishments, and control over organization of the work and the physical work environment. A distinction must be made, however, between the absolute amount of power held by the top management team and the amount of power it can actually use. While the absolute amount of power is the combination of power bases that could be used if the power-holder chose to use it, usable power is the fraction that can conceivably be used, given assumptions regarding how influence targets would react to possible influence attempts. For example, although the top management team had the power to punish those who did not cooperate during the change, it might have refrained from using coercion and punishment because the anticipated reactions would have offset any benefits from using this type of power. The main bases of power used by the Avinor top management team in this case seem to have been formal authority and information power. A top management team is usually thought to have a large amount of formal authority, as its members are situated at the top of the organizational hierarchy. In fact, position in the organizational hierarchy is often used as a proxy for formal authority in empirical research and theoretical discussions alike (e.g. Krackhardt, 1990). In addition, the top management team of Avinor had support from the majority of the board members (5 to 3 votes in support) throughout the change process. On numerous occasions the chairman of the board unequivocally stated publicly his support for the process and his trust in the Avinor leadership. Finally, the top management team, and by extension the Take-Off 05 process, was supported not only by the government, but also by a majority of the Norwegian National Assembly. In fact, the process was a response to the government's demand for more efficient air traffic control and ground service provision. However, a position at the top of the organizational hierarchy does not confer an absolute right to decide unilaterally on every issue confronting an organization. Formal authority is based on organizational members' perceptions of the domains in which a social agent (the top management team) has the right to exercise power. Organizational members may accept such a right in some areas of activity, but react sharply when attempts are made to exercise power in other areas. Additionally, the amount of formal authority may differ between members of the top management team's role set as a function of the amount of power held by different members of the role set. As power is often defined as an agent's capacity to influence another agent, it is most fruitfully seen as a relative, relational concept. This relational aspect is captured by the term 'net power', which refers to the power differential between two agents (e.g. the top management team and the air traffic controllers). In Avinor the top management team had a much higher level of formal authority over administrative and operative personnel than over the air traffic controllers because the former groups possessed less power than the latter. The Avinor top management team clearly possessed other forms of power, such as a certain amount of information-based power. Much of the information power stemmed from the management team's hiring of external consultants who had access to information about turnarounds of similar organizations in other countries. The top management team had at least partly preferential access to this information, although much of it was publicly known to any interested actor in this sector, including the air traffic controllers. Furthermore, many of the analyses provided by the top management team and the external consultants (e.g. cost projections, capacity projections, air travel demand, total effects of reorganizations, new technology and new work processes) were forcefully contested by the air traffic controllers, who performed their own, independent assessments of these issues. The top management team's upper hand with regard to information was further offset by the fact that the CEO and one of her key collaborators had no prior work experience from this sector, and while information asymmetry was in their favour for some types of information, they were novices in many other relevant knowledge domains. Control over rewards and punishments was applied to a certain extent, such as by promoting personnel who showed a clear positive attitude towards the Take-Off 05 process.

The crucial power base of the air traffic controllers was their central and non-substitutable role in the day-to-day operations of air traffic in Norway. Air traffic control is a highly specialized activity with direct repercussions on safety in the airspace. In order to become a certified air traffic controller a person must have successfully followed a mixed theoretical and practical training programme that lasts approximately three years. Furthermore, the capacity of the educational system (especially the practical training part of it) is highly limited. In fact, in the aftermath of the Take-Off 05 process, training capacity remains one of the bottlenecks. Hence, the air traffic controllers possess a unique power base when compared to other personnel, such as ground security, baggage handling, catering and administrative personnel. While other groups may also have developed negative attitudes towards the change, the air traffic controllers' capacity to act efficiently in accordance with their attitudes is a likely explanation for why the other groups did not engage in the political struggle in its early phases. Expectancy value theory of human behaviour posits that when planning a behaviour, the likelihood of influencing valued outcomes by engaging in that behaviour is a key determinant. Unless an individual, or group, perceives a link between behaviour and valued outcomes, the motivation to engage is not present in the situation.

At this point it should be noted that for both groups (i.e. the top management team and the air traffic controllers), structural rather than personal factors seemed to be the main sources of power. This mirrors the concerns that motivated Hickson *et al.* (1971, 1986) to develop a strategic contingency theory of intra-organizational power at the subunit level of analysis. They reasoned that prior work on power, based on the French and Raven (1959) conceptualization, was 'overpersonalized' and did not reflect important sources of power in organizational settings. The findings presented in this chapter are clearly consistent with this view, although much contemporary research has continued to conceptualize and measure power bases at the individual level. However, subunits' capacity for coping with environmentally generated uncertainties was a central element in this theory. In the Avinor case it seems that the two other elements in the theory – workflow centrality and non-substitutability – were the more important sources of power.

Air traffic controllers used several political tactics in order to fight against the Take-Off 05 process. Some of these tactics were used simultaneously, others sequentially, with the first preparing the ground for the second. Throughout the process (after the first three months of relative harmony) the air traffic controllers engaged in a struggle over a valid reality description. In particular, they contested the top management team's projections for future air traffic volume (which was based on a transient downturn after 9/11). According to the air traffic controllers, air traffic was likely to keep growing, and capacity needs had to be adapted to this scenario. Further, they disagreed about the benefits of closing down air traffic centres, and argued that such a move would jeopardize safety requirements. The top management team and the air traffic controllers actively used the media in order to fight over the valid description of reality. Additionally, both camps were active lobbyists and tried to convince politicians that their understanding was the most valid one. These activities went on until the top management team and the board were replaced. Meanwhile, however, the air traffic controllers made another move. It turned out that the smooth operation of air traffic control had for a long time been based on low levels of sick leave, and a considerable use of air traffic controllers' overtime. This was another use of their key power base, namely their non-substitutable role in the operations. The result of this was very strong, and led to a gradual diminution in the top management team's formal authority. For a long period, air traffic was plagued with delays and cancellations, and the media conveyed pictures of mothers with newly born babies stuck at airports on their way to visit grandparents for the Christmas holidays, and the like. The problems faced by air travellers during this period increased the media coverage, which gave the air traffic controllers increased opportunity to present their view of the Take-Off 05 process and the top management team, and the public started to put pressure on the politicians to take immediate action. Although there might have been some suspicion that the air traffic controllers were creating and using the situation for their own benefit, the board and the top management team were seen as the actors ultimately responsible, by both the public and the politicians (representing the owners). The fact that air traffic controllers consistently argued that the risk of lower safety was a potential consequence of the process could not be completely disregarded, either. In addition to the attempts to link up with external agents (government, the public), the air traffic controllers were adept at mobilizing more power by creating internal coalitions. Although reluctant at first, other groups and professions within Avinor gradually joined in, as evidenced by the fact that a joint letter of distrust in management was signed by seven different unions at one point in the process.

Conclusions

The Avinor case shows some of the limits to the effective use of formal authority in a public sector organization. Blau (1964) in his treatise defined power as the *imposition of will despite resistance*. Hence, the fact that the attempt by the Avinor top management team to impose its will was frustrated is in itself indicative of the limitations on the effective use of formal authority. Although extreme in some respects (in terms of the amount of usable power held by one important subunit, and in terms of the intermediate outcome), we think that the case is a good illustration of the context for leadership in many modern organizations. Many writers seem to think that the key characteristics that launch political struggle are likely to increase in prevalence in the future. The most important contextual factor seems to be the existence of powerful groups within the organization. In this case their power stems from highly skilled and highly specialized work roles that determine the overall performance of the organization. Their power stems from an amalgam of unique knowledge (Grant, 1991; Nonaka, 1991; Child and McGrath, 2001; Nickerson and Zenger, 2004), the proprietary right to perform specific activities within the organization, and their performance of a function that is crucial for the organization's overall effectiveness. This context is not unique to Avinor, or to air traffic control for that matter, as similar contexts can be found in many other public services such as hospitals, police organizations and universities, to mention but a few. In the private sector the context for leadership, as described in the literature on knowledge-intensive firms (e.g. Ulrich, 1998), is very similar to the one emerging from this case study. So how should change be managed in such a context? It seems to us that the high degree of dependence by the top management (or the owner) of an organization on collaboration by powerful subgroups dictates a new approach to leadership. The critical focus seems to become skilful balancing of subgroup interests as flowing from their core professional or group values on the one hand, and organizational objectives or owners' interest on the other. In fact, this case study has shown that if solutions do not take into account their effects on such subgroups' interests – and the reactions that follow – then these solutions may not be useful for achieving organizational objectives, however superior they might be in a narrow, technical sense. The leadership style that is needed in such contexts is captured by Sternberg's (1998, 2004) notion of leadership wisdom as the balancing of different consequences of a decision before a choice is made. The balancing act required is one that gives similar weight both to the consequences as seen by powerful subgroups and to the consequences for organizational performance by actors others than these powerful subgroups. If decision-making processes are to retain strong top-down elements, wisdom of this kind requires deep knowledge of the value systems held by the powerful subgroup(s). Acquisition of such knowledge does not come automatically, but is based on careful listening and interpretation of information provided when interacting with members of the subgroups (Lines, 2006). Furthermore, wisdom presupposes the insight that the achievement of organizational objectives is dependent on decisions that take into account values held by powerful subgroups. It is simply meaningless to think of an optimal solution to an organizational problem without considering the reactions of such subgroups. The application of wisdom through the balancing of owner interests with subgroup interests may have some costs, as technically superior solutions may have to be sacrificed (Barnett, 2007). However, many problems facing organizations are characterized by equifinality, and several solutions can be functionally equivalent with regard to their primary effects (cost reductions, innovation, growth, etc.) while varying considerably with respect to their relevant secondary effects on subgroup values. Hence, many problems have a portfolio of solutions from which managers may choose without sacrificing efficiency. Again, such sophisticated leadership, characterized by higher levels of wisdom, requires processes that involve the search for a number of alternative solutions to a problem, rather than processes that choose the first solution that comes to mind. The knowledge required for assessing solutions in terms of their relevant consequences is necessarily incomplete, even for the wisest leaders. This is partly because changes are subjected to sensemaking and interpretation by internal and external stakeholders. The sensemaking processes and their outcome in terms of attitudes towards change are only partly controllable by organizational leaders through planned communication and dialogue with the stakeholders. This creates a need to present and discuss proposed change solutions thoroughly before final decisions as to specific changes are made. Wise leadership in this context requires a willingness to revise – or even abandon – changes that seemed appropriate from a narrower, top-down perspective.

10 For show or for real? Organization development in the public sector

Antonie Van Nistelrooij and Harry Sminia

- Introduction
- Management of change in the public sector
- Change at The Department
- Method
- Analysis and findings
- Discussion
- Conclusions

Introduction

Within the public sector the rationale for strategic change is often directly linked to abrupt and predominantly exogenous jolts such as changed policies or legislation, technological change, management replacements, or reorganizations such as the merger or break-up of public agencies. Whenever this is the case, an organization requires decisive and large-scale strategic change to regain congruence between the organization's goals, the environment and the organization. In these instances, public sector organizations have a tendency to adopt a top-down strategic management-inspired approach to generating change (Ferlie *et al.*, 1996). The popularity of New Public Management, and especially the associated ideology of 'managerialism', has strengthened the trend of change being initiated and led from the top (Diefenbach, 2007; Ferlie *et al.*, 1996; Hood, 1991). Basically, the senior management team perceive themselves as being in the best position to initiate and implement quick and purposeful organizational change. Besides, they are considered to have the means and the position to work from a system-wide perspective that does not reflect functional or departmental biases (Conger, 2000; Jensen, 2000). However, from an organization development (OD) point of view a bottom-up approach with full participation and active involvement of all employees is seen as essential to generate commitment and ensure that the strategic reorientation actually is realized (Beer, 2000; Bennis, 2000; Cummings and Worley, 2005). Therefore, OD is being used more and more in strategic change initiatives in public sector organizations (Robertson and Seneviratne, 1995; Ferlie *et al*., 1996; Patchett, 2005; Teo and Crawford, 2005). A combination of both approaches seems to be ideal for the public sector, but pulling off the change is not an easy matter, as a number of case studies have already shown (Bate *et al*., 2000; O'Brien, 2002; Balogun and Hailey, 2004; Beer, 2001; Burnes, 2004b).

It must be said that over the past decade, an increasing dissatisfaction with traditional OD has surfaced (Worren *et al*., 1999; Bradford and Burke, 2005), as it appears to be invisible to the majority of executives while failing to generate much interest among MBA students. During the 1980s, Beer and Walton (1987) were much more positive. They concluded that OD, measured as an activity that managers and professional OD consultants do, was growing moderately. However, OD is an evolving and theoretically complex field (Cummings and Worley, 2005:30). This theoretical complexity has made it increasingly difficult to define its conceptual boundaries and to develop a unified theory of changing and developing organizations. Yet Worren *et al*. (1999) suggest there are four key dimensions. First, most authors define OD as planned interventions aimed at increasing organizational effectiveness and employee well-being (Beer and Walton, 1987; French and Bell, 1999; Beckhard, 2000; Bradford and Burke, 2005). Second, OD relies heavily on concepts and research findings from psychology and organizational behaviour (Cummings and Worley, 2005). In turn, these psychological and behavioural foundations have to do with (1) the nature of human beings within the context of organizations, (2) the motivation that drives their behaviour, (3) the resistance of such behaviour to change, and (4) groups as the focus of organization change. Third, OD is a long-term and continuous effort (French and Bell, 1999). Fourth, OD is largely focused on human relations variables (such as culture and climate, communication, leadership styles, and job satisfaction). Typical OD intervention strategies have been focused on the micro level of the organization and include process consultation, team-building, survey feedback and work restructuring (Bradford and Burke, 2005). Recently, OD has become involved with human resource management, with applied work on issues of organizational learning and knowledge management, and with the implementation of new strategic plans in organizations (Greiner and Cummings, 2005).

Reviews of OD provided by authors such as Conger and Kanungo (1988), Cotton *et al*. (1988), Ahlbrandt *et al*. (1992) and Glew *et al*. (1995) show that the mechanisms for involving people in decision-making are, at best, imperfect. To follow the reasoning of Pasmore and Fagans (1992), one cannot conclude that participation in organizations – that is, simply involving people in decision-making – will produce positive benefits to either those involved or the organization as a whole. Dachler and Wilpert (1978:1) arrived at the conclusion that '[n]o clear set of questions, let alone a set of answers, which begin to define the nature of the participation phenomenon are discernible'. The same point is made by Kanter (1982b), who believes that there are crucial perils and problems, dilemmas and decisions, that need to be addressed in managing participation in a way that produces the best results for everyone. Moreover, our own research findings (Sminia and Van Nistelrooij, 2006) suggest that the lack of preparation for participation by managers and organizational members may account for the mixed results that have been reported.

There are, of course, a number of profound differences between public and private sector organizations when it comes to realizing organizational change (Ferlie et al., 1996; Coram and Burnes, 2001; O'Brien, 2002; Härenstam et al., 2004). Not only are there different reasons for initiating change, but change concepts and approaches that are transferred from the private sector to the public sector can lead to contradictory results as well. To make the comparison, and as other contributions to the current volume have noted, public organizations have to deal with a multitude of decision-makers, a larger diversity of stakeholders, more intensive organizational dynamics and a more bureaucratic organizational design than private sector organizations. Or as Patchett (2005:598–599) puts it, 'The political nature of the legislative and representation process and the functional expert and efficiency orientation of the administrative process produce important tensions in a public-sector organization.' This particular context of a public sector organization places specific demands on the management of change, for instance, with regard to working with different authorities and with the handling of the influence of legislation and the political field of force effectively.

This chapter reports on a case study of strategic change at The Department, part of a large public sector organization in the Netherlands. The focus is on the question of whether bottom-up OD methods can be adopted alongside the strategic management-inspired approach of top-down-led change. As with so many public sector organizations, a tradition existed in this organization to initiate and manage change from the top. By incorporating OD methods in the project design, an attempt was made to avoid some of the disadvantages of the strategic management approach and to benefit from the strong points of the OD approach. What we found is that management behaviour is pivotal in reaping the benefits from OD change practices. To explain our findings we will first continue to explore the management of change in the public sector in general. Then the case study will be described briefly, as well as the methods employed. The subsequent presentation of the findings will lead to some general implications, conclusions and points for further discussion.

Management of change in the public sector

Ferlie *et al.* (1996:86) aptly described the management of change in the public sector as 'top-down radical shock strategies and the exercise of political clout'. This observation clearly fits the strategic management approach where strategic change is achieved by way of a pre-designed top-down implementation process that takes place after the content of the new strategy has been formulated (Dunphy, 2000; Balogun and Hailey, 2004; Burnes, 2004b). However, research in decision-making comparing public and private sector organizations has revealed that successful implementation in the public sector does require a bottom-up approach with some degree of employee participation (Rodrigues and Hickson, 1995; Hickson *et al.*, 2003). This provides an explanation for the growing interest in OD concepts and methods in the public sector (Patchett, 2005; Teo and Crawford, 2005). Nevertheless, what has also been found is that the introduction of OD in organizations that are accustomed to centralized control and bureaucratic and politicized working conditions may clash with the prevailing organizational culture or can even be perceived as undermining the public administration work ethos (Barnhart, 1997; O'Brien, 2002).

Both the OD and the strategic management approach to organizational change management can be considered as archetypes. Although based on plausible and legitimate premises, they will not be found in their extremes in actual practice (Beer and Nohria, 2000a). In a way, they can be considered to complement each other (Coram and Burnes, 2001; O'Brien, 2002; Hickson *et al.*, 2003; Cummings and Worley, 2005), as on their own they are insufficient for the successful implementation of strategic change (Beer, 2001; Hickson *et al.*, 2003). Conger (2000:101) even suggests that 'A purely top-down effort, in which there is little or no participation within the organization, is just as likely to end in failure as a purely bottom-up approach.' This leads to the conclusion that a combination of both approaches seems to be the most fruitful option.

There are several ways of combining different approaches to organizational change in a project. One way is to adopt a contingency perspective in which particular approaches are considered more appropriate at different stages of the change process (Huy, 2001b; Boonstra, 2004; Waldersee and Griffiths, 2004). However, Beer and Nohria (2000b) and Beer (2001) warn against such a solution of alternating different approaches through time. They argue that this leads to confusion and delay, and the process will probably suffer from the disadvantages of each approach more than it will benefit from the advantages. They do see a possibility of starting with the top-down strategic management approach to achieve a quick and definitive turnaround, followed through by an OD-informed bottom-up change programme to anchor the new way of doing things in the organization. This does require a very carefully led change programme by which confidence, commitment and trust destroyed during the first phase need to be carefully rebuilt during the second phase. The other way around, they argue, will lead to disaster: any trust, commitment and shared purpose that have been established during an initial OD initiative will be destroyed if followed up with a top-down strategic management-style turnaround. Beer and Nohria (2000b) and Beer (2000) emphasize the complementary character of strategic management and OD instead to propose the simultaneous approach to organizational change, in which the two approaches are integrated. They admit that applying this approach in practice may be challenging, but provide a number of pointers by which they say the contradiction can be managed. If one reads through their material, the following guidelines can be extracted:

- the tension between top-down and bottom-up goals needs to be confronted explicitly;
- direction needs to be set from the top and people need to be engaged from below;
- management need to embody the assumptions and styles of both approaches;
- the focus needs to be on both the organization's design and its culture;
- the change process needs to be partly planned in advance but also to allow for emergent experimentation and problem-solving.

However, the question still remains as to how this approach is to be implemented in practice. This is an especially compelling question for

public sector organizations because of their need to introduce, and interest
in introducing, bottom-up change programmes combined with their
history of top-down change efforts. What effects are exactly to be
expected when OD is introduced alongside strategic management in the
public sector? What we already know is that caution needs to be observed
in a number of respects when OD is introduced in a predominantly
strategic management-like context. First, the issues that are going to be
subject to OD need to be selected carefully and should be of real
significance. Or, as Kanter (1982a:9) pointed out, 'People are skeptical
about participation just for show, without any impact on substance.'
Second, management has to create the possibility for people to participate
and contribute to the development and implementation of the strategic
change. The expectation is that if these two recommendations, considered
the minimal requirement, are not observed, the OD part of a process of
strategic change will not have the positive effects intended.

Change at The Department

We were allowed to study a major change project at a large public sector
organization in the Netherlands that came about as a result of the merger
of seven previously separate organizations in 2002. The change project
concerned the area of disablement – more specifically, the purchase of
services from external suppliers that aim to help long-term sick and
(partly) disabled workers to reintegrate into the workforce, and the
provision of these services to workers and employers. The aim of the
project was to have a new department within the merged organization –
which we shall refer to as 'The Department' – up and running by
September 2003 and capable of handling 90 per cent of applications
within six weeks according to a generic and transparently designed work
process, accompanied by a new administrative system, potentially
affecting about 550 people within the organization.

What was required was a complete redesign of The Department's
organizational processes and administrative system dealing with the
purchase of these services. Its personnel also had to develop a working
relationship with an adjacent department that assesses the (dis)ability
levels of people on benefit. The seven previous organizations, now
merged into one, had upheld a tradition of pre-designed top-down-led
change programmes. This time, departmental management were willing
to introduce OD practices to foster employee participation because they

realized that the change project involved changes with regard to not only the strategy and structure, but also the development of new working practices and patterns of cooperation between people from the former seven organizations and between two newly formed departments.

The departmental management's willingness to work with OD methods led to what can be considered a simultaneous change approach. The project design distinguished between a 'change strand' and a 'project strand' (see Figure 10.1). The 'project strand' had to work on the organization design, the procedures, the work standards and the supporting ICT system. It was structured as an engineering project with set deadlines and specific design targets, and with people working in a strict hierarchy. The 'change strand' was supposed to feed the 'project strand' with the information required to develop the new organizational processes and administrative system, and assist in the creation of The Department. It also had to ease implementation and to improve cooperation with other departments. The 'change strand' featured a programme of OD-type interventions, based on Whole Scale Change techniques (Van Nistelrooij et al., 2004). The intention was to start this strand with different forms of large-group interventions (LGIs) (see Figure 10.1) such as conferences in order to develop the first design

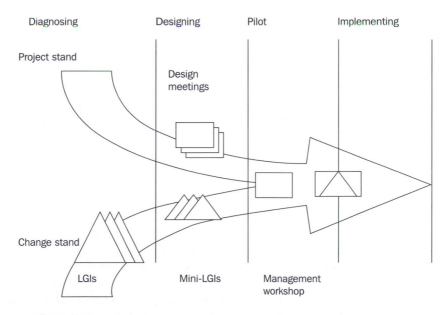

Figure 10.1 *Project design*
Note: LGI = large-group intervention.

parameters and during which the decisions on staffing of a variety of sub-projects had to be made. This was to be followed up by workshops, informative meetings and evaluative meetings to support the implementation of the newly developing organizational design. The two strands would be on separate but simultaneous tracks initially but were supposed to merge during the course of the change project.

Method

To study the course of this change project, a research methodology that allowed us to track and interpret developments over time needed to be adopted. We opted for a process approach (Mohr, 1982; Langley, 1999; Poole *et al.*, 2000), with process being defined as a sequence of events (Miles and Huberman, 1994; Van de Ven and Poole, 1995). This meant we had to concentrate on gathering data on the subsequent events that made up this change project (Peterson, 1998; Abbott, 1990). These were then coded in a theoretically meaningful way. A historical baseline could be composed by simply listing the events in the chronological order in which they occurred. To enable interpretation of the data and to analyse how a simultaneous approach to organizational change works out in practice, we needed further theory informing us how a course of events in general leads to a particular outcome.

The change project introduced new OD change methods into the organization alongside already existing strategic management practices. It was assumed that if these new methods were to be adopted successfully, they had to become institutionalized in their own right as common practices among the existing organizational routines. Looking at it this way, we see that the change project not only aimed to reorganize the department, but also had to alter the manner in which change was routinely introduced and effected in the whole organization. Barley and Tolbert proposed to study institutional change by charting flows of actions to see whether and how scripts have become subject to change over time. They define scripts as 'observable, recurrent activities and patterns of interaction characteristic of a particular setting' (1997:98). Furthermore, scripts are perceived as particular institutionalized interaction patterns, which in turn are subject to a process of structuration (Giddens, 1976). Structuration theory sees human action as shaping and being shaped by these scripts. On the one hand, these scripts prescribe what the appropriate action is in a particular situation. On the other hand, human action gives rise to the emergence and preservation of scripts when these actions change or conform to certain regularities.

We decided to single out three specific scripts in which the tensions between top-down and bottom-up change would be prominent. These scripts were labelled (1) *the power of decision script*, (2) *the project focus script*, and (3) *the participants' role script*. According to the strategic management logic, the power of decision lies with the management team. However, in line with the OD logic, the participants are supposed to be empowered to make their own decisions. With regard to *the project focus script*, the question is whether the focus of the project activities is on hierarchy and on satisfying the needs of (top) management (strategic management logic), or whether the focus is on the participants and making sure that everybody participates (OD logic). *The participants' role script* in strategic management mode expects participants to be relatively passive with regard to their involvement in the project, while the OD logic requires a more active stance from every participant. This means that the event data that were to be analysed had to reveal how these three scripts developed over time. In other words, would there be room for the OD logic next to strategic management logic with regard to these scripts over the course of the change project?

We were able to collect the raw data by recording events over the duration of the change project, either by direct observation during various meetings and gatherings or by collecting documents that were produced as a consequence of the change project. The time period over which events were recorded lasted from 1 January 2002 until 17 December 2003, resulting in a database with a total of 640 recorded events. Analysis took place by coding these events in terms of the three scripts previously identified as well as the change logic that was reflected in each event. Table 10.1 gives an indication of the coding rules utilized.

Barley and Tolbert (1997) recommend validation of the observations and conclusions with additional data. We therefore distributed a questionnaire among a sample of 152 participants in the change project in June 2003. The questionnaire was aimed specifically at measuring the perceptions and experiences of the individuals participating in the project. Questions were asked about the modes of communication, the degree to which communicated information had been received and understood, and to what degree the participants thought the goals of the project had been achieved.

Table 10.1 *Event coding rules*

SM logic	OD logic
Power of decision script *controversy*	
Management team (MT) decides if:	Participants (P) decide if:
● MT sets framework	● P decide on content and process issues
● MT sets roles and positions	● P set roles
● MT decides on what is essential	● P set purpose and results
● MT determines mode of communication	● P answer questions on content and process issues
● MT sets purpose	● emphasis is on involvement workers
● MT determines course of events	● emphasis is on discussion and decision by workers
● MT manages through results	● 'change strand' is encouraged
● MT assesses products	
● MT ignores 'change strand'	
Project focus script *controversy*	
Project is focused on MT if:	Project is focused on participants if:
● there is anticipation on expectations of MT	● there is a need to communicate with whole organization
● there is a need to convince MT	● there is a need for full participation
● there is a wish for clarity from MT	● there is a need to preserve 'change strand' consultants
● there is doubt about MT support	● there is a need to involve whole organization
● there is fear about framework already been decided upon	● there is creation of full ownership of new organization design
● there is significance put on MT statements	● new organization design is tested among workers
Participants' role script *controversy*	
Passive role participants if:	Active role participants if:
● P await MT decisions	● P make suggestions for project process and content
● P await change	● P make suggestions for new organization design
● P await communications	● P make judgements
● P refrain from judgements	● P show initiative
● documents are not distributed on time	● P make project larger
● work process has been set beforehand	● P show commitment

Analysis and findings

In keeping with the change project design, the diagnostic phase started
with three large-scale conferences. These were identical conferences
conducted within a short space of time but spread out over the country to
give every participant the opportunity to attend. These first meetings
explained and legitimized the OD part of the change process and were
mostly concerned with *the project focus script*. On many occasions the
message to the participants was that their efforts and input were going to
be considered essential to the success of the project and that they had to
take this opportunity to make their mark on the new organization. For
instance, the project manager during his presentations in the start-up
conferences emphasized the significance of this new way of achieving
change by stating, 'Let's seize the opportunity [. . .] because we have been
granted the space to create a good working process', and 'if you can blow
a hole [in the process], please do, and make the work process better', and
also 'management has decided willingly in favour of a bottom-up
approach; everyone can take part, everyone can have influence and every
voice is important' (translated from Dutch). With regard to *the power of
decision script*, however, the message was more mixed. On the one hand,
departmental management indicated they were anxious to reap the
benefits from the bottom-up approach that was designed into the project.
However, they also insisted that a number of restrictions be taken into
account and that certain requirements needed to be met. The departmental
management representative in the start-up conferences told the
participants that 'actually everything is under discussion' and 'there are
few restrictions', but also that 'I want to install regional managers' and
'I want you to meet a number of conditions', already shaping the design
and setting the boundaries before the design process had even started.

In the course of the diagnostic phase, a rift developed between The
Department and the adjacent department with which its personnel had to
forge a close working relationship. It concerned the specific content and
demarcation of the future tasks of The Department. This rift stalled the
progress of the project as a whole before management decided to
intervene in November 2002 and instructed project management to
concentrate on the design. Employees working in the adjacent department
who would have to cooperate closely with The Department, for which
new work processes were being designed, feared that too much of their
work would be transferred to The Department. A casual remark made by
an external consultant about the possibility that 90 per cent of the
workload was going to be allocated to The Department had distressed the

adjacent department's employees. The external consultant had only
made this remark to provide an example with the intention of challenging
the participants to think the unthinkable. Some time later, the '90 per
cent–10 per cent' division of tasks was believed to have the status of a
management decision – which it was not – and hence people from the
adjacent department were up in arms because they feared for their
position within the organization.

A 'kick-off' meeting on 13 January 2003 was held in order to put the
project back on track. During this meeting a new project methodology
was introduced, which was aimed at achieving substantial results. Since
the management intervention in November 2002, the rift between the two
departments had grown into somewhat of a taboo subject because
management perceived this to be the main cause of lack of progress.
Nevertheless, it remained a major concern for many of the participants.
However, during this meeting the rift was purposefully addressed and the
underlying problem and misunderstandings were dissolved. The meeting
was also used as an opportunity to mark the transition from the diagnostic
phase to the design phase of the change project. As a consequence, the
emphasis was put on the *project strand* and the design of the new work
processes (see Figure 10.2). The first results were presented to the larger
project community during a number of mini-conferences that originally

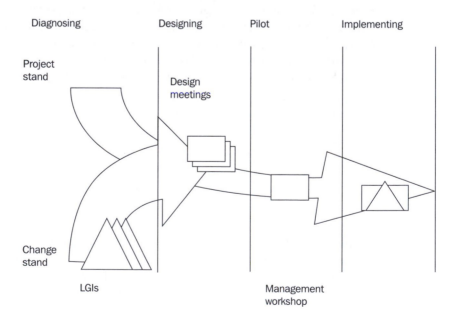

Figure 10.2 *Realized project*

had been scheduled as part of the *change strand*. The character of these mini-conferences, however, had changed considerably when compared to the original intention. The emphasis was on substance and not on process and dialogue, and participants were just asked to comment on the designs that had been drafted in the sub-projects. The overall conclusion after the last mini-conference had been held was that these first designs were too generic, somewhat incomplete and needed further elaboration. By this time it was the end of February 2003.

During this part of the design phase, events signalled all kinds of messages concerning each of the three scripts. With regard to *the power of decision script*, specifically in meetings immediately following the kick-off meeting on 13 January, departmental management further emphasized what they saw as being a good project result and stressed that they wanted results quickly, more or less signalling that they had the final say as to when choices were to be made. The messages with regard to *the project focus script* were mixed. A new change methodology had been introduced that focused on the participants and the opportunity to voice their concerns and ideas about the work process design. Project management continuously made remarks about how they were all part of the project. Nevertheless, informal comments started to become more and more laden with disappointment and reproach that the 'change strand' purpose of dialogue by way of Whole Scale Change had disappeared into the background. *The participants' role script* was particularly present during the mini-conferences. The participants seized the opportunity to comment actively on the designs, as they had been asked to do. But failures to brief the participants in advance of what was to be expected of them and failures in getting conference documents to the participants in time forced them into passivity. Departmental management also appeared to become tired of receiving critical remarks from the employees, judging from informal remarks referring to the possibility of 'boarding everything up before the mini-conferences start so that it cannot be discussed any more'.

During this phase the targets for the project strand were changed to the extent that the blueprint for The Department, including the new work process and the administrative system, had to be ready, but implementation would be limited to pilots at two separate locations as soon as possible. Also, the design phase of the change project changed character completely. In a meeting on 6 March 2003, departmental management instructed middle management of both The Department and the adjacent department directly on what they wanted, including resolving the differences between the two, and how they wanted it to be achieved.

Again the message with regard to *the power of decision script* was that it is management who make the decisions. From this moment onwards we observed hardly any events that made reference to *the project focus* or *the participants' role scripts*.

During the course of April 2003 the design phase was gradually becoming the pilot phase as a first complete work process design was being finalized and preparations were being made to test the new procedures at two selected sites. During these tests the local employees and managers who were testing things out continuously needed to change and amend the design to work out how it might become operational. By allowing this to happen, *the power of decision script* as well as *the project focus script* and *the participants' role script* appeared to be leaning towards the bottom-up approach. However, in a project management meeting on 17 June 2003 the project manager informed the participants that departmental management had decided to dissolve the change project team and that the new work processes were going to be implemented in a top-down fashion, utilizing the existing hierarchy and organization structure.

Combining the overall findings with regard to the three scripts, it appeared that the change project in this case study started off in a manner in which the bottom-up OD approach seemed to have had equal significance with the top-down strategic management approach, although the power of decision remained firmly in the hands of departmental senior management. The management intervention at the end of the diagnostic phase, emphasizing the strategic management-inspired 'project strand' over the OD-inspired 'change strand', shifted the balance between the two perspectives. During the subsequent design phase there were initially claims being made in favour of the OD perspective, but with the second management intervention in the project these claims disappeared from the process and the strategic management perspective gained the upper hand.

The results from the questionnaires confirm these observations. The targets from the original 'project strand' had by and large been reached. After the change project was officially ended with the finish of the two pilots, the new design was cascaded out over The Department. Less than 18 months after the implementation of the new operating procedures started, all offices were able to deal with 90 per cent of the applications within six weeks. Looking at the targets from the original 'change strand', however, the results lagged behind. Only 27.7 per cent of the participants confirmed an increased readiness for change and only 29.9 per cent indicated that the new operating procedures had sufficient support among the employees, with 76.9 per cent indicating that their commitment to the organization had not increased as a consequence of this change project. However, 52.2 per cent did state that communication had improved in the newly merged organization from the previous situation with seven separate organizations, but only 27.7 per cent indicated the same for the communication between The Department and adjacent department. Other aspects that the respondents felt were still worth improving were project management skills, the raising of employee commitment to the change project, and the readiness of management to listen to the shop floor.

Discussion

Can OD be introduced alongside the strategic management approach to change in the public sector? The case revealed that this is a possibility, but the role of management has proved to be essential in this. The start-up of the change project that we were able to observe showed that the OD logic had become part of the process, at least with regard to *the project focus script* and *the participants' role script*, during the first two phases. With regard to *the power of decision script*, however, the departmental practice of this being a management prerogative was being challenged throughout the project but the top team apparently felt obliged to hold on to the privilege. This was, of course, amply demonstrated by their intervention, which changed the initial project design by putting the 'project strand' first and the 'change strand' second. This did not kill off the initial enthusiasm of the workforce right away, to judge from the presence of the OD logic in events during the subsequent design phase. However, OD references with regard to *the project focus* and *the participants' role script* more or less disappeared from the scene during the remainder of the project, indicating that the strategic management logic had prevailed.

The change process encountered what appeared to be an unanticipated hurdle when the rift appeared between The Department and the adjacent department. On the one hand, this is something that could have been anticipated. When two or more organizational entities are involved in a change project, diverging interests are bound to be encountered and need to be dealt with. The way in which management in this case decided to go about it meant that ultimately they were more interested in delivering the change on time than in ensuring that everybody would have a fair chance to participate. The conflict was treated as a disturbance, slowing the process down. The pressure to deliver on time prevailed over any long-term gain in designing a more acceptable and possibly more durable solution for all of those involved, as well as over the workforce gaining experience in making bottom-up contributions to the running of this organization. By using their authority, management forced the workforce into compliance not only with regard to the newly designed work processes, but also with the top-down approach to change. Ironically, the opposing interests between the two departments were eventually reconciled with minimal interference from management.

The case discussed in this chapter demonstrates that the simultaneous approach to strategic change is not an easy matter. There are two observations that can be made as a consequence of the experience described concerning this case from the public sector. First, there is the specific role of OD in a simultaneous approach to strategic change. The plan was to utilize the results from the 'change strand' as inputs in the 'project strand' in this change project. Initially this set-up worked reasonably well. It not only resulted in the specifications for an initial design of the new work process, but also helped to staff the subsequent sub-projects. However, it became clear that departmental management was giving preference to the 'project strand' and the realization of the associated goals. Although the project was designed according to the simultaneous approach to strategic change, it appeared that members of the senior management team were working according to a contingent approach, trying to time and sequence the approach to what they perceived as the course and the requirements of the change process. The rift between the two departments and the associated delay made them reconsider their stance. To judge from the responses of the employees, the effects mentioned by Beer (2000), Beer and Nohria (2000b) and Kanter (1982b) of introducing OD into an organization but not seeing it through during the whole project affected the course and outcome. The commitment, trust and confidence that were built up initially oozed away after departmental management had intervened and started working in a top-down fashion, introducing scepticism with regard to bottom-up change altogether.

Second, the management role in creating the possibility for the employees to participate appeared to be essential for the course and the outcome of the change project. The three large-scale conferences at the beginning of the project had been an important step with regard to the level of cooperation between the various stakeholders. The results from the survey suggest that these conferences contributed to increased enthusiasm for, and commitment to, the project. However, the management intervention and the subsequent change to the project design meant that these conferences appeared to be the only occasions when the employees were able to participate fully in the project. The promises of full participation made during the starting conferences were never completely fulfilled. Some respondents in the survey complained afterwards of feeling that they had been sent away empty-handed. To that extent, the recommendations by Beer and Nohria (2000b) mentioned earlier could not be observed to have worked, as the simultaneous approach that these authors advocate was not seen through. This means that we were unable to observe workable solutions to the tensions that their recommendations imply.

The pivotal role of management in the introduction of OD change practices came to stand out during the analysis of this strategic change project in the public sector. The workforce appeared to embrace the OD methods willingly but they were not allowed to pursue them fully when management decided to intervene following the emergence of the rift between the two departments. The final success of the project with regard to the goals of the 'project strand' can be attributed to this intervention. However, by downplaying the 'change strand', the aims associated with this track within the project became largely unreachable as well. However, this was not the only effect. Management's refusal to share power with the employees and their intervention at a critical stage in the project severely hampered the dissemination of the OD logic alongside the strategic management logic. Instead, the result came out as a typical public organization initiative, where change practices are dominated by management in a true strategic management style, and employee participation, initiative and commitment remain underdeveloped.

Conclusions

This case study illustrates that management who embark on a change process of any kind are playing a two-board game. The first board concerns the change process itself, and bearing the responsibilities that they have in mind, directing the process towards a favourable outcome, or at least making sure that essential boundaries are not crossed. There is, however, a second board on which a game is played, and this game concerns the prevalent change mode in the organization: top-down, bottom-up, or perhaps an integrated simultaneous approach. Management's actions signal the direction in which they prefer the change process to proceed. Such actions also signal the type of change process they allow for. We feel that an important observation emerging from this case analysis is that as every change process proceeds over time, management must realize that they have a choice either to intervene or to let that process run its course. Whatever they decide, it signals both what they consider to be the preferred outcome and what they consider to be the preferred change approach, and both signals need to be taken into account when they decide to intervene or to let matters be. In this particular case we observed that with regard to the outcome of the change process itself, the intervention had a positive effect on the speed with which a result was produced. However, this was at the expense of the durability and acceptability of solutions to all parties. Moreover, the potential of the change initiative to contribute towards altering the change culture in this public organization has not been fulfilled. In the context of introducing more 'business-like' management in the public sector, as has been advocated under the auspices of New Public Management, it is worth observing that 'business'-like does not necessarily equate to a top-down strategic management style of change. Rather, consideration of a bottom-up OD change style also demands recognition as sound business practice because of its potential to yield worthwhile results.

11 Strategic responses to the Quality Reform: a comparative study of change in Norwegian higher education

Katarina Østergren and Inger Stensaker

- Introduction
- The Quality Reform and the HE context
- Strategic responses to planned change
- Research design
- Strategic responses and their implications
- Conclusions

Introduction

Public sector organizations have been described as being complex with multiple and sometimes conflicting goals (Lozeau *et al.*, 2002). It has often been argued that public sector organizations are subject to institutional pressure and that in the context of such pressure the quest for legitimacy leads to similarities between organizations within a field (DiMaggio and Powell, 1983). Previous research has suggested that in the face of change, public organizations respond by changing systems and structure, but without changing core features (Meyer and Rowan, 1977).

In June 2001 a government proposal for a comprehensive higher education (HE) reform – the Quality Reform – was approved by the Norwegian Parliament. The rationale behind the reform was to increase the quality of, and market response rate to, teaching and research (Bleiklie *et al.*, 2006). This chapter reports on a comprehensive study of responses to the reform in Norwegian HE. The findings indicate that the HE institutions have responded in various and proactive ways, rather than in defensive and passive ways as suggested by previous research on public sector change.

In order to explain and understand these responses, we used a strategic perspective. Although there are several key features that distinguish public organizations from private organizations (Lozeau *et al.*, 2002), strategic change theory, with its focus on agency, can help explain different responses to and outcomes of a reform. Strategic theory is based on the assumption that HE institutions can choose to respond either defensively or proactively. In a situation of change, the organizations position themselves in relation to other HE institutions in terms of market focus and product offerings. Introducing strategic choice theory in the public sector thereby captures not only passive conformity, but also active responses by organizations to such institutional pressure (Oliver, 1991).

This chapter begins with a description of the reform and the Norwegian HE context. Theory on strategic responses to change is then presented, followed by a description of the methods used to study responses to the reform. The section on findings begins with an identification and description of the three dominant strategic responses: *niche strategy*, *achieve university status* and *internationalization strategy*. A discussion of factors influencing the organizations' response to the reform follows, as well as an assessment of the consequences of each response, including organizational consequences and goal achievement – whether and how a particular response contributes (or fails to contribute) to the reaching of reform goals. Finally, the chapter presents the long-term implications expected from these strategic responses. It is argued that the responses will trigger further changes within the Norwegian HE sector.

The Quality Reform and the HE context

The move towards a European HE area is generally referred to as the Bologna process. The process is both national and European at the same time. Previously, the European HE systems consisted of three main models: (1) the German model, inherited from the Humboldtian tradition, which largely diffused across the north and east of Europe; (2) the Anglo-Saxon model, characterized by the British system; and (3) the southern model, including the mixed situation found in Southern European countries (Musselin, 2005a). The Bologna process aims at transforming HE systems by affecting their products and systems of production rather than by directly modifying their institutional setting. The ideas in the Bologna process are similar to general trends in the public sector discussed in the introductory chapter and in other contributions to this volume, often labelled New Public Management

(NPM). The focus is on increased autonomy, stronger decentralized leadership and increased transparency. The idea is to decentralize the responsibility from the state to the universities but at the same time increase audit and control of their actions (Østergren *et al.*, 2007).

The Norwegian government is known for being a slow reformer compared to other European countries (Bleiklie, 2005), but this trend has changed with the radical Quality Reform (QR), which followed from a report (NOU 14:2000) by a government-appointed commission (the Mjøs Commission). The reform, as it was passed by Parliament, consisted of three main components: (1) structural change, (2) increased internationalization, and (3) new governance forms, including a new financing system.

The *structural component* of the QR involved implementing the recommendation of the Bologna declaration, which was a new degree structure called the '3 + 2 + 3' system, which indicates the duration of the bachelor, Master's and doctoral degree programmes. The reform emphasized the responsibility of the institutions for the efficiency and success of the programmes delivered and the need to introduce modern teaching methods, frequent feedback to students, longer teaching semesters and portfolio evaluation. The main goal was to make the degree studies more efficient by decreasing the length of the degree programmes, increasing compliance with programme schedules and increasing the completion of study programmes.

Increased internationalization aimed particularly at increasing and facilitating the mobility of bachelor degree students, for instance, by offering a three- to six-month period of study abroad. However, internationalization as a process had wider ramifications and profound consequences not only for the way in which universities would go about their daily activities within research, teaching and institutional management, but also for the understanding of what academic activity and universities are all about. The directly observable international and European element in the QR was unprecedented in the history of Norwegian university policy.

New governance forms changed the formal status of HE institutions in relation to central government, as well as leadership structures at all levels within the institutions. In addition, an incentive-based funding system was introduced to stimulate institutions to respond to new demands and expectations from students, society and industry. While financing used to be based on input, such as the number of students accepted into the institution, production (output) created the new basis for financing.

The reform ideas are in line with contemporary views on how public organizations should be organized (Musselin, 2005a). Similar ideas can also be found in public administration in general, both in European and in other countries. Modern universities in countries with traditions of academic freedom and autonomy are in a process of profound change with global reach, and they are affected by what we may call changing HE regimes (Deem, 2004). The regime change characterizes the pattern of ideological, political, juridical and financial pressure that shapes HE systems and their institutions.

The HE sector in Europe has been described as a major international market that is under development. Meyer (2002a) argues that these processes indicate a more profound movement in the direction of increasing convergence in models of HE worldwide. Others modify or even reject the idea of convergence, and emphasize that all systems of HE exist in a specific historical and cultural context, and that the features of the various national systems must be understood in relation to their respective context in order to grasp their real nature (Musselin, 2000). It seems fair to say that these institutions are no longer (or not to the same extent as previously) collegiate bodies of professors in which other employee groups and students are excluded from decision-making bodies. Since the 1970s, institutions have undergone two important transformations in Europe (Bleiklie, 2005; Musselin, 2005b). First, they became democratized, and the decision-making bodies included all major employee groups. Second, external interests, such as funding bodies, regional actors, managers, etc., have in various ways gained a stronger foothold in university governance and increasingly became represented on university boards.

Consequently, two things have happened. First, institutions have been reformed from autonomous collectives to stakeholder organizations (Neave, 2002). One of the major shifts in power relationships in and around universities that follows from this transformation is that universities and individual academics are expected to serve the expressed needs of stakeholders for research and educational services. This is a fundamental shift from a situation where decisions about research and teaching were left to the professional judgement of academics. Some researchers argue that this shift is necessary but that the commitment to the new forms of control of professionals will not succeed if the controls become too tight (Meyer, 2002b). Recent research presents evidence of negative internal consequences of controls and audits (see, for example, By *et al.*, 2008), and Anderson (2006) emphasizes the difficulty of keeping the professionals' identity as professional workers rather than as production workers.

Second, the values of academic institutions have been called into question, and they are often accused of having unclear aims, or at least not communicating aims clearly. Universities are criticized for being self-serving and not useful enough to society. Since the late 1980s the environment has become more fluid as student populations have risen sharply; funding conditions, legislative conditions and steering mechanisms have changed; external demands and internal pressures for organizational reforms have mounted; and internationalization and globalization have created new pressures – both real and perceived.

In turn, these developments have prompted a series of reform attempts (Bleiklie, 2005). Universities have tried to adapt by aiming to expand the capacity for applied research; providing education to a growing and increasingly diverse student body; expanding their sources of revenue; organizationally strengthening leadership functions; and making their operations and performance transparent to the public. These developments create leadership challenges, which cannot necessarily be met merely by finding the best reform measures for making universities more efficient or useful. Although university reformers emphasize goals of improved efficiency and higher quality (and these are no doubt legitimate concerns), current changes within and around HE institutions suggest that a deep value shift is taking place. A shift towards a more business-like leadership ideal has appeared at the expense of authority based on academic excellence or social values such as democracy and provision of welfare services (Clark, 1998). Universities are now expected to be managed on the basis of predefined strategies in a more or less competitive market (see, for example, de Boer and Goedegebuure, 2001; de Boer, 2002).

The new values that are in the process of replacing the former ones are not clearly identified or specified, and hence they are still contested. Therefore, universities are not only faced with challenges that increase the need for leadership. The conditions for collective leadership have deteriorated as the elite autonomy that underpins institutional leadership appears to have been reduced. It is argued, among reformers, that a new type of leadership is needed to mobilize universities to meet the challenges raised by the changes in the HE sector. However, the particular mix of values that underpins leadership is in flux, and despite a general ideological movement towards business enterprise ideals, it is far from obvious how HE institutions will respond to a more competitive environment.

The nature of the changes can thus be summarized as a shift towards more business thinking, and the reform is embedded in and involves fundamental shifts in values, which is increasing organizational uncertainty about what responses will be perceived as legitimate. In the next section we present strategic change theory and different responses to planned radical change, such as the reform we described earlier.

Strategic responses to planned change

During large-scale planned change, such as a government reform, the norms within a field or sector are subject to change, and this creates uncertainty and ambiguity about the future 'rules of the game', but it also provides an opportunity for affecting future institutional norms. In the absence of clear institutional norms and processes, it is not always clear what actions will be perceived as legitimate. Organizations, public as well as private, that are subject to externally initiated large-scale changes that upset the institutional norms can respond in various ways. In presenting different responses to change, we primarily draw on strategic literature and research that focus on changes that are imposed on an organization (or in our case, HE institution) by an external force, in this case the government. This is conducive to an episodic view on change. Episodic change can be triggered by changes in the competitive environment, technological innovation or international trends. On the basis of such triggers, corporate and top management initiate change and impose new strategies and ideas on divisions and departments within the organization, which again respond to the external pressure for change in various ways (Oliver, 1991; Fox-Wolfgramm *et al.*, 1998; Kostova and Roth, 2002; Lozeau *et al.*, 2002). Through their responses, individuals and organizations actively shape the outcome of a reform or change initiative (Balogun and Johnson, 2004; Balogun, 2006; Lozeau *et al.*, 2002; Stensaker and Falkenberg, 2007). Hence, understanding responses to external pressure for change is crucial in order to understand and explain change outcomes.

One stream of literature within strategic change has identified different responses to change, which in essence are aimed at avoiding change. Such defensive responses can take several forms, and they include both passive and active strategies. Passive strategies and responses can imitate other institutions (that are perceived as legitimate or that are known and trusted) (Oliver, 1991), or comply with reform intentions but do a minimum of what is required, such as making superficial changes (Kostova and Roth,

2002; Lozeau *et al.*, 2002; Knights and McCabe, 1998), or making incremental changes (Fox-Wolfgramm *et al.*, 1998). This response is well known to institutional theorists. Some organizations try more actively to alter or modify decisions to change by using such strategies as bargaining and negotiating with institutional stakeholders or contesting and attacking (Oliver, 1991) change ideas and/or change initiators. More manipulative strategies include corrupting new ideas to reinforce previous practices (Lozeau *et al.*, 2002). An example of such corruption would be to relabel old practices and thus attempt to hide the fact that nothing has changed in the organization. Finally, some managers choose to loosen the institutional attachments by exiting the domain (Oliver, 1991). These rather defensive responses have been found in in-depth studies of large-scale change imposed by external forces or agents (Kostova and Roth, 2002; Lozeau *et al.*, 2002; Knights and McCabe, 1998; Fox-Wolfgramm *et al.*, 1998; Oliver, 1991). However, when faced with external pressure to change, organizations can respond *either* defensively, by trying to maintain the status quo and making only minimal changes, *or* proactively, by viewing change as an opportunity to pursue a new strategy.

In-depth and theoretically based studies of proactive responses are rare; therefore we draw more broadly on strategic theory and the positioning perspective to address more proactive and opportunity-based responses to imposed change. One of the core perspectives within strategy is Porter's (1979) positioning school, which views organizational responses in terms of how institutions position themselves in relation to others in the industry or sector.

In HE, the geographical background of students might determine which market an organization focuses on in terms of education, while different study programmes reflect the 'product lines'. Research is another 'product' that most HE institutions offer. Positioning theory assumes that changes in the environment trigger opportunities for strategic and competitive behaviour, such as repositioning. For example, the market can be expanded geographically by targeting new groups of students or by targeting new customer segments (such as executive students). The product portfolio can also be expanded or changed by introducing new study programmes (new master programmes) and/or new areas of focus (such as sports management), for either teaching, research or both. Changes in products and markets can aim to broaden the scope, but also to narrow it by focusing on a niche. Positioning the organization in a competitive market involves distinguishing one's organization from the competitors.

Porter (1979) introduces three generic strategies: cost leadership, differentiation and niche strategy. Differentiation and niche strategies are most relevant in the HE context, because HE tuition is free in Norway. Differentiation means to distinguish one's institution from other HE institutions on the basis of quality (of research and/or teaching), innovation, or customer focus. In the case of HE, students can be viewed as the customers.[1] Niche means to focus on specific geographical areas or specific products. In addition to understanding the nature of these responses and their effect on change outcome, it is important to understand why an organization responds in a certain way. According to Porter (1979), the performance of organizations within a specific sector, such as HE, depends on the intensity of the competition within the sector. Organizations will attempt to position themselves in ways that reduce (1) the intensity of competition from their rivals, (2) the power of suppliers and customers, and (3) the threat of substitutes and/or new rivals.

The response to external pressure for change will be based on an assessment of the competitive environment, and will aim to position the focal organization in the best possible way, given certain industry characteristics. However, HE institutions in Norway have no history of competition. The institutions have historically held different roles with responsibility for various geographical areas in Norway. While the reform itself introduces a competitive and strategic way of thinking, we have to keep in mind that this has not been the traditional way of thinking about the sector and how to organize institutions that offer higher education and research. Organizational responses may therefore be based on factors other than mere competitive concerns.

Organizational responses to external pressure for change have also been explained by less competitively focused factors such as the *nature of the institutional pressure* itself (Oliver, 1991). In situations of institutional reforms this would be the goals and content of the reform. Contextual factors found to influence responses to pressure for change include the *receptivity of the organization* (Kostova and Roth, 2002). Other explanations for responses combine content and context and focus on the *compatibility between corporate initiatives (or reform goals) and the organizational context*. For example, this can be compatibility with organizational goals (Lozeau *et al.*, 2002), current power structures (Lozeau *et al.*, 2002; Knights and McCabe, 1998) or organizational identity (Fox-Wolfgramm *et al.*, 1998). Existing research also points out that changes that are perceived as forced can create resistance (Kostova and Roth, 2002) and that relational issues such as trust between those who initiate and formulate change and those who are set to implement it (Kostova and Roth, 2002) can affect the responses to change. Although less focused on purely competitive reasons for different strategic responses, most of these studies have been conducted in business contexts, such as banks (Fox-Wolfgramm *et al.*, 1998) and multinational corporations (Kostova and Roth, 2002), but there are also studies from the public sector focusing on examples such as hospitals (Lozeau *et al.*, 2002).

Research design

This study is part of a larger research programme focusing on all universities and university colleges in Norway and how they have implemented the QR. The analysis of strategic responses is based on a comparative case study with a combination of qualitative and quantitative data that were collected through three data sources: (1) a national survey of employees at universities and university colleges in 2004, (2) a national survey of chancellors and directors in 2005, and (3) a multiple case study with qualitative in-depth data from seven HE institutions.

The first survey was sent to the total population of employees in Norwegian universities and university colleges, and aimed to capture employee perceptions of the implications of the reform. A 60 per cent response rate was obtained. The second survey was sent to the total population of rectors and directors in the Norwegian HE sector and aimed to obtain management perceptions. This survey obtained an 86 per cent response rate. We used data from these surveys to identify different strategic responses to the reform. The strategic responses were developed inductively through an iterative process of comparing and contrasting statements about product and market focus and changes therein. Three broad categories seemed to cover the most typical responses among the total population of HE institutions. While all the institutions could be placed in one of the three categories of responses, one institution, a private university college, responded completely differently from these three responses. The findings reported here do not include this institution, as the emphasis is on dominant responses.

A case study was then conducted in order to flesh out the three strategic responses. Seven HE institutions were selected, based on an assessment of typical representatives of the respective responses. We targeted two large and traditional universities in larger cities (case 'uni A' and 'uni B'), four medium-sized university colleges from different parts of the country ('med A', 'med B', 'med C' and 'med D'), and one small, rural university college ('rur A'). We conducted a total number of 150 interviews across these seven institutions, targeting academic and administrative personnel at various organizational levels in the time period 2003–2006. The interviews typically lasted between one and two hours. This chapter is primarily based on the top management responses, as they tended to put greater emphasis on strategic issues. In the analysis, data were coded in terms of how the institutions positioned themselves: whether they were entering new markets and/or launching new study programmes or research areas, or focusing more narrowly on specific markets and/or products.

Strategic responses and their implications

The data analysis suggests that HE institutions responded with one of the following three strategies: by focusing on a niche, changing status or internationalizing. Below, each of the strategic responses is fleshed out by first describing the response and then identifying which institutions responded in this way. Finally, the reasons for, and consequences of, different responses are discussed.

Figure 11.1 shows that prior to the reform, HE institutions were divided into two main camps: the universities, with broad geographical focus and emphasis on research-based teaching on the one hand; and the university colleges, with a narrower geographical focus and more focus on teaching than research on the other hand. The QR led to two types of movement among institutions within this second group. A few institutions (such as 'rur A') chose to narrow their focus further, while a more common response (such as by 'med A', 'med B' 'med C' and 'med D') was to move towards the other main camp – that of the universities. Hence, four institutions responded to the QR by changing their status and increasing their market and product offerings, becoming more similar to the universities. While this may lead to institutional convergence, the universities did not remain completely static. As Figure 11.1 shows, they explicitly focused more on the international arena in both teaching and research. Overall, however, the number of institutions targeting national and international student segments (the upper right-hand quadrant in Figure 11.1) has increased dramatically, with only a few institutions specifically choosing a narrow strategy. In what follows, the three main strategies are presented in more detail.

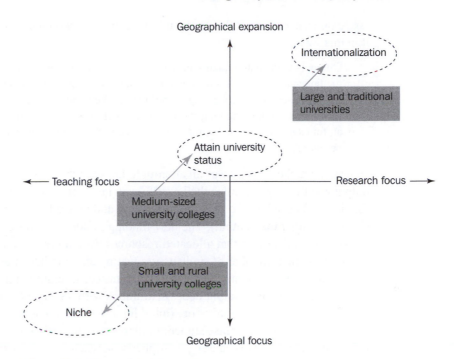

Figure 11.1 *Three strategic positions*

Niche strategy

Some institutions responded to the reform by choosing a niche strategy. This means narrowing the product line or focusing on a specific group of students. The niche strategy was particularly common among university colleges that already had a rather narrow geographical and product scope. One example is 'rur A'. The staff viewed their institution as an important actor for the region and emphasized the continued contribution to the immediate environment. While the focus was regional, specific research and teaching areas were sometimes targeted for specialization among the regions. One university college in our larger sample focused on logistics, an area where it had developed high competence and that offered a Ph.D. programme. Similar patterns, with ambitions for one or two Ph.D. programmes, could be seen among other university colleges that opted for a niche strategy.

A central goal for small rural university colleges has been to increase their number of students. The challenge of obtaining enough students was evident before the QR, but the new funding model, where the university colleges benefit from the number of students who earn study credits or take exams, accentuated this challenge. One of the respondents expressed it in this way:

> Output is defined as a quality measure. . . . This has consequences for the financial side. . . . There should be a quota in terms of how many students each university college should have. We hope that the government is thinking long-term, so that it will be possible to study at, for example, ['rur A']. Otherwise the research environment could be ruined.

Hence, the niche strategy was an attempt to increase the focus on student output and thereby minimize the loss of financial resources. Previously, funding had been based on a larger lump sum and on student enrolment (i.e. input rather than output). The new funding system was more transparent in the sense that allocated resources were more closely related to output, such as number of students graduating and number of research publications. However, student output generates considerably higher revenues than research output does. Institutions with a strained financial situation, such as 'rur A', therefore opted for a regional focus in a continued attempt to increase student numbers and, in so doing, gain financial resources. This caused an emphasis on teaching at the expense of research. As a consequence, several highly productive researchers have left the university colleges.

The niche strategy has contributed to the teaching goals within the reform as it entails an increase in students in one discipline or area (for example, teacher or nurse programme). In terms of research, however, the niche strategy has led to reduced research, as departments with few students have been closed down, despite their having extensive research outputs. One of the risks of the niche strategy is that the university colleges will not attract enough students and therefore fail to attract the resources required in order to survive in the HE market. A possible scenario, based on historical experience, is that if the strategy fails, the Ministry of HE will provide extra budgetary resources. If the aim with the competitive element in the QR is to force HE to be attractive to students, then such actions could be counter-productive in the long run.

Achieve university status

A number of HE institutions responded to the QR by attempting to achieve university (rather than university college) status. This is a proactive strategy that demands substantial resources and efforts from the management, as the 'university' label, according to the new regulations, requires that the institution offer a minimum of four doctoral programmes and five Master's programmes.

More than half of the university colleges in Norway either had the stated ambition of becoming a university in their strategy documents or were in the process of evaluating how to become a university. Several university colleges in the case study opted for this strategic response. In some institutions, the work needed to become a university had been going on for several years and the QR merely provided an opportunity to push this work further. One of the respondents explained that they had already produced material with the new 'university' name, although they had yet to achieve the status.

While increased status was an obvious motive for this response, there were no immediate financial incentives related to becoming a university. On the contrary, this was a costly strategy, as substantial resources had to be spent on training staff, and reviewing and upgrading educational programmes to the required level. However, there may be expectations of future financial benefits as the social democratic government that came to power in 2006 has already discussed the potential for extra resources for newly established universities.

Two tactics for achieving university status appear in the data. Some institutions, such as 'med A', chose to develop the necessary competences and meet the requirements by themselves. Another tactic, employed, for example, by 'med D', was to enter into an alliance with another university college. Our data suggest that when the university college could handle the financial burden of achieving the university status by itself, then it would do so. These institutions were generally situated in medium-sized cities. If the financial resources were lacking, strategic alliances were used as a vehicle to secure the necessary resources for obtaining university status. It is interesting to note that university colleges in the large cities (such as Oslo and Bergen) did not attempt to become universities. One reason for this could be that the university colleges in cities with already established universities were reluctant to enter into more direct competition with these.

Although becoming a university required increased focus on research, implementation was costly. It was not possible to get any extra funding for this purpose from the government. Hence, in order to generate funding for new programmes and research, the focus on teaching escalated:

> . . . more large lectures; we feel great pressure to get the
> students through our programme. Otherwise we do not get the
> money.

Resources had to be reallocated from the existing bachelor programmes
to the development of the new Master's and doctoral programmes. Many
of the respondents were critical of the new strategy and claimed that it
was problematic that employees teaching at the bachelor level were
'paying' for the development of new programmes. Some of the
respondents wanted instead to continue as a university college, and
one of the respondents stated:

> The dean did not follow employees' suggestions. We did not want a
> doctoral programme, not everyone liked it . . . much of the resources
> are kept at the central level. Less of the QR resources have been
> distributed to the departments.

Not only were resources reallocated to the development of Master's and
doctoral programmes, but also the number of students was increased.
This created pressure on the staff, as is illustrated in the following
quotations: 'The Quality Reform is more of everything'; 'The number of
students has increased dramatically'. As a result, employee satisfaction
showed mixed results in several of these institutions and a number of
respondents questioned whether this in fact could lead to better-quality
teaching.

The 'achieve university status' strategy contributed to the reform goals
through the increased output of graduates at bachelor level. However,
this involved a risk. Increasing the number of students at the bachelor
level in order to get enough resources to develop Master- and
doctoral-level courses can reduce the quality of lower-level courses
as fewer contact hours between the lecturers and students will
negatively affect those students who need close supervision to master
and complete their education. Another risk with the 'achieve university
status' strategy is based on the need for competent staff. The strategy
creates greater competition for research staff, and, although the number
is increasing, there are not too many people in Norway with Ph.D.s.
Therefore, sometimes the same employees can be found employed at
several institutions (employees are allowed to work part time in addition
to their permanent position). One consequence of this can be that the
employees do not contribute much to the university college as such, but
offer their name and list of publications to the highest bidder in order to
provide extra resources. The role of associated researchers then becomes

more of a legitimating role than a real contribution to the educational environment as such.

International strategy

The third response to the QR among HE institutions was to explicitly pursue an international strategy. This strategy manifested itself through expressions of international goals, such as aiming to become one of the best universities in Europe or in the world. Thus, the competitive arena has been expanded from a national market to the international HE market. Institutions that opted for an international strategy also participated in international ranking systems and emphasized student exchange programmes as well as attracting international students. The expanded market notion also manifested itself in research, through competition for EU funding and increased focus on publications in international journals. The latter can also be viewed as a response to the new funding system, which is partly based on the amount of international publications.

The institutions that responded with international strategies were mainly the old universities in the larger cities and the specialist university colleges such as business schools. These institutions have generally been considered as having high status because they offer both Master- and Ph.D.-level degrees. It is interesting to note that it is the universities, with their favourable historical positions, that have been most sceptical towards the QR. Resistance can be expected if their status is threatened or diluted, for instance, by the entry of new actors, such as the university colleges. However, the threat of loss of status was rarely mentioned as a reason for scepticism. Instead, our data suggest that three main factors triggered resistance: uncertainty about the future quality of HE, threats to academic freedom and threats of losing the open universities (universities that are open, meaning free of charge for everyone in Norway with a high school diploma).

Many of the university employees expressed doubts as to how the QR would increase the quality of HE. For them the reform meant more standardization and focus on student output. Some of the respondents expressed the increased focus on standardization and financial issues in this way: 'Management and funding are put together', or 'We will get a university that is more commercialized and streamlined'.

Academic freedom has been highly valued in Norway's universities. The most common understanding among Norwegian academics seems to be that the researcher should be at liberty to choose which courses to teach and which areas and topics to research. This perception of a right to 'academic freedom' has been described as an obstacle to change by some of the reformers. One way to deal with this has been to change the leadership and to move away from elected leaders (among equals) towards employing full-time leaders (e.g. heads of department and similar positions). The idea has been to strengthen the role of the leader and to emphasize strategic decisions, sometimes at the expense of academic freedom. While there has been much debate and scepticism about this issue, some respondents were more optimistic and expressed their expectations of the new leadership roles in this way: 'Full-time leaders have to make the unpopular decisions.'

One important difference between HE organizations in Norway and those in the rest of Europe is that Norwegian HE organizations are not allowed to charge students a fee. The Norwegian HE system is also based on free access for everyone with a high school certificate (although many programmes have only a limited number of places). Therefore, the conditions differ from those in many other countries in the need to attract students. Some respondents explained that the focus on becoming 'the best' was perceived as a contradiction to the idea of universities as open to everyone.

Despite the expressed resistance to the QR, universities responded by a slight repositioning. There were several reasons for this response. First, the universities had high status nationally and had long traditions of international ties. Regardless of national reforms and suchlike, they were more subject to international pressure to make changes than, for instance, university colleges. Hence, the universities reacted to the increased pressure from the European Union and the Bologna declaration to create a more competitive European market in higher education and it was more difficult for large universities and business schools to disregard the increasing international focus, for example, on educational rating lists. Second, at the national level the Ministry of Education made it its ambition to make the HE system in Norway one of the best in the world. 'Centres of excellence' were established for research, and this generated competition among the large universities and specialist university colleges. These centres were provided with extra funding for ten years and were thus an important source of research funding, which increased the push for further internationalization.

In order to compete in the national and international arena in both research and teaching, several universities reorganized and reduced the number of departments substantially. This implies a shift from more specialist departments to less specialist departments. Our data indicate that one reason for this was a belief in scale as the means for developing strong and internationally competitive research environments. Another reason that was stated involved cost reductions: 'The Quality Reform and mergers between departments have been closely related.' This trend towards less specialized departments was found in all the universities that chose an international strategy except for one institution, which had reduced the number of departments just before the QR was introduced. The same patterns were found in the specialized university colleges (business schools, etc.). One of the more proactive tactics for increased emphasis on international high-quality research was found in 'uni A', where the number of students enrolled was deliberately reduced in order to increase quality and accentuate its role as a research university.

The international strategy contributed to the reform goal by increasing both student and research outputs. Effectiveness is the main challenge with this strategic response. High-quality research can be difficult to define and measure. There is a risk that we will see the production of a large amount of scientific work, but of low quality. Another risk with the international strategy is that it may create a division between teachers and researchers, since the best researchers will focus on research (for example, in centres of excellence) and the best teachers will focus on teaching. While this may optimize each activity, it may also contradict traditional goals of research-based teaching at Norwegian HE institutions.

Comparing responses and long-term effects

In summary, we found that small and rural HE institutions opted predominantly for a niche strategy, medium-sized institutions in cities that did not have traditional universities opted for improving their status by becoming universities, while the traditional universities and specialized institutions aimed for an international strategy. The different responses can in part be explained by looking at the existing financial resources within an institution as well as its size, history and status.

Some of the HE institutions (such as 'rur A') had limited financial resources, hence their responses were limited. No matter how good their track record on teaching and research, unless they had sufficient resources they could neither opt for becoming a university nor enter the international arena and compete in international rankings. The niche strategy was therefore the only viable strategy for small university colleges with limited financial resources.

Small institutions with greater resources could opt for increasing their status by becoming a university. For the university colleges with sufficient resources, the QR with its competitive elements provided an opportunity to make changes that had been planned for a long time. As Kingdon (1984) argued, a reform can provide a window of opportunity to achieve university status. However, small institutions were not able to become universities on their own, but had to enter into alliances with other institutions.

The institutions with the strongest finances were the traditional universities. Because of their history and high status, these institutions did not feel that their future financial security was threatened in the same way as did the smaller institutions. The large, traditional universities therefore had the most options in terms of strategic responses. Their historical role also made them attentive to international trends and demands. Hence, despite widespread scepticism and perhaps some constraints based on their long-standing high status, these institutions responded by increasing their focus on research and developing a number of new programmes.

Our findings indicate that all three responses contributed in the short term to the overall goals of the reform (increasing the quality of teaching and research), but along different dimensions. Although one might argue that there is a convergence within HE, with more institutions becoming similar to the universities, the findings we have presented suggest that the gap between small and rural university colleges and medium-sized and large institutions is widening. One might, then, ask what the long-term consequences for the HE sector will be.

Because of increased rivalry and competition, strategic positioning theory would predict that organizations must either differentiate themselves clearly in terms of research and teaching focus, or there will be a consolidation in which some organizations merge and some may even disappear. This is primarily because of limitations in terms of students and researchers, as there are not enough students or researchers in the Norwegian market to make too many 'similar' HE institutions viable.

Because of the limited market size, greater differences in terms of financial resources can be expected and there will be increased room for manoeuvre for those that increase their income. One possible scenario is that the large organizations will become even larger, while the small will become even smaller or simply cease to exist. Finally, a market perspective is built on the idea that the fittest will survive. The underlying assumption seems to be that a high production of graduates will lead to high quality and that a high production of research outcomes will ensure high-quality research. However, our findings indicate that it can be challenging to focus simultaneously on high-quantity *and* high-quality education and research.

Conclusions

We have explored how HE institutions in Norway responded to a government-led Quality Reform initiated by the Bologna process. The aim was to improve the quality of HE through structural and financial changes. A central element in the transformation of HE concerns the creation of a competitive market for higher education. The idea is that increased competition will result in improved quality. When faced with changes that implied increased competition, business thinking and fundamental changes in the sources of financing, the Norwegian HE institutions responded not passively and defensively, but rather proactively and by positioning themselves in different ways in order to meet future challenges. In accordance with traditional strategy theory, the institutions reacted to the new market conditions by actively and strategically positioning themselves. This study has identified three different positions that institutions took as a response to the QR: adopting a niche strategy, achieving university status and adopting an international strategy. The way in which any particular institution responded depended on factors such as its existing financial resources, size, and previous history and status. While all three strategies at one level or another contributed to the reform goals, they also brought less intended effects that may, in the long run, serve to go against some of the intentions of the reform.

The long-term consequences of these three strategies have yet to be seen. According to strategic theory and the positioning perspective, the competition among these institutions will intensify, as many university colleges come to resemble the universities. Unless they can all generate revenues, the question is whether all of the current organizations will remain in the market. Such a situation may lead to the request for additional financial support from the government. The competition for students, staff and financial resources depends among other things on the relatedness of different study programmes. It also depends on the extent to which the new universities manage to develop their core competences and create competitive advantages within specific disciplines. The competition for financing by attracting an increased number of students will not be the most challenging, however, particularly if foreign students continue to gain free access to Norwegian HE and as long as financial resources are ploughed into the sector. The fiercest competition is likely to be within the market for competent researchers. Currently, there are not enough academics within the Norwegian market to fill the positions available. In the past it has been challenging to attract foreign researchers to Norway, as wage levels and status within academia are relatively low compared to those in other countries.

In other words, when Norwegian HE starts to compete in the European HE arena, this can be understood as a first step towards a global market for HE – not only when it comes to students, but also when it comes to researchers. Halvorsen (2005) refers to the growing market of HE as 'knowledge shopping'. The findings in our study show that Norwegian HE institutions have responded proactively in order to change their strategic position. The traditional role of the university, as a creator of nation-states' identity, is under transformation into a role as a creator of global public space and common global values. The nation-state has previously been an important guardian of free access to knowledge, as well as the freedom of knowledge producers. Hence, this study directs attention to consequences of the HE sector becoming a global product in a global marketplace.

By way of implications for further research on governance in the public sector, this study emphasizes the need to pay greater attention to use of global standards, such as the Bologna process, and how they are used in order to change both national systems and their interaction with the systems of other nations rather than treating standards as something given.

Note

1 The conceptualization of students as consumers has triggered a heated debate, as has the notion of hospital patients as consumers of health services. One reason for the debate is that viewing students as consumers brings with it a number of associations and implications, such as the idea that 'the customer is always right'. For the purpose of analysis the students are viewed as the customers here. The primary point is not, however, to defend the conceptualization of students as customers, with all of its implications.

12 Changing organizational values and actions in public services: a longitudinal empirical analysis

Richard M. Walker and

Fariborz Damanpour

- Introduction
- Public services improvement strategy
- Change in public service organizations
- Methods
- Findings
- Discussion and conclusions

Introduction

Swathes of management reforms have swept through Western democratic countries over the past two decades, resulting in changes in management, organization and service delivery (Pollitt and Bouckeart, 2000). Reforms have sought to change the values and actions of public organizations, placing emphasis at various points on competition and privatization, customer focus, innovation, decentralization, and partnerships. Analyses of such changes are often limited to case studies, and we know little about how public organizations and public servants have changed.

In this chapter we will use a four-year panel of data from English local governments to explore the changes in management reform values and actions. The focus will be upon the programme of management reform referred to as the United Kingdom Labour government's public service improvement strategy. This is a top-down change programme that, because of the centralized nature of English public service, uses legislation and oversight to achieve implementation. We are particularly interested in the gap between perceptions of attitudes (values) and behaviour (actions) as expressed by public managers in public sector organizations. Do attitudes change over time and do they change positively in response to the management reforms rolled out by higher levels of government? Do behaviours change over time, again in the anticipated direction? Do expressed attitudes differ from behaviours over time? And how do public managers' perceptions of management reform change: radically, incrementally or in a bumpy fashion? The data used to explore these questions are drawn from an electronic survey conducted from 2001 to 2004 that includes 677 cases and over 300 organizations. The survey measured values and actions for the key areas of the Labour government's reform agenda: choice, devolution, flexibility and minimum standards. Our analysis includes nine measures under these headings: competition, continuous improvement, corporateness, customer focus, devolution to the front line, innovation, entrepreneurial behaviour, partnership and performance measurement.

The balance of the chapter is set out thus: in the next section we outline the policy arena and the details of the United Kingdom Labour government's public service improvement strategy that was launched in the late 1990s under the leadership of Prime Minister Blair. We follow this with a discussion of change in organizations and then outline our methods, including our units of analysis, data and measures. Findings suggest that organizational change is more likely to be found in attitudes or values than in behaviours and actions, and that change in both values and actions increases over time. Although change in organizations usually occurs incrementally, we found that the largest changes are recorded between the first and subsequent years of our sample, suggesting that perhaps without continued urgency for change, motivation to change may be reduced over time. In conclusion we discuss the implications of these findings for theory and practice.

Public services improvement strategy

Under the leadership of Prime Minister Tony Blair, the Labour government's public services improvement strategy was outlined on a number of occasions. The first articulation was in a Fabian Society booklet by the Prime Minister (Blair, 2002) entitled *The Courage of Our Convictions: Why Reform of the Public Services is the Route to Social Justice*. The framework was subsequently developed and presented, along with examples of successful reform, by the Prime Minister's Office for Public Service Reform (OPSR, 2002, 2003) (the OPSR was disestablished in May 2007 and the responsibilities for public service reform transferred to other parts of the Cabinet Office and government departments. For an assessment of the consequences of this regime, see Walker and Boyne (2006)).

Labour's strategy sought to achieve excellence in public service delivery by way of four principles of reform: (1) guaranteed national standards of service through rational planning, (2) devolution and delegation, (3) flexibility and incentives, and (4) enhanced choice for the consumer (Blair, 2002; OPSR, 2002, 2003). The OPSR (2002:11) argued that '[t]he starting point must be that the public has a right to good quality education, to healthcare, to law and order, to local authority services. . . . Wherever they live, citizens should be able to rely on good quality public services.' This high-quality level was to be achieved through a 'national framework of standards and accountability with floor targets beneath which no public service should fall' (Blair, 2002:21). The performance of local government has been assessed since the early 1990s. Targets for all authorities are currently specified through the Best Value regime (OPSR, 2002) and measured by Best Value Performance Indicators (Office of the Deputy Prime Minister, 2000). Performance targets were set to ensure national standards were achieved (OPSR, 2002), and performance management systems (OPSR, 2002) were the route to success. The director of the OPSR (Thompson, 2002) argued that service providers need measurement and control systems that enable managers to review and analyse how resources are spent and what results are achieved.

Excellence was to be achieved through the devolution and delegation of power to the local level. Blair (2002:23) argues that '[t]he evidence is overwhelming that front-line leadership makes a critical difference to the quality of public services'. Achieving the benefits of devolved and delegated public services was believed to require change at two levels. First, central government controls would be relaxed to ensure that organizational leaders (e.g. headteachers of schools or chief executives of local authorities) were given powers to manage effectively. In the local government arena, extra freedoms and flexibilities were intended to release councils from 'unnecessary restrictions and controls' (OPSR, 2002:16). Second, within organizations at the service delivery level, where customer pressure is brought to bear, further devolution and delegation were required. The emphasis is upon resolving problems as near to the front line as possible or, as the OPSR (2003) puts it, 'leading from the front line'. In short, devolved management seeks to ensure that service providers 'shape services around the needs and aspirations of customers and communities' (OPSR, 2002:16).

Reform of professionals also seeks to ensure that service providers become more responsive to the demands of users. In return for higher investment in public services, the government expected 'higher standards of professional engagement [. . .] and new flexibility in the professions that breaks down old working practices, old demarcations' (Blair, 2002:27). Three specific reforms were advocated to achieve such flexibilities and incentives: 'reducing bureaucratic demarcations, restrictive practices and red tape; incentives and rewards for front-line staff; and inspirational leadership and management' (OPSR, 2002:18). To tackle red tape, 'innovation needs to be promoted, encouraging staff to find new ways of responding to customer demands' (OPSR, 2002:19). Alongside innovation, cooperation between services is singled out because 'public services work best when they work together' (OPSR, 2002:19). Monetary and non-monetary incentives are advocated so that people choose to work in the public rather than the private or non-profit sector. Substantial emphasis is placed on non-monetary rewards to ensure that 'people feel valued at work [and are] treated fairly' (OPSR, 2002:21). Finally, inspirational leadership and management are singled out as a mechanism to drive improvement: 'Public services reform requires support for and development of excellent leaders capable of tackling poor management and inspiring ambitious performance' (OPSR, 2002:21).

Expanding 'choice' is the final part of the Labour government's public service improvement rubric. Choice is defined in two ways: choice between providers and suppliers of public services, and choice within each service for users. Choice between providers implies the introduction of contestable public service markets, with the voluntary and private sectors actively encouraged to play a role in service delivery (Blair, 2002:30). Choice through contestability is believed to drive up performance across the sector: 'Widening the market to create more suppliers of public services (contestability) can improve the quality of management and value for money' (OPSR, 2002:24). Greatest weight is attached to working with the private sector: 'public–private partnerships increase investment, with the private sector investment additional to that provided by the public sector (rather than instead of it as before)' (OPSR, 2002:25). Choice within services reflects the needs and demands of users for the type of service they wish to receive. Examples include choices within the curriculum at school and opportunities to access different types of health care services (Blair, 2002:30). The OPSR (2002:24) argues that 'where customers have different requirements, there should be more diversity of service provision, with customers involved in the design so that the services are as responsive as possible'.

The centralized nature of English government suggests that it is very likely that reforms in the areas of choice, flexibility, minimum standards and devolution would be transmitted around the social system of English public services and that local authorities (the unit of analysis in the chapter) would adopt these reforms. A key question is concerned with the nature of the adoption of these changes and the extent to which authorities present themselves as having changed, perhaps seeking legitimacy, and the degree to which they have. We go on to discuss the likely nature of change in these public service organizations in the next section.

Change in public service organizations

Types of organizational change

Chapter 1 outlined key dimensions of change as discussed in the organizational change literature. Here, we consider in more detail some of these dimensions as they relate to this study. Broadly, change can be defined as a planned or unplanned response to the external or internal pressures and forces (Jick and Peiperl, 2003). It continues to be a topic of interest in management research because organizations are continuously pressured to change by modifying their strategies, structures and processes in order to remain effective in an environment characterized by technological change, globalization, deregulation and resource scarcity (Pettigrew *et al.*, 1992; Pollitt and Bouckeart, 2000; Wischnevsky and Damanpour, 2006). Studies of the management of change in organizations report that the impetus for organizational change includes the occurrence of environmental change (Burke, 2002; Lawrence and Lorsch, 1967), pressures to improve organizational performance (Wischnevsky and Damanpour, 2006; Zajac and Kraatz, 1993) and the installation of new leaders or major changes in the top executive team (Sherman and Chaganti, 1998; Virany *et al.*, 1992). Overall, independent of the event or condition that triggers change, research suggests that the intended goal of changing an organization is to enable it to adapt to new external and/or internal conditions and to maintain or improve its level of performance (Burke, 2002; Pettigrew *et al.*, 2001; Wischnevsky and Damanpour, 2006).

Change theorists often distinguish between two types of change: first-order change, which involves modifications in a system that do not affect its key parameters; and second-order change, which entails a transformation of the fundamental properties of the system (Burke, 2002; Wischnevsky and Damanpour, 2005). In organizational studies, second-order change has been characterized in different ways, including core feature change, organizational transformation, and configuration or archetype change (Hannan and Freeman, 1984; Miller and Friesen, 1984; Romanelli and Tushman, 1994; Wischnevsky and Damanpour, 2005). Following theories in biology, psychology and sociology, some management scholars have proposed that fundamental organizational change occurs in short periods of discontinuous, revolutionary change, which punctuate long eras of relative stability typified by incremental, convergent changes (Gersick, 1988). However, how second-order change is achieved is mainly a subject of theoretical interest and has received limited empirical scrutiny. Historically, studies of organizational change have adopted the evolutionary view of change (Burke, 2002; Haveman *et al.*, 2001). Influenced by Darwinian gradualism, evolutionary views assume that organizational change is incremental and continuous, and that fundamental differences result from the accumulation of small changes over long periods (Wischnevsky and Damanpour, 2005).

The way organizations adopt change will most likely vary according to the rate of occurrence of change in their external environment. By's (2005) review of organizational change management categorizes change by its rate of occurrence into five types: discontinuous, incremental, bumpy incremental, continuous and bumpy continuous change. In this chapter we are not concerned with continuous or bumpy continuous changes, as they take place at the sub-organizational level within departments and subunits (By, 2005). Discontinuous change is a second-order change and is marked by radical and swift changes in organizational core features (i.e. simultaneous changes in structure, strategy and processes). It is likely to occur in response to extreme environmental shocks of the scale of Hurricane Katrina in the United States during 2006 and SARS in Asia in 2003. Programmes of management reform often build upon prior practice and are not likely to be discontinuous in their nature. We focus on By's (2005) two categories of incremental change as they are more likely to be typified by a system-wide programme of reform that is led from a higher level of government to a lower one. Incremental change 'is concerned with organisation-wide strategies and the ability to constantly adapt these to the demands of both the external and internal environment', whereas bumpy incremental change 'is characterised by periods of relative peacefulness punctuated by acceleration in the pace of change' (By, 2005:372).

Organizational change and performance

A recent review of the literature on the relationship between organizational transformation and performance identified three theoretical perspectives that portray, albeit differently, the relationship between change and performance (Wischnevsky and Damanpour, 2006). These authors state that according to the *rational perspective*, organizational change is an adaptive and deliberate process that is planned by decision-makers who seek the explicit goal of either closing a perceived performance gap or seizing an attractive opportunity to boost performance (By, 2005; Wischnevsky and Damanpour, 2006). On the contrary, according to the *population ecology perspective*, organizational change is hampered by inertia, which could lead to 'a diminution in an organization's ability to perform reliably and accountably, and thus – eventually – to performance declines' that may raise the chances of organizational failure (Wischnevsky and Damanpour, 2006:110). Finally, according to the *institutional perspective*, organizational change is driven by pressures to conform to industry, professional and societal patterns (Wischnevsky and Damanpour, 2006).

The improvement strategy in public services can be attributed to rational and institutional perspectives of organizational change and performance (Ashworth *et al.*, 2007). (We do not consider the population ecology perspective because it views changes in organization-wide strategy and structure as negatively impacting the ability of an organization to maintain high levels of sustained performance (Wischnevsky and Damanpour, 2006).) Both perspectives postulate that change aims to maintain the organization–environment fit to help the organization remain viable and effective. However, whereas the rational perspective emphasizes factors in the environment that relate to demands for efficiency and effectiveness in the production and exchange of products and services in markets, the institutional perspective emphasizes factors that relate to demands for conformity to rules and norms in order to obtain legitimacy and resources (Scott, 1992; Wischnevsky and Damanpour, 2006). As DiMaggio and Powell (1983) articulate, institutional isomorphism may come about as a result of three different types of pressures or forces. (Isomorphism is a central concept in the institutional perspective and is defined as 'a constraining process that forces one unit in a population to resemble other units that face the same set of environmental conditions' (DiMaggio and Powell, 1983:149).) The first are external pressures on dependent organizations that need resources and legitimacy (*coercive isomorphism*). The second are pressures arising from the adoption of innovation and new routines by elite and leading organizations in the industry or organizational population (*mimetic isomorphism*). The third are pressures related to adhering to professional standards (*normative isomorphism*) (Wischnevsky and Damanpour, 2006:109–110).

The first and fourth principles of public service reform stated above can relate to both perspectives. They reflect the rational perspective because a planned change regime is initiated and monitored externally by central government to direct and motivate public service organizations to become more effective and perform better by improving the quality and quantity of the services they provide to their clients and customers. The reform principles also reflect (1) the coercive isomorphism of the institutional perspective, because public service organizations depend on the government for resources; and (2) mimetic isomorphism, because these organizations eventually need to improve the delivery and quality of their services somewhat to imitate those that are innovators or early adopters of management reform.

Models of organizational change and performance have generally followed the open system and contingency theories of organizations (for a review of models of organizational change, see Burke, 2002). They assume that organizational effectiveness requires both internal and external alignments; thus, successful implementation of organizational change involves simultaneous changes in multiple organizational dimensions. For example, the Burke–Litwin model considers the impetus from the external environment as the 'input', improvements in the performance of the organization due to change as the 'output', and corresponding changes in leadership, strategy, structure and processes as the 'throughput' of the organizational change process (Burke, 2002:198–201). The second and third principles of public service reform, including delegation of power to the local authorities and provision of incentives and flexibility for innovation and change, exemplify the throughputs. The Burke–Litwin model identifies organizational leadership as the primary dimension that is alerted and influenced by environmental forces for change. Organizational leaders in turn influence and change the other organizational dimensions (e.g. strategy, administrative processes, work-unit climate, rewards) to provide internal and external alignments necessary for individual, unit and organizational performance.

Managing organizational change

Damanpour and Schneider (2006:220) observe that organizational managers, especially top managers, heavily influence organizational capabilities by establishing organizational culture, motivating and enabling organizational members, and building capacity for change and innovation (Chaganti *et al.*, 2005; Elenkov *et al.*, 2005; Hambrick and Mason, 1984; Yukl, 1999). Top managers' responsibilities include modulating the process of scanning the external environment, formulating policy to respond to environmental change, and allocating and controlling resources for meeting the performance goals (Damanpour and Schneider, 2006). Managers are a potent force for or against change and innovation because they are mainly responsible for encouraging the values and attitudes that should prevail across the organization in support of innovation and change (Bantel and Jackson, 1989; Elenkov *et al.*, 2005). Thus, their personal characteristics, especially their attitude towards change, influence organizational culture and climate conducive to reform, innovation and change (Damanpour and Schneider, 2006; Hoffman and Hegarty, 1993; West and Anderson, 1996).

The Burke–Litwin model similarly emphasizes the role of top managers, especially transformational leaders, in shaping organizational culture and work-unit climate, development of vision, mission and strategies, and adoption of administrative systems and incentives for motivating organizational members for the successful implementation of change (Burke, 2002).

In this chapter we focus on managers' attitude towards change and the corresponding actions taken to implement organizational change. Studies of leadership behaviour have identified 'change-oriented' behaviour as a unique dimension distinct from traditional 'task-oriented' and 'employee-oriented' behaviours (Ekvall and Arvonen, 1991; Yukl, 1999). It entails a manager who takes long-term perspectives, describes appealing visions, encourages and accepts new ideas, and forges agreements and approvals with people inside and outside of the organization to initiate and implement change (Damanpour and Schneider, 2006; Ekvall and Arvonen, 1991; Yukl, 1999). Studies of organizational innovation and change also report that managers' favourable attitude towards change facilitates all phases of the process of innovation or change. For example, in a study of local government organizations in the United States, Damanpour and Schneider (2006) found that top managers' favourable attitude towards competition and entrepreneurship, two aspects of public services management reform, positively affect the initiation, adoption and implementation of innovation.

Methods

Unit of analysis

This study is situated in the English local government sector. English local governments are politically elected bodies with a Westminster-style cabinet system of political management. They are multi-purpose authorities delivering education, social services, regulatory services (such as land-use planning), housing, libraries, leisure services and welfare benefits in specific geographical areas. London boroughs, metropolitan boroughs and unitary authorities deliver all of these services in urban areas. In rural areas a two-tier system prevails, with county councils administering education and social services, and district councils providing environmental and welfare services, while some regulatory functions such as land-use planning are shared. In the two-tier system, county councils' expenditure is around three times that of district councils, given their delivery of education and social services. In many cases, district councils have outsourced services such as public housing provision and management and leisure services, and thus play a residual role. Authorities are not all-purpose; for example, health care is provided by health authorities. They employ professional career staff and receive around two-thirds of their income and guidance on the implementation of legislation from the central government.

Data

Within each local authority, data were collected from multiple informants at the corporate and service levels. This strategy was adopted to address the weakness of prior studies that have utilized elite surveys, which typically collect evidence on organizational leaders' aspirations rather than actual changes in organizational behaviour, and overlook the range of different perceptions within organizations (Bowman and Ambrosini, 1997; Walker and Enticott, 2004; Brewer, 2006). Two echelons were used to overcome the sample bias problem faced in surveying large numbers of informants from one organizational level. Corporate officers and service officers were selected because research has shown that attitudes differ between hierarchical levels within organizations (Aiken and Hage, 1968), and has been confirmed for this dataset (see Walker and Brewer, 2008; Walker and Enticott, 2004; Walker et al., 2007). Corporate officers included the chief executive officer and members of the senior management team, and the service officers were constituted of directors of service areas (such as the Director of Education or the Director of Social Services) and assistant directors (including the Head of Benefits and Revenue and the Head of School Improvement). For this sample, a simple organizational mean would drown out the voices of the smaller numbers of corporate officers surveyed. Therefore, an organizational mean for our measures of values and action was derived from a mean of individual corporate officers in each authority and a mean of individual service officers in each local government. This method of calculating an organizational mean maintains variations across organizations and converts categorical measures to continuous ones.

Data are taken from the 'The Long Term Evaluation of Best Value and Its Impact' dataset, an electronic survey of English local authorities. The survey explored informants' perceptions of organization and management, notably culture, structure, strategy-making and strategy content, drivers of service improvement, background variables and the management reform regime called 'Best Value' (Boyne et al., 2004). A copy of the full questionnaire is available on request from the authors. In each authority, questionnaires were sent to up to three corporate officers and four service officers (the chief officer and three front-line supervisory officers) in each of seven service areas (education, social care, land-use planning, waste management, housing, libraries and leisure, and benefits). All survey questions were in the form of a Likert-type scale, and informants were asked to rate their authority (for corporate officers) or service (for service officers) on seven points that ran from 1 (disagreement) to 7 (agreement).

At the core of the 'Best Value' survey is a representative sample of 102 English local authorities. Representativeness is based upon background variables including deprivation, population and performance (see Martin et al., 2003). The survey was conducted annually from 2001 to 2004. Table 12.1 outlines the number of authorities, the officer echelons and the number of individuals who responded to the survey. In 2001 a census was undertaken of all 386 English local authorities, and responses were received from 314, a response rate of 81.3 per cent. In 2002 and 2003 the 102 core representative authorities were sampled; all responded in 2002, and four did not respond in 2003 (Table 12.1). The 2004 survey was administered to 175 authorities (the 102 representative

Table 12.1 *Year-on-year organizational and echelon responses to the Best Value survey*

	2001	2002	2003	2004
Number of organizations	314	102	98	163
Respondents				
Corporate officers	534	209	208	242
Service officers	1,821	999	820	975
Total individual respondents	2,355	1,308	1,028	1,217

authorities plus all other upper-tier councils), and responses were received from 163 authorities – a response rate of 93 per cent.

Measures

The measures selected in this study relate to the United Kingdom Labour government's local government modernization agenda (LGMA) (DETR, 1998) during the years of the first Blair government. The overall objectives of the LGMA are to improve services, to increase the accountability of local government and to increase public participation and confidence in it. These objectives are intrinsically linked to the public service improvement strategy. The survey instrument focused on the service improvement branch of this reform strategy, a performance improvement regime called Best Value that expected continuous improvement in cost-effectiveness and service standards (DETR, 1998). Improvement was to be achieved by internal organizational processes including corporate management, consultation with stakeholders, users and citizens, establishing the competitiveness of services, comparisons through techniques such as benchmarking, challenging and questioning service requirements, and strategic plans that outlined the routes to improved performance.

The Best Value regime emphasized change in values and actions by promoting organizational cultures and encouraging change to structures, processes and strategies (Boyne *et al.*, 2004). Analysis of the LGMA and its service improvement facets, together with the measures available in the Best Value survey, led to the identification of nine pairs of variables representing values and actions. Respondents to the survey were asked to agree or disagree with the value or attitude statements. For the action or behaviour statements, respondents were asked to consider whether or not the topic was a major part of the organization's approach to management, organization or service delivery. These variables offer two measures of choice (one competition and one user) labelled *competition* and *customer focus*, one of devolution (*devolution to the front line*), one of minimum standards (*performance management*) and five of flexibility, majoring on the improvement aspects (labelled *continuous improvement, corporateness, innovation, entrepreneurial behaviour* and *partnership*). Table 12.2 lists the Labour government's public service improvement

Table 12.2 *Management reform value and action labels and measures*

Management reform category	Value measures	Action measures
Choice		
Competition	The service welcomes private sector involvement and partnership	Contracting out or outsourcing (e.g. the same or similar service delivered by another agency under contract)
Customer focus	Most managers place the needs of users first and foremost when planning and delivering services	Working more closely with users
Devolution		
Devolution to the front line	Control is devolved to service managers	Decentralization (e.g. organizing services on a neighbourhood basis)
Flexibility improvement		
Continuous improvement	There is a strong focus on continuous improvement in our service	New approaches to improvement (e.g. EFQM, re-engineering, charter marks)
Corporateness	The authority's mission, values, objectives are clearly and widely understood and owned by all staff in the service	Enhanced coordination and joint working with other departments
Innovation	The service is at the forefront of innovative approaches	Providing new services to new users
Entrepreneurial behaviour	The service is prepared to take risks	Developing new methods of raising income (e.g. charging for services)
Partnership	Strategy is made in consultation with our external stakeholders (e.g. users, other agencies, etc.)	Developing local strategic partnerships (e.g. voluntary partnerships to coordinate funding, policy, implementation, etc.)
Minimum standards		
Performance measurement	There is a well-developed framework of clear performance measurement and targets to drive what we do	The introduction of new management information systems (e.g. performance management systems)

categories, the variable names and the measures of values and actions used in this study. It is important to note that these measures are illustrative of the reform agenda and do not intend to be comprehensive and have been validated in other studies (see Walker and Enticott, 2004).

Findings

We first independently examined changes in values and actions over time. Tables 12.3 and 12.4 report the means and results of ANOVA tests. Then we examined values at each year and actions at the subsequent year.

Table 12.3 *Means and differences (ANOVA) in value statements of reform categories over time*

Management reform category	2001	2002	2003	2004	F	Differences
	1	2	3	4		
Competition	4.28 (0.98)	5.44 (0.66)	5.58 (0.59)	5.51 (0.64)	127.15***	1-2, 1-3, 1-4
Customer focus	5.25 (0.66)	5.33 (0.53)	5.36 (0.56)	5.48 (0.60)	5.18**	1–4
Devolution to the front line	5.01 (0.87)	5.19 (0.56)	5.28 (0.58)	5.20 (0.62)	4.64**	1–3, 1–4
Continuous improvement	5.28 (0.75)	5.67 (0.62)	5.88 (0.59)	6.02 (0.57)	51.43***	1–2, 1–3, 1–4, 2–4
Corporateness	4.47 (1.01)	4.94 (0.86)	5.04 (0.79)	5.29 (0.71)	33.95***	1–2, 1–3, 1–4, 2–4
Innovation	4.62 (0.93)	5.03 (0.78)	5.20 (0.73)	5.18 (0.72)	23.47***	1–2, 1–3, 1–4,
Entrepreneurial behaviour	4.37 (0.92)	5.16 (0.72)	5.20 (0.67)	5.05 (0.68)	50.33***	1–2, 1–3, 1–4,
Partnership	5.26 (0.71)	5.35 (0.61)	5.51 (0.54)	5.41 (0.61)	4.35**	1–3
Performance measurement	4.92 (0.91)	5.25 (0.74)	5.50 (0.72)	5.71	36.86***	1–2, 1–3, 1–4, 2–4

Note: ** $p < 0.01$, *** $p < 0.001$.

Table 12.5 presents the result of three independent sample t-tests of values at t and actions at $t + 1$: 2001–2002, 2002–2003 and 2003–2004.

First we discuss the univariate trajectories over the four-year period for the nine measures of organizational values and actions (Tables 12.3 and 12.4). Five of the values measure increase over the four-year period (*competition, customer focus, continuous improvement, corporateness* and *performance measurement*) and the remaining four variables rise for three years and drop in the last year (Table 12.3). The actions display a more complicated pattern. Two measures rise over the four years (*innovation* and *entrepreneurial behaviour*); four rise for three years and then drop in the last year (*competition, devolution to the front line, corporateness* and *partnership*); one (*continuous improvement*) rises for three years and then

Table 12.4 *Means and differences (ANOVA) in action statements of reform categories over time*

Management reform category	2001	2002	2003	2004	F	Differences
	1	2	3	4		
Competition	3.39 (1.20)	3.92 (0.96)	3.95 (1.02)	3.76 (0.94)	.99	
Customer focus	4.78 (0.94)	5.27 (0.59)	5.19 (0.72)	5.18 (0.70)	15.86***	1–2, 1–3, 1–4
Devolution to the front line	2.53 (1.27)	2.97 (1.13)	3.19 (1.15)	3.10 (1.06)	12.83***	1–2, 1–3, 1–4
Continuous improvement	4.42 (1.19)	4.64 (0.84)	4.78 (0.85)	4.78 (0.88)	5.90***	1–3, 1–4
Corporateness	5.20 (0.87)	5.40 (0.56)	5.53 (0.68)	5.44 (0.66)	6.76***	1–3, 1–4
Innovation	3.47 (1.00)	3.87 (0.66)	4.03 (0.83)	4.25 (0.83)	29.83***	1–2, 1–3, 1–4, 2–4
Entrepreneurial behaviour	3.94 (1.09)	4.21 (0.78)	4.19 (0.85)	4.23 (0.90)	4.51**	1–4
Partnership	5.06 (0.94)	5.50 (0.64)	5.65 (0.58)	5.26 (0.74)	16.72***	1–2, 1–3, 1–4, 3–4
Performance measurement	5.56 (0.85)	5.24 (0.78)	5.40 (0.67)	5.35 (0.76)	5.51***	1–2, 1–4

Note: * $p < 0.05$, ** $p < 0.01$, *** $p < 0.001$.

remains unchanged; and one (*customer focus*) rises for two years and then flattens out (Table 12.4). Finally, *performance measurement* offers a brief roller-coaster ride dropping from year one to two, and then rising again before marginally falling again (Table 12.4). Only two of the variables display the same pattern for values and actions: *devolution to the front line* and *partnership* rise for three years and show falls in the final year (Tables 12.3 and 12.4).

Second, the means of these score are typically above the mid-point on our Likert scale (= 4.0). All the value statements are greater than 4, and mean scores for four of the measures (*customer focus*, *devolution to the front line*, *continuous improvement* and *partnership*) are greater than 5 for the four-year period. The picture is again a little more complex for actions. Three variables (*corporateness*, *partnership* and *performance measurement*) register mean scores over 5. However, two variables (*competition* and *devolution*) record mean scores below 3 for the four-year period, suggesting that respondents did not agree that these actions were a central part of their approach. *Customer focus* and *continuous improvement* recorded mean scores above 4, and saw rises in the extent to which actions were implemented. For the final two actions (*entrepreneurial behaviour* and *innovation*), they moved from not being a major part of the organizations' activities (below the mid-point) in the earlier years to becoming a more important part of their activities (above the mid-point) in the later years.

In summary, analysis of the univariate data suggests that change has been more clearly registered in attitudes than in behaviours, though the pattern is not consistent across all the public management reform variables. For only two variables (*competition* and *customer focus*) were the means for actions greater than the values. Given these uncertain results at this stage, we now go on to examine whether change through time is a product of random noise or whether some more fundamental changes are taking place.

Tables 12.3 and 12.4 also present the results of ANOVA analysis. The tables report the F-value and level of statistical significance for each of the two-year pairs of the nine reform categories over four years. If there are statistically significant differences over the time period this is indicated by the stars against the F-score. The final columns of Tables 12.3 and 12.4 report the differences between the two-year pairs.

The F-score for each value statement is high and all of the differences are statistically significant at the 0.01 or 0.001 level (Table 12.3). This suggests that there is change in the value statements over time. The differences between two-year pairs reveal some interesting patterns of change. In total there are 25 statistically significant differences, of which 22 are between 2001 and subsequent years. Between 2001 and 2002 there are six differences; between 2001 and 2003, and 2001 and 2004, there are eight differences in each case. This implies that values in 2002 to 2004 have changed markedly from those in 2001. As observed above, although some means fall from 2003 to 2004, the differences between 2001 and 2004 remain large enough to be significant. Moreover, there were no statistically significant differences between 2003 and 2004, and only three between 2002 and 2004 (*continuous improvement, corporateness* and *performance measurement*). Overall, we take these results to suggest that in the majority of organizations managers' attitudes changed between 2001 and 2002, and hardened from 2003 onwards.

Turning to Table 12.4, the ANOVA results for the actions reveal a more complex pattern, duplicating as would be expected our discussion on the univariate analysis. The results show that behaviour towards competition did not change from year to year as the F-score is not statistically significant for competition (Table 12.4). From the 21 statistically significant differences between years for the action measures, 19 are between year 2001 and subsequent years. Similar sets of relationships are portrayed for actions as were for values. Between 2001 and 2002 we see five differences, and between 2001 and 2003 six; however, all variables (except competition) differ by mean between 2001 and 2004. Of the remaining two statistically significant differences, one is between 2002 and 2004 (*innovation*), which shows an increase, and the other between 2003 and 2004 (*partnership*), which registers the only fall in actions in our sample.

To examine effects of changes in values on subsequent changes in actions, we ran a series of t-tests comparing values at t and actions at $t + 1$ (Table 12.5). The results more clearly support our contention that changes in values outstrip changes in actions. Of the 27 tests we ran, 25 are statistically significant ($p < 0.05$). Of these, 21 are positive, indicating that the means for the values are greater than the means for the actions. Only four are negative, showing actions to be higher than values. For the *corporateness* variable the sign is negative for every time period. This would suggest that coordination and joint working among departments within a local authority are greater than changes in values regarding a common ownership of organizational mission and objectives. It is permissible that this is because there was a higher level of agreement on

Table 12.5 Differences between values and action: t-tests for adjacent years

Management reform category	Values 01– actions 02 t-score	Values 02– actions 03 t-score	Values 03– actions 04 t-score
Competition	13.90***	24.15***	28.80***
Customer focus	8.05***	2.38*	5.94***
Devolution to the front line	33.51***	23.42***	26.98***
Continuous improvement	16.45***	17.18***	24.71***
Corporateness	–13.23***	–7.93***	–5.50***
Innovation	22.37***	19.68***	19.58***
Entrepreneurial behaviour	9.42***	14.78***	13.51***
Partnership	2.67	–3.03**	0.90
Performance measurement	–9.15***	0.93	4.87***

Note: * $p < 0.05$, ** $p < 0.01$, *** $p < 0.001$.

this measure prior to our study. This alludes to a limitation of this chapter, because we do not have data to establish a clear pre-management reform baseline from which changes in values and changes in actions can be projected. That said, the results of these t-tests are quite consistent: values outstrip actions 84 per cent of the time. This leads towards the conclusion that public service organizations are more amenable to changes in values than actions, and that this occurs in a consistent fashion through time. The implications of these findings for studying change in public organizations are now discussed.

Discussion and conclusions

In this chapter we have examined a programme of management reform or change initiated by the Blair government in the late 1990s. We studied the implementation of the public service improvement strategy in English local governments for the period 2001 to 2004. The results show more rapid change in relation to values or attitudes by public service organizations than in relation to actions or behaviours. These observations generally suggest that (1) public management reform is a top-down planned change where local authorities are put under institutional pressure to conform, and (2) its adoption occurs incrementally by the changing first of organizational values and then of behaviours.

The evidence we have garnered would support the hypothesis that the change in English local authorities is a bumpy incremental change (By, 2005). We are a little hesitant in drawing firm conclusions because of the lack of a clear baseline in our study. Nonetheless, if we look at the results of the ANOVA tests in Tables 12.3 and 12.4, we note 46 statistically significant differences between pairs of years for organizational values and actions. Of these 46 differences, only five are for differences that do not include year 1 (2001), while 34 are for differences between year 1 and year 2 (2002). This suggests that there was clearly a bump following our measurement in year 1; there is acceleration in organizations' change attitudes and behaviours, with all management reform categories, bar that for performance measurement actions, moving on an upward or positive trajectory. Reductions in action on performance measurement are likely to result from earlier implementation of performance measurement IT systems that once in place should not require additional investment. Furthermore, performance measurement has been a long-running theme in the various forms of reform and change promulgated in English local governments since the early 1990s. Overall, our findings suggest that change in public service organizations occurred as the central government anticipated, because local governments aligned their attitudes and behaviours with the central government's intents.

Second, we conclude that these reforms travel in a sequential form, from reform → values → behaviours. That is, management reform forced from outside (in this case by central government) affects managers' and organizational values (or their attitude towards change), which in turn affects organizational actions (changes in strategy, structure, etc.) to help implement the reform. This would support the notion of planned change in organizations, whether business or public. Planned change has been criticized for focusing on the small scale, for requiring extensive knowledge by managers and common agreement on the change strategy (see By, 2005). These criticisms are predominantly to do with the political characteristics of planning rather than the technical aspects, and it is the technical facets that create obstacles to planned change (Boyne *et al.*, 2004). Our analysis suggests that local governments have mainly overcome the technical problems and have adopted the management reforms. This has occurred because local authorities operate in a social system of many actors, where central government is one of the key actors. The central government has substantial influence over local governments through allocating approximately three-quarters of their budgets, passing legislation that has to be implemented by them, and offering guidance and enforcement on the adoption of new programmes and approaches.

In addition to these levers, central government also runs – through its agent the Audit Commission – a competitive benchmarking scheme that rewards achievements in service delivery and management approaches and capacity. From this standpoint it is not surprising that local governments respond to the demands of this key external constituency and adopt the policies promoted by the central government.

Third, building upon the coercive and reward powers of central government noted above, there are some variations in our findings that would add support to the importance of institutional perspective of organizational change. Most notably, the results suggest that values are affected more than actions. This suggests that (1) management attitudes can be influenced more easily (perhaps because of the need to manage upwards to central government), and (2) the transition of managerial attitude to organization action takes more time and is more difficult because actions for change require buy-in from organizational members and their cooperation and commitment to the reform. In short, the process of reform is slow and the occurrence of change takes time. Nevertheless, interpretation of these findings from the institutional perspective suggests that the organizations in our sample are seeking legitimacy – making changes that give the appearance of full compliance with central government intent, rather than making sweeping changes in behaviours that deviate from it. This is not surprising, because, for example, the local governments in our sample are controlled not only by Labour administrations but also by Conservatives, Liberal Democrats and Independents, who may not be willing adopters of reforms promoted by a different political party. Despite some mimetic and normative isomorphic pressures, our argument above alludes mainly to coercive isomorphism in English local government as central government is able to exercise power over lower levels, thereby guaranteeing change in the anticipated direction. However, after four years, organizational attitudes towards the reform agenda outstrip actions. Organizations can talk the talk but they do not fully walk the walk – implying that central powers are insufficient to bring about change across all localities.

In keeping with the contextual aspects of organizational change discussed in previous contributions to the current volume, these findings might, of course, be a product of the peculiarities of English local government. In less centralized systems, change may pan out in less planned, bumpy and coercive patterns. Further research in different locations with different organizations would assist in developing knowledge on how change occurs in public services. In addition, research on this topic would need to include attitudes and behaviours of non-managers to help us attain a clearer understanding of the depth to which a top-down planned change penetrates organizational actions and behaviours. What is clear, however, is that attitudes change prior to behaviours. Those interested in designing programmes of management reform should be cognizant of this finding when implementing such programmes and expect that it will take time after the initial shock for reforms to roll out in the ways anticipated by those leading the reform. To address the bumpiness of the management reform categories reported in this chapter, it is likely that continued emphasis on the reform programme is required by those leading change in public service organizations.

Part IV
Conclusions

13 Organizational change management in public services: key findings and emerging themes

Calum Macleod and Rune Todnem By

- Introduction
- The limits to comparative analysis of change in public services
- An international dimension to change in public service organizations?
- Conclusions

Introduction

Sifting through the debris of 'ruined hopes' precipitated by the disintegration of an ill-starred initiative by the US Economic Development Agency to provide permanent employment opportunities for minorities in the city of Oakland, California, Pressman and Wildavsky's (1973) seminal study on public policy implementation concluded that 'the apparently simple and straight-forward is really complex and convoluted'. The same might reasonably be said of efforts to initiate and manage change in organizations generally and those involved in the delivery of public services in particular (Randall, 2004). Indeed, a striking feature of the literature on contemporary organizational change management is the extent to which it mirrors aspects of the earlier public policy implementation literature, both in its preoccupations regarding the efficacy of top-down and bottom-up change management processes and in the wide range of variables it identifies as significant in shaping the management of change. Similar trends are also detectable in the current volume. In this final chapter we consider the limits to directly comparative analysis in the study of organizational change management and discuss their implications for students and practitioners of change in public services. We then examine the extent to which change management in contemporary public service organizations has an international dimension, before offering some concluding observations.

The limits to comparative analysis of change in public services

As earlier chapters testify, the complex and often highly contested (in both academic and practical terms) arena of organizational change indicates that any claims as to the 'best' way to manage that process in relation to public services should be treated with a healthy dose of scepticism by academics and practitioners alike. There are several reasons for this.

First, and perhaps most fundamentally, all organizational change is shaped to a greater or lesser degree by the *context* in which it occurs. As is illustrated in this volume, the formulation and implementation of change initiatives in public service organizations is influenced by complex horizontal and vertical relationships between macro-level *external* socio-economic, cultural and political variables and micro-level *internal* cultural, structural and process variables (encompassing resource allocation, values, behaviour, authority, legitimacy and power relationships). Identifying and mapping these complex webs of external and internal variables and analysing their interrelationships to create convincing narratives of cause and effect in individual change contexts is difficult enough. Attempting to replicate that process across national public services boundaries in search of universal change management truths is virtually impossible, owing to the volume of variables and their often distinctive characteristics within particular national settings.

The significance of context in public services has been alluded to time and again in earlier chapters. Perrott's (see Chapter 3) account of managing public sector organizations in environmental turbulence is underpinned by the scope for fluctuations in the broad operating environment and focuses on senior management's capacity to respond strategically to such fluctuations. However, what causes such environmental fluctuations may vary internationally, or indeed *between* public services in particular countries. By way of an example of the lack of theoretical uniformity in this broad field of inquiry, both Østergren and Stensaker (see Chapter 11), in their account of the Norwegian higher education sector's response to the 'Bologna process', and Walker and Damanpour (see Chapter 12), in their analysis of changes to values and actions in English local government, speculate as to the extent to which national styles of government influence the outcomes of change that they respectively uncover. Contextual factors are even more to the fore in Cameron and Green's (see Chapter 2) discussion of leadership and change in the public sector. A central thrust of their analysis is that senior public sector managers need to apply varying leadership styles that can be adapted to the particular change contexts in which they find themselves operating.

Thus, context clearly matters to the management of organizational change. Indeed, we submit that despite the blurring of edges between the public and private sectors, contextual issues arguably matter more for change management in the public sector than is the case elsewhere. This is due to its fundamentally different objectives, accountability arrangements and ethos, together with the specific characteristics of public goods and services that lead them to define key aspects of the relationship between the state and civil society.

Limitations in scope for undertaking directly comparative analysis are further compounded by differences in the *types* of change initiatives and their *scope*. As is discussed in Chapter 1, the change management literature makes important distinctions in terms of *rate of change of occurrence* (broady, discontinuous, incremental and continuous), *how change occurs* (broadly, planned and emergent) and *scale of change* (fine-tuning, incremental adjustment, modular transformation and corporate transformation). These classifications are useful in that they provide academic and practical order to an otherwise conceptually dense and bewilderingly complex morass of 'change' activity. However, they offer little comfort for anyone under the illusion that a grand overarching theory of organizational change management is tantalizingly close to hand.

Directly related to the above, a plurality of *theoretical perspectives* also makes direct comparative analysis of organizational change management problematic. In this collection alone, a vast expanse of theoretical terrain has been reconnoitered, ranging from strategic change theory to rational and institutional perspectives with numerous variations in between. Without wishing to oversimplify, one can classify this plurality of theoretical perspectives as broadly 'top-down' or broadly 'bottom-up' in orientation. While such plurality performs a vital analytical function in opening up new avenues of inquiry and explanation for the management of change initiatives and processes, it comes at the price of a discordant theoretical fragmentation familiar to policy implementation scholars.

In their review of the aspects of policy implementation to which 'top-down' and 'bottom-up' policy implementation theorists attribute objective or relativist (subjective) status, Linder and Peters (1987) argue that top-down theorists focus on the extent to which means (in the form of policy programmes) achieve desired ends and in identifying ways in which implementation can be made more 'rational'. In contrast, bottom-up theorists' attribution of relativistic status to policy muddies the analytic waters somewhat. As Linder and Peters (1987:121) state,

> The meaning assigned to policy then depends not only on where one looks but on when, as well as whom, one asks. All at once, policy as a phenomenon is opened to uncertainty, variability and contingency. In effect, it becomes an artefact whose form can be interpreted only in contextual terms, relative to both its functions and stage of development.

Substitute 'change' for 'policy' in the above quotation and the parallels in terms of theoretical divergence and the issues that divergence presents for organizational change management studies become readily evident. The management of organizational change *is* highly dependent on context, as we have noted. But the analytical cleavage between 'top-down' and 'bottom-up' (or planned and emergent) change processes raises thorny academic questions regarding the focus of inquiry and equally thorny practical questions concerning the parameters of discretion and power within public service organizations and concerning what constitutes change 'success', and by whose measure.

Finally, differences in the *units of analysis* deployed in the study of organizational change further impede the scope for comparative analysis of the phenomenon within a public services context. Permutations of such units vary, but Pollitt and Bouckaert (2004:5) usefully and succinctly differentiate between perspectives on change as those emanating from 'above' or 'outside' (encompassing the political perspectives of governments and politicians along with the perspectives of other elite decision-makers) and those emanating from 'inside' or 'below' (focusing on groups and individuals within the public services organizations which have an interest in promoting or blocking particular change initiatives).

The focus throughout this volume has predominantly been on what happens *inside* public service organizations in terms of the management of change. In the final section of this chapter we draw some overarching conclusions in that regard. First, we consider the extent to which there is an international dimension to change in public service organizations.

An international dimension to change in public service organizations?

Given the limitations that exist to directly comparative analysis of organizational change in public services, is it reasonable to suggest that

there is an international dimension to that phenomenon? We believe that
there is a general direction of travel internationally in that regard but that
there are important nuances of approach linked directly to the types of
contextual socio-economic, cultural and political issues discussed in the
previous section.

As is noted in Chapter 1, perspectives on the relationship between
politics, administration and management in the design, delivery and
evaluation of public services have changed significantly since the
mid-1970s for a variety of socio-economic and political reasons. Much of
this reconfiguration of perspectives on public services was fuelled by the
neo-liberal thinking of the New Right, fiscal crisis and growing alarm at
the perceived inability of governments to deliver on what they promised.
As a consequence, and as is also noted in Chapter 1, traditional
differentiating lines between the public and private sectors have become
blurred in key respects relating to arrangements for financing and
delivering public goods and services in particular. Important
distinguishing characteristics of public goods and services do remain
largely intact in that they continue to offer collective benefits to society
and remain non-exclusive in that an individual's access to such goods and
services is not dependent on his or her ability to pay, as is the case in
private market transactions. Nevertheless, how such public goods and
services are to be organized and managed, and to what ends, has
increasingly occupied governments of whatever political hue
internationally since the 1980s, and continues to do so.

At the forefront of this ongoing public services reform agenda has been
the application of a variety of managerialist techniques and principles
under the broad rubric of New Public Management (NPM) within the
public services contexts of a considerable number of liberal democratic
states. Indeed, the continuing influence of NPM as a driving force for
organizational change is noted in a number of the contributions to this
volume. For example, Perrott's (see Chapter 3) discussion in Part II on
managing public sector organizations in environmental turbulence
highlights the development of NPM as one source of that turbulence.
Meanwhile, Burnes' (see Chapter 7) presentation of the case for planned
organizational change in the public sector focuses on the National Health
Service in the United Kingdom, itself one of the first public services to
comprehensively experience the application of NPM principles in
practice. Furthermore, in both Østergren and Stensaker's (see Chapter 11)
account of change in the Norwegian higher education sector, and Lofquist
and Lines' (see Chapter 9) analysis of an aborted change management

initiative in the Norwegian civil aviation industry, concerns with generating competition, ensuring greater cost-effectiveness and stimulating responsiveness to customer demands are all linked to the rise of NPM.

Even in cases where the managerialist prescriptions of NPM have not been so overtly discernible, there has been a broader common agenda of international dimensions revolving around the four 'Es' of efficiency, effectiveness, economy and equity in which improved performance and quality of service loom large. Aspects of this modernizing agenda for public services inform the structural and process reorganization of administering Dutch collective employee benefit regulations which Van Nistelrooij and Sminia (see Chapter 10) examine in Part III. Moreover, concerns with the four 'Es' remain highly visible in change contexts where NPM appears to have receded from its high-watermark in terms of shaping public services delivery, as Walker and Damanpour's (see Chapter 12) discussion of the impacts of modernization on changing values and actions in English local government well illustrates.

Conclusions

The introductory chapter of this volume posed the question as to why the management of organizational change in public services is apparently so challenging. The ensuing contributions go some way towards shedding light on that fundamental question. They illustrate that many of the challenges of public service change management relate to issues of *control*, *power*, *values*, *authority* and *legitimacy* within public service organizations, set against the backdrop of broader macro-level socio-economic, cultural and, above all, *political* factors. Indeed, we are of the view that the relationship between politics and public services is central to any attempts to understand and explain the dynamics of organizational change in public services in whatever context. As we have noted, the ways in which public goods and services should be delivered and what they should achieve have been central to the recalibration of the relationship between the state and society across international boundaries dating back to at least the early 1980s. What began as academic debates have transmuted into political questions with often strong ideological undercurrents. Fused with the neo-liberalism of the New Right and subsequent efforts to modernize public services by reconnecting them in terms of flexibility, choice and responsiveness to people's needs and aspirations, such questions have succeeded in making change arguably one of the few constants in the organizational life of public services.

Mindful of our own earlier comments regarding the perils of attempting to shoehorn directly comparative analysis into contexts where there is little or no theoretical or practical fit, we offer the following concluding observations on organizational change management in public services.

Chapter 1 quotes former United Kingdom Prime Minister Tony Blair's 'scars on my back' speech in which he bemoaned the difficulties in trying to achieve change in the public sector and public services. Indeed, a number of contributions in this volume cite deficits between the original (top-down) objectives of change and the extent to which these were achieved in practice (see Chapters 9, 10 and 12). Such deficits are perhaps not altogether surprising. Thirty years ago, Gunn's (1978) list of ten necessary preconditions for 'perfect implementation', based on Hood's (1976) original five-component model of 'perfect administration', provided insights that are readily transferable to the closely related field of organizational change management. These preconditions include:

1 that circumstances external to the implementing agency do not impose crippling constraints;
2 that adequate time and sufficient resources are made available to the programme;
3 that the required combination of resources is actually available;
4 that the policy to be implemented is based on a valid theory of cause and effect;
5 that the relationship between cause and effect is direct and that there are few, if any, intervening links;
6 that dependency relationships are minimal;
7 that there is understanding of, and agreement on, objectives;
8 that tasks are fully specified in correct sequence;
9 that there is perfect communication and coordination;
10 that those in authority can demand and obtain perfect compliance.

There is more than a hint of 'straw man' status to Gunn's (1978) model. However, it does illustrate the difficulties associated with attempting to implement change initiatives as well as providing useful clues as to why so many of these initiatives seem to deviate from their objectives when viewed from a top-down or planned change perspective. All too often in reality the above conditions fail to be satisfied: adequate resources for change are in short supply; change is often not thought through in terms of cause and effect; dependency relationships are widespread and at risk of rupture; understanding of and agreement with change objectives is not secured, because of the existence of conflicting values and agendas; communication and coordination are poor; and compliance cannot be obtained, owing to concentrations of power among key groups.

There is no elixir with which to magically cure these supposed ills that beset change management initiatives. Instead, scholars and practitioners of organizational change in public services should remain attuned to the significance of context and contingency in developing, leading and implementing change management initiatives. In this regard, the concepts of *change readiness* and *capacity* are significant (see By *et al.*, 2008), continuous change readiness being a requirement for creating and sustaining organizational capacity to implement successfully a series of changes over time if and when required. Jones *et al.* (2005:362) define change readiness as

> the extent to which employees hold positive views about the need for organizational change (i.e. change acceptance), as well as the extent to which employees believe that such changes are likely to have positive implications for themselves and the wider organization.

Change capacity has been defined by Klarner *et al.* (2008:58) as an 'organization's ability to develop and implement appropriate organizational changes to constantly adapt to its environment'.

Change readiness and capacity can be created, enhanced and sustained by adopting Armenakis *et al.*'s (1993), and Armenakis and Harris' (2002) change message model. This model identifies five questions requiring to be answered in relation to the change message:

- discrepancy (*is change required and is it legitimate?*);
- appropriateness (*is this the right change option?*);
- efficacy (*is it realistic?*);
- principal support (*are senior stakeholders committed to this change?*);
- personal valence (*what are the benefits for individuals and groups within the organization?*).

According to Armenakis *et al.* (1993), Armenakis and Harris (2002) and By (2007), this message, when created, can be communicated through a mix of direct communication; attitudes, behaviour and actions; by providing the views of others; and positive change empowerment – organizations encouraging, facilitating and acknowledging real empowerment where employees are given the opportunity and choice to influence and implement organizational change.

In summary, it should be acknowledged that no change initiative can be value free, no matter what its proponents may suggest. Therefore, what is essential to the success and sustainability of any change initiative is that the decision to initiate change in the first place is based on sound knowledge of cause and effect, together with an understanding of the distinctiveness of the public sector's purpose, the conditions of its strategic and operating environment, and its tasks (Rose and Lawton, 1999). Moreover, as power is inherent to change, organizations need to ensure that individuals and groups are not allowed to initiate change on the basis of their own aspirations. In managing organizational change in public services it is crucial to have clear accountability for change and strong evidence that the change to be implemented is in the best interests of the organization in question, and, most importantly of all, in the best interests of the public that it serves.

References

Abbott, A. (1990). A primer on sequence methods. *Organization Science*, *1*, 375–392.

Abercrombie, N., Hill, S. and Turner, B. S. (1980). *The Dominant Ideology Thesis*. London: Allen and Unwin.

Abrahamson, E. (1996). Management fashion. *Academy of Management Review*, *21*(1), 254–285.

Ahlbrandt, R. S., Leana, C. R. and Murrel, A. J. (1992). Employee involvement programmes improve corporate performance. *Long Range Planning*, *25*(5), 91–98.

Aiken, M. and Hage, J. (1968). Organizational interdependence and intra-organizational structure. *American Sociological Review*, *33*, 912–930.

Alford, J. (2002). Defining the client in the public sector: a social-exchange perspective. *Public Administration Review*, *62*(3), 337–346.

Allport, G. W. (1948). Foreword. In: G. W. Lewin and G. W. Allport (eds), *Resolving Social Conflict*. London: Harper and Row.

Alvesson, M. and Willmott, H. (1992). Critical theory and management studies: an introduction. In: M. Alvesson and H. Willmott, *Critical Management Studies*. London: Sage.

Anderson, G. (2006). Carving out time and space in the managerial university. *Journal of Organizational Change Management*, *19*(5), 578–592.

Ansoff, H. I. (1965). *Corporate Strategy*. New York: McGraw-Hill.

Ansoff, H. I. (1980). Strategic issue management. *Strategic Management Journal*, *1*, 131–148.

Ansoff, H. I. (1987). The emerging paradigm of strategic behavior. *Strategic Management Journal*, *8*, 501–515.

Ansoff, H. I. and McDonnell, E. J. (1990). *Implementing Strategic Management*. Englewood Cliffs, NJ: Prentice Hall.

Argyris, C. (1977). Double-loop learning in organizations. *Harvard Business Review*, September–October, 115–125.

Argyris, C. (1990). *Overcoming Organizational Defenses*. Needham, MA: Allyn and Bacon.

Armenakis, A. A. and Harris, S. G. (2002). Crafting a change message to create transformational readiness. *Journal of Organizational Change Management*, *15*(2), 169–183.

Armenakis, A. A., Harris, S. G. and Mossholder, K. W. (1993). Creating readiness for organizational change. *Human Relations*, *46*(6), 681–703.

Ashworth, R., Boyne, G. A. and Delbridge, R. (2007). Escape from the iron cage? Organizational change and isomorphic pressures in the public sector. *Journal of Public Administration Research and Theory*, DOI 10.1093/jopart/mum038.

Avinor (2003). Take-Off 05 Summary Report – Design phase.

Bacharach, S. B. and Lawler, E. J. (1998). Political alignments in organizations: contextualization, mobilization and coordination. In: R. M. Kramer and M. A. Neale (eds), *Power and Influence in Organizations*. Thousand Oaks, CA: Sage.

Back, K. W. (1992). This business of topology. *Journal of Social Issues*, *48*(2), 51–66.

Balogun, J. (2003). From blaming the middle to harnessing its potential: creating change intermediaries. *British Journal of Management*, *14*(1), 69–83.

Balogun, J. (2006). Managing change: steering a course between intended strategies and unanticipated outcomes. *Long Range Planning*, *39*, 29–49.

Balogun, J. and Hailey, V. H. (2004). *Exploring Strategic Change*, 2nd edn. Harlow, UK: Prentice Hall.

Balogun, J. and Johnson, G. (2004). Organizational restructuring and middle manager sensemaking. *Academy of Management Journal*, *47*, 523–549.

Balogun, J. and Johnson, G. (2005). From intended strategies to unintended outcomes: the impact of change recipient sensemaking. *Organization Studies*, *26*, 1537–1601.

Bamford, D. R. and Forrester, P. L. (2003). Managing planned and emergent change within an operations management environment. *International Journal of Operations and Production Management*, *23*(5), 546–564.

Bandura, A. (1977). *Social Learning Theory*. Englewood Cliffs, NJ: Prentice Hall.

Bantel, K. A. and Jackson, S. E. (1989). Top management and innovations in banking: does the composition of the top management team make a difference? *Strategic Management Journal*, *10*(S), 107–124.

Barber, R., Jonathan D., Boote, J. D. and Cooper, C. L. (2007). Involving consumers successfully in NHS research: a national survey. *Health Expectations*, *10*(4), 380–391.

Bargal, D. and Bar, H. (1992). A Lewinian approach to intergroup workshops for Arab-Palestinian and Jewish youth. *Journal of Social Issues*, *48*(2), 139–154.

Bargal, D., Gold, M. and Lewin, M. (1992). The heritage of Kurt Lewin: introduction. *Journal of Social Issues*, *48*(2), 3–13.

Barker, J. R. (1999). *The Discipline of Teamwork: Participation and Concertive Control*. London: Sage.

Barley, S. R. and Tolbert, P. S. (1997). Institutionalization and structuration: studying the links between action and institution. *Organization Studies*, *18*(1), 93–117.

Barnett, M. L. (2007). Stakeholder influence capacity and the variability of financial returns to corporate social responsibility. *Academy of Management Review*, *32*(3), 794–816.

Barnhart, T. (1997). Save the bureaucrats (while reinventing them). *Public Personnel Management*, *26*, 7–14.

Bartunek, J. M. (1984). Changing interpretive schemes and organizational restructuring: the example of a religious order. *Administrative Science Quarterly*, *29*, 355–372.

Bass, B. M. and Avolio, B. J. (1990). The implications of transactional and transformational leadership for individual, team and organizational development. *Research in Organizational Change and Development*, *4*, 231–272.

Bate, P., Kahn, R. and Pyle, A. J. (2000). Culturally sensitive structuring: an action-research based approach to organization development and design. *Public Administration Quarterly*, *23*, 445–470.

Beckhard, R. (2000). What is organization development? In: J. R. P. French, C. H. Bell and R. A. Zawacki (eds), *Organization Development and Transformation: Managing Effective Change*, 5th edn. New York: McGraw-Hill.

Beckhard, R. and Harris, R. (1987). *Organizational Transitions*. Reading, MA: Addison-Wesley.

Beer, M. (2000). Research that will break the code of change: the role of useful normal science and usable action science. In: M. Beer and N. Nohria (eds), *Breaking the Code of Change*. Boston: Harvard Business School Press.

Beer, M. (2001). How to develop an organization capable of sustained high performance: embrace the drive for results-capability development paradox. *Organizational Dynamics*, *29*, 597–619.

Beer, M. and Nohria, N. (eds) (2000a). *Breaking the Code of Change*. Boston: Harvard Business School Press.

Beer, M. and Nohria, N. (2000b). Cracking the code of change. *Harvard Business Review*, *78*, 133–141.

Beer, M. and Walton, A. E. (1987). Organization change and development. *Annual Review of Psychology*, *38*, 339–367.

Beer, M., Eisenstat, R. A. and Spector, B. (1990). Why change programs don't produce change. *Harvard Business Review*, *68*(6), 158–166.

Behn, R. D. (1980). Leadership for cut back management: the use of corporate strategy. *Public Administration Review*, *40*(6), 613–620.

Belbin, M. (1981). *Management Teams: Why They Succeed or Fail*. Oxford: Butterworth-Heinemann.

Bennett, R. (1983). *Management Research*. Management Development Series, 20. Geneva: International Labour Office.

Bennis, W. (2000). Leadership of change. In: M. Beer and N. Nohria (eds), *Breaking the Code of Change*. Boston: Harvard Business School Press.

Benson Report on the National Trust (1968). *Report by the Council's Advisory Committee on the Trust's Constitution, Organization and Responsibilities*. London: National Trust.

Beresford, P. (2007). User involvement, research and health inequalities: developing new directions. *Health and Social Care in the Community*, *15*(4), 306–312.

Bernstein, L. (1968). *Management Development*. London: Business Books.

Biddle, B. J. (1979). *Role Theory: Expectations, Identities, and Behaviors*. New York: Academic Press.

Blair, T. (2002). *The Courage of Our Convictions: Why Reform of the Public Services Is the Route to Social Justice*. Fabian Ideas 603. London: Fabian Society.

Blau, P. (1964). *Exchange and Power in Social Life*. New York: Wiley.

Bleiklie, I. (2005). Academic leadership and emerging knowledge regimes. In: I. Bleiklie and M. Henkel (eds), *Governing Knowledge: A Study of Continuity and Change in HE*. Dordrecht, the Netherlands: Springer.

Bleiklie, I., Ringkjøp, H. E. and Østergren, K. (2006). Nytt regime i variert landskap: ledelse og styring av universiteter og høyskoler etter kvalitetsreformen (New regime in a heterogeneous landscape: management and control of universities and university colleges). *Report No. 9 of the Evaluation of the Quality Reform*. Bergen, Norway: Rokkansenteret.

Boer, H. de (2002). On nails, coffins and councils. *European Journal of Education*, *37*, 7–20.

Boer, H. de and Goedegebuure, L. (2001). On limitations and consequences of change: Dutch university governance in transition. *Tertiary Education and Management*, *7*(2),163–180.

Bolchover, D. (2005). *The Living Dead – Switched Off, Zoned Out: The Shocking Truth about Office Life*. Chichester, UK: Capstone.

Boonstra, J. (2004). Conclusion: some reflections and perspectives on organizing, changing, and learning. In: J. Boonstra (ed.), *Dynamics of Organizational Change and Learning*. Chichester, UK: John Wiley.

Bovaird, T. and Russell, K. (2007). Civil service reform in the UK, 1999–2005. *Public Administration*, *85*(2), 301–328.

Bower, J. L. (1970). *Managing the Resource Allocation Process*. Boston: Harvard Business School.

Bower, J. L. and Gilbert, C. G. (eds) (2005) *From Resource Allocation to Strategy*. Oxford: Oxford University Press.

Bowman, C. and Ambrosini, V. (1997). Using single respondents in strategy research. *British Journal of Management*, *8*, 119–132.

Boyne, G. (2002). Public and private management: what's the difference? *Journal of Management Studies*, *39*(1), 97–122.

Boyne, G. A., Martin, S. and Walker, R. M. (2004). Explicit reforms, implicit theories and public service improvement. *Public Management Review, 6,* 189–210.

Bradford, D. L. and Burke, W. W. (eds) (2005). *Reinventing Organization Development: Addressing the Crisis, Achieving the Potential.* San Francisco: John Wiley.

Braynion, P. (2004). Power and leadership. *Journal of Health Organization and Management, 18*(6), 447–463.

Bresnen, M., Goussevskia, A. and Swan, J. (2004). Embedding new management knowledge in project-based organizations. *Organization Studies, 25*(9),1535–1555.

Brewer, G. A. (2006). All measures of performance are subjective: more evidence on U.S. federal agencies. In: G. A. Boyne, K. J. Meier, L. J. O'Toole, Jr and R. M. Walker (eds), *Public Service Performance.* Cambridge: Cambridge University Press.

Brookfield, S. D. (2005). *The Power of Critical Theory for Adult Learning and Teaching.* Maidenhead, UK: Open University Press.

Brown, S. L. and Eisenhardt, K. M. (1997). The art of continuous change: linking complexity theory and time-paced evolution in relentlessly shifting organizations. *Administrative Science Quarterly, 42*(1), 1–34.

Bruch, H. and Sattelberger, T. (2001). The turnaround at Lufthansa: learning from the change process. *Journal of Change Management, 1*(4), 344–363.

Buchanan, D. and Boddy, D. (1992). *The Expertise of the Change Agent.* Englewood Cliffs, NJ: Prentice Hall.

Buchanan, D. and Badham, R. (1999). Politics and organizational change: the lived experience. *Human Relations, 52*(5), 609–629.

Buchanan, D., Claydon, T. and Doyle, M. (1999). Organisation development and change: the legacy of the nineties. *Human Resource Management Journal, 9*(2), 20–37.

Buchanan, D. A., Addicott, R., Fitzgerald, L., Ferlie, E. and Baeza, J. I. (2007). Nobody in charge: distributed change agency in healthcare. *Human Relations, 60*(7), 1065–1090.

Burglemann, R. A. (1983). A process model of internal corporate venturing in the diversified major firm. *Administrative Science Quarterly, 28,* 223–244.

Burke, W. W. (2002). *Organization Change: Theory and Practice.* Thousand Oaks, CA: Sage.

Burnes, B. (1996). No such thing as . . . a 'one best way' to manage organizational change. *Management Decision, 34*(10), 11–18.

Burnes, B. (2004a). Kurt Lewin and the planned approach to change: a re-appraisal. *Journal of Management Studies, 41*(6), 977–1002.

Burnes, B. (2004b) *Managing Change: A Strategic Approach to Organizational Dynamics,* 4th edn. Harlow, UK: Pearson.

Burnes, B. (2007). Kurt Lewin and the Harwood studies: the foundations of OD. *Journal of Applied Behavioral Science, 43*(2), 213–231.

Burnham, J. (1941). *The Managerial Revolution*. New York: John Day.

Burns, T. (1961). Micropolitics: mechanisms of institutional change. *Administrative Science Quarterly*, 6(3), 257–281.

By, R. T. (2005). Organisational change management: a critical review. *Journal of Change Management*, 5(4), 369–380.

By, R. T. (2007). Ready or not . . . *Journal of Change Management*, 7(1), 3–11.

By, R. T., Diefenbach, T. and Klarner, P. (2008). Getting organizational change right in public services: the case of European higher education. *Journal of Change Management*, 8(1), 21–35.

Caldwell, R. (2005). Things fall apart: discourses on agency and change in organizations. *Human Relations*, 58(1), 83–114.

Caldwell, R. (2006). *Agency and Change*. London: Routledge.

Caldwell, R. (2007). Agency and change: re-evaluating Foucault's legacy. *Organization*, 14(6), 769–791.

Cameron, E. and Green, M. (2008). *Making Sense of Leadership: Exploring the Five Key Roles Used by Effective Leaders*. London: Kogan Page.

Camillus, J. C. and Datta, D. (1991). Managing strategic issues in a turbulent environment. *Long Range Planning*, 24(2), 67–74.

Carnall, C. A. (2007). *Managing Change in Organizations*, 5th edn. Harlow, UK: FT Pearson Prentice Hall.

Carson, P. P., Lanier, P. A., Carson, K. D. and Birkenmeier, B. J. (1999). A historical perspective on fad adoption and abandonment. *Journal of Management History*, 5(6), 320–333.

Cartwright, D. (ed.) (1952). *Field Theory in Social Science*. London: Social Science Paperbacks.

Castells, M. (2000). *The Rise of the Network Society*, vol. 1, *The Information Age: Economy, Society and Culture*, 2nd edn. Oxford: Blackwell.

Chaganti, R., Damanpour, F. and Mankelwicz, J. (2005). CEOs' power cycle and corporate performance cycles: an examination of the relationship between changes in power and changes in performance. In: M. A. Rahim and R. T. Golembiewski (eds), *Current Topics in Management*, 10. Piscataway, NJ: Transaction.

Chapman, L. (1978). *Your Disobedient Servant*. London: Chatto and Windus.

Chiapello, E. and Fairclough, N. (2002). Understanding the new management ideology: a transdisciplinary contribution from critical discourse analysis and new sociology of capitalism. *Discourse and Society*, 13(2), 185–208.

Child, J. and McGrath, R. G. (2001). Organizations unfettered: organizational forms in an information-intensive economy. *Academy of Management Review*, 44(6), 1135–1148.

Clark, B. R. (1998). *Creating Entrepreneurial Universities*. Oxford: IAU Press/Pergamon.

Clark, P. (2003). *Organizational Innovations*. London: Sage.

Clarke, P. and Trebilcock, C. (eds) (1997). *Understanding Decline: Perceptions and Realities of British Economic Performance*. Cambridge: Cambridge University Press.

Clarke, T. and Clegg, S. R. (1999). Changing paradigms in public service management. *Administrative Theory and Praxis*, *21*(4), 485–489.

Clegg, C. and Walsh, S. (2004). Change management: time for a change! *European Journal of Work and Organizational Psychology*, *13*(2): 217–239.

Clegg, S. R., Courpasson, D. and Phillips, N. (2006). *Power and Organizations*. London: Sage.

Coch, L. and French, J. R. P. (1948). Overcoming resistance to change. *Human Relations*, *1*, 512–532.

Cohen, L., Duberley, J. and McAuley, J. (1999). Fuelling discovery of monitoring productivity: research scientists' changing perceptions of management. *Organization*, *6*(3), 473–498.

Collins, D. (1998). *Organizational Change*. London: Routledge.

Committee on Standards in Public Life (1995). *First Report of the Committee on Standards in Public Life*. Cmnd. 2850–I. London: HMSO.

Common, R. K. (1998). Convergence and transfer: a review of the globalisation of new public management. *International Journal of Public Sector Management*, *11*(6), 440–450.

Conger, J. A. (2000). Effective change begins at the top. In: M. Beer and N. Nohria (eds), *Breaking the Code of Change*. Boston: Harvard Business School Press.

Conger, J. A. and Kanungo, R. N. (1988). The empowerment process: integrating theory and practice. *Academy of Management Review*, *13*(3), 471–482.

Contu, A. and Willmott, H. (2004). Re-embedding situatedness: the importance of power relations in learning theory. *Organization Science*, *14*(3), 283–296.

Coopey, J. and Burgoyne, J. (2000). Politics and organizational learning. *Journal of Management Studies*, *37*(6), 869–885.

Cope, S., Leishman, F. and Starie, P. (1997). Globalization, new public management and the enabling state futures of police management. *International Journal of Public Sector Management*, *10*(6), 444–460.

Coram, R. and Burnes, B. (2001). Managing organizational change in the public sector: lessons from the privatization of the Property Service Agency. *International Journal of Public Sector Management*, *14*, 94–110.

Cotton, J. L., Vollrath, D. A., Froggatt, K. L., Lengnick-Hall, M. L., and Jennings, K. R. (1988). Employee participation: diverse forms and different outcomes. *Academy of Management Review*, *13*(1), 8–22.

Courpasson, D. (2000). Managerial strategies of domination: power in soft bureaucracies. *Organization Studies*, *21*(1), 141–161.

Crisp, N. (2002). Introduction. *Department of Health: Code of Conduct for NHS Managers*. London: Department of Health.

Cummings, T. G. and Huse, E. F. (1989). *Organization Development and Change*, 4th edn. St Paul, MN: West.

Cummings, T. G. and Worley, C. G. (1997). *Organization Development and Change*, 6th edn. Cincinnati, OH: Southwestern College Publishing.

Cummings, T. G. and Worley, C. G. (2005). *Organization Development and Change*, 8th edn. Mason, OH: Southwestern College Publishing.

Currie, G. (1999). The influence of middle managers in the business planning process: a case study in the UK NHS. *British Journal of Management*, *10*(2), 141–155.

Currie, G. and Procter, S. (2005). The antecedents of middle managers' strategic contribution: the case of a professional bureaucracy. *Journal of Management Studies*, *42*(7), 1325–1356.

Cyert, R. M. and March, J. G. (1963). *A Behavioral Theory of the Firm*. Engelwood Cliffs, NJ: Prentice Hall.

Dachler, H. P. and Wilpert, B. (1978). Conceptual dimensions and boundaries of participation in organizations: a critical evaluation. *Administrative Science Quarterly*, *23*(1), 1–39.

Damanpour, F. and Schneider, M. (2006). Phases of the adoption of innovation in organizations: effects of environment, organization, and top managers. *British Journal of Management*, *17*, 215–36.

Dawson, P. (1994). *Organizational Change: A Processual Approach*. London: Paul Chapman.

Deem, R. (2001). Globalisation, new managerialism, academic capitalism and entrepreneurialism in universities: is the local dimension still important? *Comparative Education*, *37*(1), 7–20.

Deem, R. (2004). The knowledge worker, the manager-academic and the contemporary UK university: new and old forms of public management? *Financial Accountability and Management*, *20*(2), 107–128.

Deem, R. and Brehony, K. J. (2005). Management as ideology: the case of 'new managerialism' in higher education. *Oxford Review of Education*, *31*(2), 217–235.

Deetz, S. A. (1985). Critical-cultural research: new sensibilities and old realities. *Journal of Management*, *11*(2), 121–136.

Denhardt, J. V. and Denhardt, R. B. (2007). *The New Public Service*. Armonk, NY: M. E. Sharpe.

Dent, E. B. and Goldberg, S. G. (1999). Challenging resistance to change. *Journal of Applied Behavioral Science*, *35*(1), 25–41.

Department of Health (2000). *The NHS Plan: A Plan for Investment; A Plan for Reform*. London: The Stationery Office.

Department of Health (2001). *Implementation Programme for the NHS Plan*. London: The Stationery Office.

Department of Health (2002). *Code of Conduct for NHS Managers*. London: Department of Health.

Derthick, M. (1972). *New Towns In-Town: Why a Federal Program Failed*. Washington, DC: Urban Institute.

DETR (1998). *Modernising Local Government: Local Democracy and Community Leadership*. London: Department of the Environment, Transport and the Regions.

Dickens, L. and Watkins, K. (1999). Action research: rethinking Lewin. *Management Learning*, *30*(2), 127–140.

Diefenbach, T. (2005). Competing strategic perspectives and sense-making of senior managers in academia. *International Journal of Knowledge, Culture and Change Management*, *5*(6), 126–137.

Diefenbach, T. (2007). The managerialistic ideology of organisational change management. *Journal of Organizational Change Management*, *20*(1), 126–144.

Diefenbach, T. (2008). Are case studies more than sophisticated story telling? Methodological problems of case studies mainly based on semi-structured interviews. *Quality and Quantity*, online first edition.

Diefenbach, T. (2009). *Management and the Dominance of Managers*. London: Routledge.

DiMaggio, P. J. and Powell, W. W. (1983). The iron cage revisited: institutional isomorphism and collective rationality in organization fields. *American Sociological Review*, *48*(2), 147–160.

Doherty, T. L. and Horne, T. (2002). *Managing Public Services: Implementing Change – A Thoughtful Approach*. London: Routledge.

Dunphy, D. and Stace, D. (1993). The strategic management of corporate change. *Human Relations*, *46*(8), 905–918.

Dunphy, D. C. (2000). Embracing the paradox: top-down versus participative management of organizational change: a commentary on Conger and Bennis. In: M. Beer and N. Nohria (eds), *Breaking the Code of Change*. Boston: Harvard Business School Press.

Dutton, J. E. (1988). Perspectives on strategic issue processing: insights for a case study. *Advances in Strategic Management*, *5*, 223–244.

Dutton, J. E. and Duncan, R. B. (1987). The creation of momentum for change through the process of strategic issue diagnosis. *Strategic Management Journal*, *8*, 279–295.

Dutton, J. E., Fahey, L. and Narayanan, V. K. (1983). Toward understanding strategic issue diagnosis. *Strategic Management Journal*, *4*, 307–323.

Eadie, D. C. (1989). Identifying and managing strategic issues: from design to action. In: J. Rabin, G. J. Miller and W. B. Hildreth (eds), *Handbook of Strategic Management*. New York: Marcel Dekker.

Eden, C. and Huxham, C. (1996). Action research for the study of organizations. In: S. R. Clegg, C. Hardy and W. R. Nord (eds), *Handbook of Organization Studies*. London: Sage.

Ekvall, G. and Arvonen, J. (1991). Change-centered leadership: an extension of the two-dimensional model. *Scandinavian Journal of Management*, *7*, 17–26.

Elden, M. and Chisholm, R. F. (1993). Emerging varieties of action research: introduction to the special issue. *Human Relations*, *46*(20), 121–142.

Eldrod, P. D. II and Tippett, D. D. (2002). The 'Death Valley' of change. *Journal of Organizational Change Management*, *15*(3), 273–291.

Elenkov, D. S., Judge, W. and Wright, P. (2005). Strategic leadership and executive innovation influence: an international multi-cluster comparative study. *Strategic Management Journal*, *26*, 665–682.

Ellis, S. (1998). A new role for the Post Office: An investigation into issues behind strategic change at Royal Mail. *Total Quality Management*, *9*(2/3), 223–234.

Exworthy, M. and Halford, S. (eds) (1998). *Professionals and the New Managerialism in the Public Sector*. Maidenhead, UK: Open University Press.

Ferdinand, J. (2004). Power, politics and state intervention in organizational learning. *Management Learning*, *35*(4), 435–450.

Ferlie, E., Ashburner, L., Fitzgerald, L. and Pettigrew, A. M. (1996). *The New Public Management In Action*. Oxford: Oxford University Press.

Finkelstein, S. (1992). Power in top management teams: dimensions, measurement, and validation. *Academy of Management Journal*, *35*, 505–538.

Floyd, S. W. and Wooldridge, B. (1992). Middle management involvement in strategy and its association with strategic type. *Strategic Management Journal*, *13*, 153–167.

Floyd, S. W. and Wooldridge, B. (1994). Dinosaurs or dynamos? Recognizing middle management's strategic role. *Academy of Management Executive*, *8*(4), 47–57.

Floyd, S. W. and Wooldridge, B. (1997). Middle management's strategic influence on organizational performance. *Journal of Management Studies*, *34*(3), 465–485.

Floyd, S. W. and Wooldridge, B. (2000). *Building Strategy from the Middle*. London: Sage.

Floyd, S. W., Wooldridge, B. and Schmid, T. (2008). A middle management perspective: current contributions, synthesis and future research. *Journal of Management*, forthcoming.

Flynn, N. (1993). *Public Sector Management*, 2nd edn. Hemel Hempstead, UK: Harvester Wheatsheaf.

Flynn, N. (2002). *Public Sector Management*, 4th edn. Harlow, UK: FT Prentice Hall.

Fogel, W. and Lewin, D. (1974). Wage determination in the public sector. *Industrial and Labor Relations Review*, *27*(April), 410–431.

Foucault, M. P. (1980). *Power/Knowledge: Selected Interviews and Other Writings 1972–1977*. Brighton: Harvester Press.

Foucault, M, (2000). *Michel Foucault: The Essential Works*, vol. 3, *Power*. London: Allen Lane.

Fournier, V. and Grey, C. (2000). At the critical moment: conditions and prospects for critical management studies. *Human Relations*, *53*(1), 7–32.

Fox-Wolfgramm, S. J., Boal, K. B. and Hunt, J. G. (1998). Organizational adaptation to institutional change: a comparative study of first-order change in prospector and defender banks. *Administrative Science Quarterly*, *43*, 87–126.

Fredrickson, H. G. (1980). *New Public Administration*. Tuscaloosa, AL: The University of Alabama Press.

French, J. R. P. and Raven, B. H. (1959). The bases of social power. In: D. Cartwright (ed.), *Studies of Social Power*. Ann Arbor, MI: Institute for Social Research.

French, W. L. and Bell, C. H. (1973). *Organization Development*. Englewood Cliffs, NJ: Prentice Hall.

French, W. L. and Bell, C. H. (1984). *Organization Development*, 4th edn. Englewood Cliffs, NJ: Prentice Hall.

French, W. L. and Bell, C. H. (1995). *Organization Development*, 5th edn. Englewood Cliffs, NJ: Prentice Hall.

French, W. L. and Bell, C. H. (1999). *Organizational Development: Behavioral Science Interventions for Organization Improvement*, 6th edn. Englewood Cliffs, NJ: Prentice Hall.

Frost, P. J. and Egri, C. P. (1991). The political process of innovation. *Research in Organization Behavior*, 13, 229–295.

Fulton, Lord (1968). *The Civil Service: Report of the Committee*. Cmnd 3638. London: HMSO.

Gaebler, T. and Osborne, D. (1992). *Reinventing Government: How the Entrepreneurial Spirit is Transforming the Public Sector*. Reading, MA: Addison-Wesley.

Garfinkel, H. (1967). *Studies in Ethnomethodology*. Englewood Cliffs, NJ: Prentice Hall.

Gergin, J.K. (2001). *Constructionism in Context*. London: Sage.

Gerhart, B., Milkovich, G. T. and Murray, B. (1992). Pay, performance, and participation. In: D. Lewin, O. S. Mitchell and P. D. Sherer (eds), *Research Frontiers in Industrial Relations and Human Resources*. Madison, WI: Industrial Relations Research Association.

Gersick, C. J. G. (1988). Time and transition in work teams: toward a new model in group development. *Academy of Management Journal, 31*, 9–41.

Giddens, A. (1976). *New Rules of Sociological Method*. New York: Basic Books.

Giddens, A. (1984). *The Constitution of Society*. Cambridge: Polity Press.

Giddens, A. (1991). *Modernity and Self-Identity*. Cambridge: Polity Press.

Gill, R. (2003). Change management – or change leadership? *Journal of Change Management, 3*(4), 307–318.

Gioia, D. A. and Chittipeddi, K. (1991). Sensemaking and sensegiving in strategic change. *Strategic Management Journal, 12*, 433–448.

Glew, D. J., O'Leary-Kelley, A. M., Griffin, R. W. and Van Fleet, D. D. (1995). Participation in organizations: a preview of the issues and proposed framework for future analysis. *Journal of Management, 21*(3), 395–421.

Graetz, F. (2000). Strategic change leadership. *Management Decision, 38*(8), 550–562.

Grant, R. M. (1991). The resource-based theory of competitive advantage: implications for strategy formulation. *California Management Review, 33*(3), 114–135.

Grant, R. M. (2003). Strategic planning in a turbulent environment: evidence from the oil majors. *Strategic Management Journal, 24*(6), 491–517.

Gray, A. and Jenkins, B. (1994). Public administration and government. *Parliamentary Affairs, 47*(4), 1–22.

Greiner, L. and Cummings, T. G. (2005). OD: wanted more alive than dead! In: D. L. Bradford and W. W. Burke (eds), *Reinventing Organization Development: Addressing the Crisis, Achieving the Potential.* San Francisco: John Wiley.

Grey, C. (1999). We are all managers now; we always were: on the development and demise of management. *Journal of Management Studies, 36*(5), 561–585.

Griffin, R. (2006). Ideology and culture. *Journal of Political Ideologies, 11*(1), 77–99.

Gronn, P. (2002). Distributed leadership as a unit of analysis. *Leadership Quarterly, 13*, 423–451.

Grundy, T. (1993). *Managing Strategic Change.* London: Kogan Page.

Gunn, L. A. (1978). Why is implementation so difficult? *Management Services in Government, 33*, 169–176.

Hague, M. S. (2001). The diminishing publicness of public service under the current mode of governance. *Public Administration Review, 61*(1), 65–82.

Hales, C. (1999). Why do managers do what they do? Reconciling evidence and theory in accounts of managerial work. *British Journal of Management, 10*, 335–350.

Halvorsen, T. (2005). *Identity Formation or Knowledge Shopping: Education and Research in the New Globality.* SIU report series. Bergen, Norway: SIU.

Hambrick, D. and Mason, P. (1984). Upper echelons: the organization as a reflection of its top managers. *Academy of Management Review, 9*, 193–206.

Hamilton, M. (1987). The elements of the concept of ideology. *Political Studies, 35*(1), 18–38.

Hannan, M. T. and Freeman, J. (1984). Structural inertia and organizational change. *American Sociological Review, 49*, 149–164.

Härenstam, A., Bejerot, E., Leijon, O., Schéele, P., Waldenström, K. and MOA Research Group (2004). Multilevel analysis of organizational change and working conditions in public and private sector. *European Journal of Work and Organizational Psychology, 13*, 305–343.

Harrison, S. and Mort, M. (1998). Which champions, which people? Public and user involvement in health care as a technology of legitimation. *Social Policy and Administration, 32*(1), 60–70.

Hartley, J. F. (1983). Ideology and organizational behaviour. *International Studies of Management and Organization, 13*(3), 7–34.

Hatch, M. J. (1997). *Organization Theory: Modern, Symbolic and Postmodern Perspectives.* Oxford: Oxford University Press.

Haveman, H. A., Russo, M. V. and Meyer, A. D. (2001). Organizational environments in flux: the impact of regulatory punctuations on organizational domains, CEO succession, and performance. *Organization Science, 12*, 253–273.

Hayes, J. (2002). *The Theory and Practice of Change Management.* Basingstoke, UK: Palgrave Macmillan.

Hellawell, D. and Hancock, N. (2001). A case study of the changing role of the academic middle manager in higher education: between hierarchical control and collegiality? *Research Papers in Education*, *16*(2), 183–197.

Heller, F. (1970). Group feed-back analysis as a change agent. *Human Relations*, *23*(4), 319–333.

Hendry, C. (1996). Understanding and creating whole organizational change through learning theory. *Human Relations*, *48*(5), 621–641.

Hickson, D. J., Hinings, C. R., Lee, C. A., Schneck, R. E. and Pennings, J. M. (1971). A strategic contingencies theory of intraorganizational power. *Administrative Science Quarterly*, *16*(2), 216–229.

Hickson, D. J., Butler, R. J., Cray, D., Mallory, G. R. and Wilson, D. C. (1986). *Top Decisions: Strategic Decision Making in Organizations*. San Francisco: Jossey-Bass.

Hickson, D. J., Miller, S. J. and Wilson, D. C. (2003). Planned or prioritized? Two options in managing the implementation of strategic decisions. *Journal of Management Studies*, *40*, 1803–1836.

Hill, P., O'Grady, A., Millar, B. and Boswell, K. (2000). The Patient Care Development Programme: organisational development through user and staff involvement. *International Journal of Health Care Quality Assurance*, *13*(4), 153–161.

Hindess, B. (1986). Interests in political analysis. In: J. Law (ed.), *Power, Action and Belief: A New Sociology of Knowledge?* Sociological Review Monograph 32. London: Routledge and Kegan Paul.

Hoffman, R. C. and Hegarty, W. H. (1993). Top management influence on innovations: effects of executive characteristics and social culture. *Journal of Management*, *19*, 549–574.

Hoggett, P. (1996). New modes of control in the public service. *Public Administration*, *74*, 9–32.

Hood, C. C. (1976). *The Limits of Administration*. London: John Wiley.

Hood, C. (1991). A public management for all seasons? *Public Administration*, *69*, 3–19.

Hood, C. and Peters, G. (2004). The middle aging of New Public Management: into the age of paradox? *Journal of Public Administration Research and Theory*, *14*(3), 267–282.

Horton, S. (2006). New Public Management: its impact on public servant's identity: an introduction to this symposium. *International Journal of Public Sector Management*, *9*(6), 533–542.

Huczynski, A. and Buchanan, D. (2001). *Organizational Behaviour*, 4th edn. Harlow, UK: FT Prentice Hall.

Humphrey, M. (2005). (De)contesting ideology: the struggle over the meaning of the struggle over meaning. *Critical Review of International Social and Political Philosophy*, *8*(2), 225–246.

Hutton, W. (1995). *The State We're In*. London: Cape.

Huy, Q. N. (2001a). In praise of middle managers. *Harvard Business Review*, September, 73–79.

Huy, Q. N. (2001b). Time, temporal capability and planned change. *Academy of Management Review, 26*, 601–623.

Huy, Q. N. (2002). Emotional balancing of organizational continuity and radical change: the contribution of middle managers. *Administrative Science Quarterly, 47*(1), 31–69.

ICAO (2002). *International Civil Aviation Organization Meeting of Directors of Civil Aviation of Caribbean Region (CAR/DCA/1)* (Grand Cayman, Cayman Islands, 8–11 October 2002).

Iles, V. and Sutherland, K. (2001). *Managing Change in the NHS: Organisational Change: A Review for Health Care Managers, Professionals and Researchers*. London: NCC SDO.

Ingraham, P. W. (1993). Of pigs in pokes and policy diffusion: another look at pay-for-performance. *Public Administration Review, 53* (March/April), 348–356.

Jacques, R. (1996). *Manufacturing the Employee: Management Knowledge from the 19th to 21st Centuries*. London: Sage.

Jarzabkowski, P., Balogun, J. and Seidl, D. (2007). Strategizing: the challenges of a practice perspective. *Human Relations, 60*(1), 5–27.

Jensen, M. C. (2000). Value maximization and the corporate objective function. In: M. Beer and N. Nohria (eds), *Breaking the Code of Change*. Boston: Harvard Business School Press.

Jick, T. D. and Peiperl, M. A. (2003). *Managing Change: Cases and Concepts*. New York: McGraw-Hill.

Jones, R. A., Jimmieson, N. L. and Griffiths, A. (2005). The impact of organizational culture and reshaping capabilities on change implementation success: the mediating role of readiness for change. *Journal of Management Studies, 42*(2), 361–386.

Joyce, P. (2000). *Strategy in the Public Sector: A Guide to Effective Change Management*. Toronto: John Wiley.

Kallinikos, J. (2004). The social foundations of bureaucratic order. *Organization, 11*(1), 13–36.

Kanter, R. M. (1982a). Dilemmas of management participation. *Organization Dynamics, 11*, 5–27.

Kanter, R. M. (1982b). The middle manager as innovator. *Harvard Business Review*, July–August, 95–105.

Kanter, R. M. (1986). The reshaping of middle management. *Management Review, 75*(1), 19–20.

Kanter, R. M., Stein, B. A. and Jick, T. D. (1992). *The Challenge of Organizational Change*. New York: The Free Press.

Karp, T. (2005). Unpacking the mysteries of change: mental modelling. *Journal of Change Management, 51*, 87–96.

Kellough, E. J. and Selden, S. C. (1997). Pay for performance systems in state government. *Review of Public Personnel Administration, 17* (winter), 5–21.

Kerr, S. and Jermier, J. M. (1978). Substitutes for leadership: their meaning and measurement. *Organizational Behavior and Human Performance, 22*(3), 375–403.

Kieser, A. (1997). Rhetoric and myth in management fashion. *Organization, 4*(1), 49–74.

King, A. (1975). Overload: problems of governing in the 1970s. *Political Studies, 23*, 284–296.

Kingdon, J. W. (1998). *Agendas, Alternatives, and Public Policies.* New York: HarperCollins.

Kippenberger, T. (1998a). Planned change: Kurt Lewin's legacy. *The Antidote, 14*, 10–12.

Kippenberger, T (1998b). Managed learning: elaborating on Lewin's model. *The Antidote, 14*, 13.

Kirkpatrick, I., Ackroyd, S. and Walker, R. (2005). *The New Managerialism and Public Service Professions.* New York: Palgrave Macmillan.

Klarner, P., Probst, G. and Soparnot, R. (2008). Organizational change capacity in public services: the case of the World Health Organization. *Journal of Change Management, 8*(1), 57–72.

Knights, D. and McCabe, D. (1998). When 'life is but a dream': obliterating politics through business process reengineering? *Human Relations, 51*, 761–798.

Kostova, T. and Roth, K. (2002). Adoption of an organizational practice by subsidiaries of multinational corporations: institutional and relational effects. *Academy of Management Journal, 45*, 215–233.

Kotter, P. (1996). *Leading Change.* Boston: Harvard Business School Press.

Krackhardt, D. (1990). Assessing the political landscape: structure, cognition, and power in organizations. *Administrative Science Quarterly, 35*, 342–369.

Laffont, J. J. (2001). *Incentives and Political Economy.* Oxford: Oxford University Press.

Lane, J. K. (2005). *Public Administration and Public Management.* London: Routledge.

Langley, A. (1999). Strategies for theorizing from process data. *Academy of Management Review, 24*, 691–710.

Lasswell, H. D. (1936). *Politics: Who Gets What, When, How?* New York: McGraw-Hill.

Lau, E. (2000). *Government of the Future.* Paris: Organisation for Economic Co-operation and Development.

Lawler, J. and Hearn, J. (1995). UK public sector organisation: the rise of managerialism and the impact of change on social services departments. *International Journal of Public Sector Management, 8*(3), 7–16.

Lawrence, P. R. and Lorsch, J. W. (1967). *Organizations and Environments: Managing Differentiation and Integration.* Boston: Graduate School of Business Administration, Harvard University.

Le Grand, J. (2007). The politics of choice and competition in the public services. *Political Quarterly, 78*(2), 207–213.

Leigh, A. (2003). Thinking ahead: strategic foresight and government. *Australian Journal of Public Administration*, *62*(2), 3–10.

Levine, H. Z. (1997). New strategies for public pay: rethinking government compensation programs. *Compensation and Benefits Review*, *29* (November/December), 75–87.

Levy, D. L., Alvesson, M. and Willmott, H. (2001). Critical approaches to strategic management. Paper presented at the Critical Management Studies Conference 2001, conference stream: Strategy, 2001.

Lewin, D. (1974). The prevailing wage principle and public wage decisions. *Public Personnel Management*, *3* (November–December), 473–485.

Lewin, D. (1987). Technological change in the public sector: the case of sanitation service. In: D. B. Cornfield (ed.), *Workers, Managers, and Technological Change: Emerging Patterns of Labor Relations*. New York: Plenum, 281–309.

Lewin, D. (2003). Incentive compensation in the public sector: evidence and potential. *Journal of Labor Research*, *24*, 597–619.

Lewin, D. and Mitchell, D. J. B. (1995). *Human Resource Management: An Economic Approach*, 2nd edn. Cincinnati, OH: Southwestern.

Lewin, K. (1939). When facing danger. In: G. W. Lewin (ed.) (1948), *Resolving Social Conflict*. London: Harper and Row.

Lewin, K. (1943). Psychological ecology. In: D. Cartwright (ed.) (1952), *Field Theory in Social Science*. London: Social Science Paperbacks.

Lewin, K. (1946). Action research and minority problems. In: G. W. Lewin and G. W. Allport (eds) (1948), *Resolving Social Conflict*. London: Harper and Row.

Lewin, K. (1947a). Group decision and social change. In: T. M. Newcomb and E. L. Hartley (eds), *Readings in Social Psychology*. New York: Henry Holt.

Lewin, K. (1947b). Frontiers in group dynamics. In: D. Cartwright (ed.) (1952), *Field Theory in Social Science*. London: Social Science Paperbacks.

Lewin, K. (1951). *Field Theory in Social Science*. New York: Harper and Row.

Likert, R. (1961). *New Patterns of Management*. New York: McGraw-Hill.

Linder, S. H. and Peters, B. G. (1987). Relativism, contingency and the definition of success in implementation research. *Policy Studies Review*, *7*(1), 116–127.

Lines, R. (2005). The structure and functioning of attitudes towards organizational change. *Human Resource Development Review*, *4*, 8–32.

Lines, R. (2006). The dual role of values in reactions to organizational change. In: R. Lines, I. Stensaker and A. Langley (eds), *New Perspectives on Organizational Change and Learning*. Bergen, Norway: Fagbokforlaget.

Lines, R. (2007). Using power to install strategy: the relationships between expert power, position power, influence tactics and implementation success. *Journal of Change Management*, *7*(2), 143–170.

Llewellyn, S. (2007). Introducing the agents . . . *Organizational Studies*, *28*(2), 133–153.

Lozeau, D., Langley, A. and Denis, J. (2002). The corruption of managerial techniques. *Human Relations*, *55*, 537–564.

Luecke, R. (2003). *Managing Change and Transition*. Boston: Harvard Business School Press.

McAuley, J., Duberley, J. and Cohen, L. (2000). The meaning professionals give to management . . . and strategy. *Human Relations*, *53*(1), 87–116.

McLaughlin, K., Osborne, S. P. and Ferlie, E. (eds) (2002). *New Public Management: Current Trends and Future Prospects*. London: Routledge.

Maitlis, S. and Lawrence, T. B. (2007). Triggers and enablers of sensegiving in organizations. *Academy of Management Journal*, *50*, 57–84.

Mantere, S. (2007). Role expectations and middle manager strategic agency. *Journal of Management Studies*, *45*(2), 294–316.

Markóczy, L. (2001). Consensus formation during strategic change. *Strategic Management Journal*, *22*, 1013–1031.

Marrow, A. J. (1969). *The Practical Theorist: The Life and Work of Kurt Lewin*. New York: Teachers College Press (1977 edition).

Marsden, D. and Belfield, R. (2007). Pay for performance where output is hard to measure: the case of performance pay for school teachers. In: D. Lewin and B. E. Kaufman (eds), *Advances in Industrial and Labor Relations*, *15*, 1–34.

Martin, R. R., Manning, K. and Ramaley, J. A. (2001). The self-study as a chariot for strategic change, *New Directions for Higher Education*, *113*, 95–115.

Martin, S., Walker, R. M., Ashworth, R., Boyne, G. A., Enticott, G., Entwistle, T. and Dawson, L. (2003). *The Long Term Evaluation of Best Value and Its Impact: Baseline Report*. London: Office of the Deputy Prime Minister.

Massey, A. and Pyper, R. (2005). *Public Management and Modernisation in Britain*. Basingstoke, UK: Palgrave Macmillan.

Meehan, R. H. (1991). Strategic total compensation planning in the public sector. *Compensation and Benefits Management*, *7* (summer), 10–17.

Merton, R. (1968). *Social Theory and Social Structure*. New York: The Free Press.

Meyer, J. W. (2002a). Globalization and the expansion and standardization of management. In: K. Sahlin-Andersson and L. Engwall (eds), *The Expansion of Management Knowledge: Carriers, Flows and Sources*. Stanford, CA: Stanford University Press.

Meyer, H. D. (2002b). From 'loose coupling' to 'tight management'? Making sense of the changing landscape in management and organization theory. *Journal of Educational Administration*, *40*(6), 515–520.

Meyer, J. W. and Rowan, W. R. (1977). Institutionalized organizations: formal structure as myth and ceremony. *American Journal of Sociology*, *83*, 340–363.

Miles, M. B. and Huberman, A. M. (1994). *Qualitative Data Analysis*, 2nd edn. Thousand Oaks, CA: Sage.

Milkovich, G. T. and Newman, J. M. (1999). *Compensation*. Burr Ridge, IL: Irwin/McGraw-Hill.

Milkovich, G. T. and Stevens, J. (2000). From pay to rewards: 100 years of change. *American Compensation Association Journal*, *9* (first quarter): 6–18.

Miller, D. and Friesen, P. (1984). *Organizations: A Quantum View*. Englewood Cliffs, NJ: Prentice Hall.

Miller, S. J., Hickson, D. J. and Wilson, D. C. (1996). Decision-making in organizations. Reprinted in: G. Salaman (ed.) (2002), *Decision Making for Business*. London: Sage, for The Open University.

Mintzberg, H. (1975). The manager's job: folklore and fact. *Harvard Business Review*, *53*(4), 49–61.

Mintzberg, H. (1979). *The Structuring of Organizations*. Englewood Cliffs, NJ: Prentice Hall.

Mintzberg, H. (1983). *Power in and around Organizations*. Englewood Cliffs, NJ: Prentice Hall.

Mintzberg, H. (1985). The organization as political arena. *Journal of Management Studies*, *22*(2), 133–154.

Mintzberg, H. (1994). Rethinking strategic planning: Part I: Pitfalls and fallacies. *Long Range Planning*, *27*(3), 12–21.

Mitchell, D. J. B., Lewin, D. and Lawler, E. E. (1990). Alternative pay systems, firm performance, and productivity. In: A. S. Blinder (ed.), *Paying for Productivity: A Look at the Evidence*. Washington, DC: Brookings Institution Press.

Mizruchi, M. S. (1992). *The Structure of Corporate Political Action*. Cambridge, MA: Harvard University Press.

Mohr, L. B. (1982). *Explaining Organizational Behavior: The Limits and Possibilities of Theory and Research*. San Francisco: Jossey-Bass.

Montanari, J. R. and Bracker, J. S. (1986). The strategic management process at the public planning unit level. *Strategic Management Journal*, *7*, 251–265.

Moran, J. W. and Brightman, B. K. (2001). Leading organizational change. *Career Development International*, *6*(2), 111–118.

Morrill, C., Zald, M. N. and Rao, H. (2003). Covert political conflict in organizations: challenges from below. *Annual Review of Sociology*, *29*(1), 391–415.

Musselin, C. (2000). Do we compare societies when we compare national university systems? In: M. Maurice and A. Sorge (eds), *Embedding Organizations*. Amsterdam: John Benjamins.

Musselin, C. (2005a). Change or continuity in HE governance? Lessons drawn from twenty years of national reforms in European countries. In: I. Bleiklie and M. Henkel (eds), *Governing Knowledge: A Study of Continuity and Change in HE*. Dordrecht, the Netherlands: Springer.

Musselin, C. (2005b). Is the Bologna process a move towards a European HE area? Conference paper at the third Conference on Knowledge and Politics, University of Bergen, Norway, 18–20 May.

Musson, G. and Duberley, J. (2007). Change change or be exchanged: the discourse of participation and the management of identity. *Journal of Management Studies*, *44*(1), 143–164.

Myers, F. and MacDonald, C. (1996). Power to the people? Involving users and carers in needs assessments and care planning – views from the practitioner. *Health and Social Care in the Community, 4*(2), 86–95.

Nash, M. (1996). Consumers without teeth: can probation service 'clients' have a say in the service they receive? *International Journal of Public Sector Management, 9*(4), 12–19.

Neave, G. (2002). The stakeholder perspective historically explored. In: J. Enders and O. Fulton (eds), *Higher Education in a Globalizing World*. International Trends and Mutual Observations. Dordrecht, the Netherlands: Kluwer.

Newell, H. and Dopson, S. (1996). Muddle in the middle: organizational restructuring and middle management careers. *Personnel Review, 1*(4), 4–20.

Newton, J. (2003). Implementing an institution-wide learning and teaching strategy: lessons in managing change. *Studies in Higher Education, 28*(4), 427–441.

NHS Executive (1996). *Patient Partnership*. London: Department of Health.

Nickerson, J. A. and Zenger, T. R. (2004). A knowledge-based theory of the firm: the problem-solving perspective. *Organization Science, 15*(6), 617–632.

Nonaka, I. (1988). Toward middle-up-down management: accelerating information creation. *Sloan Management Review, 29*(3), 9–18.

Nonaka, I. (1991). The knowledge-creating company. *Harvard Business Review, 69*(6), 96–104.

Nonaka, I. and Takeuchi, H. (1995). *The Knowledge-Creating Company: How Japanese Companies Create the Dynamics of Innovation*. Oxford: Oxford University Press.

Nonaka, I., Toyama, R. and Konno, N. (2000). SECI, *ba* and leadership: a unified model of dynamic knowledge creation. *Long Range Planning, 33*(1), 5–34.

Nutt, P. C. and Backoff, R. W. (1987). A strategic management process for public and third sector organizations. *American Journal of Planning, 53*(1), 44–57.

O'Brien, G. (2002). Participation as the key to successful change: a public sector case study. *Leadership and Organizational Development Journal, 23*, 442–455.

OECD (1993). *Managing with Market-Type Mechanisms*. Paris: Organisation for Economic Co-operation and Development.

Office of the Deputy Prime Minister (2000). *Best Value Performance Indicators for 2000/2001*. London: Office of the Deputy Prime Minister.

Office of the Deputy Prime Minister (2005). *An Organisational Development Resource Document for Local Government*. Wetherby, UK: ODPM Publications.

Office of Public Service Reform (2002). *Reforming Our Public Services: Principles into Practice*. London: Office of Public Service Reform.

Office of Public Service Reform (2003). *Leading from the Front Line*. London: Office of Public Service Reform.

Oliver, C. (1991). Strategic responses to institutional processes. *Academy of Management Review, 16*, 145–179.

Osborne, D. and Gaebler, T. (1992). *Reinventing Government: How the Entrepreneurial Spirit is Transforming the Public Sector*. Reading, MA: Addison-Wesley.

Osborne, D. and Plastrik, P. (1997). *Banishing Bureaucracy: The Five Stages for Reinventing Government*. New York: Addison-Wesley.

Østergren, K, Boni, S. Danishevski, K. and Kaarbøe, O. (2007). Implementation of health care decentralization. In: R. B. Saltman, V. Bankauskaite and K. Vrangbæk (eds), *Decentralization in Health Care*. New York: Open University Press.

Palese, M. and Crane, T. Y. (2002). Building an integrated issue management process as a source of sustainable competitive advantage. *Journal of Public Affairs*, *2*(4), 284–292.

Parker, M. (2002). *Against Management: Organisation in the Age of Managerialism*. Cambridge: Polity.

Parkin, J. (1994). *Public Management*. Sydney: Avebury.

Pascale, R. (1990). *Managing on the Edge: How the Smartest Companies Use Conflict to Stay Ahead*. London: Viking.

Pasmore, W. A. and Fagans, M. R. (1992). Participation, individual development, and organizational change: a review and synthesis. *Journal of Management*, *18*(2), 375–397.

Patchett, R. R. (2005). Organization development in the public sector. In: T. G. Cummings and C. G. Worley (eds), *Organization Development and Change*. Mason, OH: Southwestern College Publishing.

Perrott, B. E. (1996). Managing strategic issues in the public service. *Long Range Planning*, *29*(3), 337–345.

Peters, T. and Waterman, R. H. (1982). *In Search of Excellence: Lessons from America's Best-Run Companies*. London: Harper and Row.

Peterson, M. F. (1998). Embedded organizational events: the units of process in organization science. *Organization Science*, *9*, 16–33.

Pettigrew, A. M. (1973). Decision-making as a political process. Reprinted in: G. Salaman (ed.), *Decision Making for Business*. London: Sage, for the Open University.

Pettigrew, A. M. (1992). On studying managerial elites. *Strategic Management Journal*, *13*, 163–182.

Pettigrew, A. M. (2003). Strategy as power, process and change. In: S. Cummings and D. Wilson (eds), *Images of Strategy*. Oxford: Wiley Blackwell.

Pettigrew, A. M., Ferlie, E. and Mckee, L. (1992). *Shaping Strategic Change*. London: Sage.

Pettigrew, A. M., Woodman, R. W. and Cameron, K. S. (2001). Studying organizational change and development: challenges for future research. *Academy of Management Journal*, *44*, 697–713.

Pilgrim, D. and Waldron, L. (1998). User involvement in mental health development: how far can it go? *Journal of Mental Health*, *7*(1), 95–104.

Plowden, Lord (1961). *Control of Public Expenditure*. Cmnd 1432. London: HMSO.

Poister, T. H. and Streib, G. D. (1999). Strategic management in the public sector. *Public Productivity and Management Review, 22*(3), 308–325.

Pollitt, C. (1990). *Managerialism and the Public Services: The Anglo-Saxon Experience*. Oxford: Basil Blackwell.

Pollitt, C. and Bouckaert, G. (2000). *Public Management Reform: A Comparative Analysis*. Oxford: Oxford University Press.

Pollitt, C. and Bouckaert, G. (2004). *Public Management Reform: A Comparative Analysis*, 2nd edn. Oxford: Oxford University Press.

Poole, M. S., Van de Ven, A. H., Dooley, K. and Holmes, M. E. (2000). *Organizational Change and Innovation Processes: Theory and Methods for Research*. Oxford: Oxford University Press.

Poole, M., Mansfield, R. and Gould-Williams, J. (2006). Public and private sector managers over 20 years: a test of the convergence thesis. *Public Administration, 84*(4), 1051–1076.

Porter, M. (1979). How competitive forces shape strategy. *Harvard Business Review* (March/April), 137–145.

Poulton, B. C. (1999). User involvement in identifying health needs and shaping and evaluating services: is it being realised? *Journal of Advanced Nursing, 30*, 1289–1296.

Pressman, J. and Wildavsky, P. (1973). *Implementation*. Berkeley: University of California Press.

Preston, L. E. and Post, J. E. (1975). *Private Management and Public Policy: The Principle of Public Responsibility*. Englewood Cliffs, NJ: Prentice Hall.

Pugh, D. S. (1993). Understanding and managing organizational change. In: C. Mabey and B. Mayon-White (eds), *Managing Change*, 2nd edn. London: Paul Chapman, for the Open University.

Rainey, H. G. and Bozeman, B. (2000). Comparing public and private organizations: empirical research and the power of the a priori. *Journal of Public Administration Research and Theory, 10*(2), 447–469.

Rainey, H. G., Backoff, R. W. and Levine, C. H. (1976). Comparing public and private organizations. *Public Administration Review, 36*(1), 233–244.

Randall, J. (2004). *Managing Change/Changing Managers*. London: Routledge.

Ranson, S. and Stewart, J. (1994). *Management in the Public Domain: Enabling the Learning Society*. Basingstoke, UK: Palgrave Macmillan.

Redman, T., Wilkinson, A. and Snape, E. (1997). Stuck in the middle: managers in building societies. *Work, Employment and Society, 11*(1), 101–114.

Risher, H. W. (1999). Are public employers ready for a 'new pay' program? *Public Personnel Management, 28* (fall), 323–343.

Risher, H. W., Fay, C. H. and Shrader, A. (1997). *New Strategies for Public Pay: Rethinking Government Compensation Programs*. San Francisco: Jossey-Bass.

Robertson, P. J. and Seneviratne, S. J. (1995). Outcomes of planned organizational change in the public sector: a meta-analytic comparison to the private sector. *Public Administration Review, 55*, 547–558.

Rodrigues, S. B. and Hickson, D. J. (1995), Different organizations, differing reasons for success. *Journal of Management Studies, 32*, 655–679.

Rokeach, M. (1973). *The Nature of Human Values*. New York: The Free Press.

Romanelli, E. and Tushman, M. L. (1994). Organizational transformation as punctuated equilibrium: an empirical test. *Academy of Management Journal, 37*, 1141–1166.

Rose, A. and Lawton, A. (1999). *Public Services Management*. Harlow, UK: FT Prentice Hall.

Rouleau, L. (2005). Micro-practices of strategic sensemaking and sensegiving: how middle managers interpret and sell change every day. *Journal of Management Studies, 42*(7), 1413–1441.

Rush, B. (2004). Mental health service user involvement in England: lessons from history. *Journal of Psychiatric and Mental Health Nursing, 11*(3), 313–318.

Salancik, G. R. and Pfeffer, J. (1978). A social information processing approach to job attitudes and task design. *Administrative Science Quarterly, 23*, 224–253.

Sarker, A. E. (2006). New public management in developing countries: an analysis of success and failure with particular reference to Singapore and Bangladesh. *International Journal of Public Sector Management, 19*(2), 180–203.

Savage, G. T., Nix, T. W., Whitehead, C. J. and Blair, J. D. (1991). Strategies for assessing and managing organisational stakeholders. *Academy of Management Executive, 5*(2), 61–75.

Schein, E. H. (1988). *Organizational Psychology,* 3rd edn. Englewood Cliffs, NJ: Prentice Hall.

Schein, E. H. (1996). Kurt Lewin's change theory in the field and in the classroom: notes towards a model of management learning. *Systems Practice, 9*(1), 27–47.

Scott, W. R. (1992). *Organizations: Rational, Natural, and Open Systems*. Englewood Cliffs, NJ: Prentice Hall.

Seldon, A. (2005). *Blair*. London: The Free Press.

Semler, R. (1989). Managing without managers. *Harvard Business Review* (September–October), 76–84.

Senge, P., Ross, R., Kleiner, A., Roberts, C., Roth, G. and Smith, B. (1999). *The Dance of Change*. London: Nicholas Brealey.

Senior, B. (2002). *Organisational Change*, 2nd edn. London: Prentice Hall.

Shattock, M. (2003). *Managing Successful Universities*. Maidenhead, UK: Society for Research into Higher Education and Open University Press.

Shaw, P. (2002). *Changing Conversations in Organizations*. London: Routledge.

Sherman, H. and Chaganti, R. (1998). *Corporate Governance and the Timeliness of Change: Reorientation in 100 American Firms*. Westport, CT: Quorum.

Shrivastava, P. (1986). Is strategic management ideological? *Journal of Management, 12*(3), 363–377.

Siegel, P. A., Post, C., Brockner, J., Fishman, A. Y. and Garden, C. (2005). The moderating influence of procedural fairness on the relationship between work–life conflict and organizational commitment. *Journal of Applied Psychology*, *90*(1), 13–24.

Simon, B. and Oakes, P. (2006). Beyond dependence: an identity approach to social power and domination. *Human Relations*, *59*(1), 105–139.

Simpson, B. (2008). Re-viewing 'role' in processes of identity construction. *Organization*, *15*(1), 29–50.

Sminia, H. and Van Nistelrooij, A. T. M. (2006). Strategic management and organization development: planned change in a public sector organization. *Journal of Change Management*, *6*(1), 99–113.

Smith, M. K. (2001). Kurt Lewin: groups, experiential learning and action research. *The Encyclopedia of Informal Education*, 1–15, available at www.infed.org/thinkers/et-lewin.htm.

South, J. (2007). Bridging the gap? A critical analysis of the development of the Patient Advice and Liaison Service (PALS). *Journal of Health Organization and Management*, *21*(2), 149–165.

Spencer-Matthews, S. (2001). Enforced cultural change in academe: a practical case study: implementing quality management systems in higher education. *Assessment and Evaluation in Higher Education*, *26*(1), 51–59.

Starling, G. (2005). *Managing the Public Sector*, 7th edn. Belmont, CA: Thompson Wadsworth Publishing.

Starr, M. A. (2004). Reading *The Economist* on globalisation: knowledge, identity, and power. *Global Society*, *18*(4), 373–396.

Staw, B. M. and Epstein, L. D. (2000). What bandwagons bring: effects of popular management techniques on corporate performance, reputation, and CEO pay. *Administrative Science Quarterly*, *45*(3), 523–556.

Steger, M. (2005). From market globalism to imperial globalism: ideology and American power after 9/11. *Globalizations*, *2*(1), 31–46.

Stensaker, I. and Falkenberg J. (2007). Making sense of different responses to corporate change. *Human Relations*, *60*, 137–177.

Sternberg, R. J. (1998). A balance theory of wisdom. *Review of General Psychology*, *2*, 347–365.

Sternberg, R. J. (2004). Why smart people can be so foolish. *European Psychologist*, *9*(3), 145–150.

Stewart, J. and Kringas, P. (2003). Change management: strategy and values in six agencies from the Australian public service. *Public Administration Review*, *63*(6), 675–688.

Stickland, F. (1998). *The Dynamics of Change: Insights into Organisational Transition from the Natural World*. London: Routledge.

Suddaby, R. and Greenwood, R. (2005). Rhetorical strategies of legitimacy. *Administrative Science Quarterly*, *50*(1), 35–67.

Swedberg, R. (2005). Can there be a sociological concept of interest? *Theory and Society*, *34*(4), 359–390.

Talbot, C. (2001). UK public services and management (1979–2000): evolution or revolution? *International Journal of Public Sector Management*, *14*(4), 281–303.

Teo, S. T. and Crawford, J. (2005). Indicators of strategic HRM effectiveness: a case study of an Australian public sector agency during commercialization. *Public Personnel Management*, *34*, 1–16.

Therborn, G. (1980). *The Ideology of Power and the Power of Ideology*. London: Verso NLB.

Thomas, R. and Dunkerley, D. (1999). Careering downwards: middle management in the downsized organisation. *British Journal of Management*, *10*(2), 157–169.

Thompson, V. A. (1961). Hierarchy, specialization, and organizational conflict. *Administrative Science Quarterly*, *5*(4), 485–521.

Thompson, W. (2002). *Managing Change to Improve Public Services: Top Down or Bottom Up?* London: Office of Public Service Reform. Retrieved from www.opsr.gov.uk (accessed 25 August 2004).

Towles, R. D. (2003). The changing landscape of government competition. *Contract Management*, *43*(10), 6–11.

Tsamenyi, M., Cullen, J. and González, J. M. G. (2006). Changes in accounting and financial information system in a Spanish electricity company: a new institutional theory analysis. *Management Accounting Research*, *17*(4), 409–432.

Turnbull, S. (2001). Corporate ideology: meanings and contradictions for middle managers. *British Journal of Management*, *12*(3), 231–242.

Tushman, M. L. and O'Reilly, C. A. (1997). *Winning through Competition: A Practical Guide to Leading Organizational Change and Renewal*. Boston: Harvard Business School Press.

Tyler, T. R. (1994). Governing amid diversity: can fair decision-making procedures bridge competing public interests and values? *Law and Society Review*, *28*, 701–722.

Ulrich, D. (1998). Intellectual capital = competence × commitment. *Sloan Management Review*, *39*(2), 15–27.

US Department of Labour, Bureau of Labor Statistics (2005). *Monthly Labor Review*, 128 (February).

Van de Ven, A. H. and Poole, M. S. (1995). Explaining development and change in organizations. *Academy of Management Review*, *20*, 510–540.

Van Loon, R. (2001). Organizational change: a case study. *Innovative Higher Education*, *25*(4), 285–301.

Van Nistelrooij, A. T. M., De Vries, C. and Minkema, D. (2004). Dialogue and Whole Scale Change: a combination of democratic participation and planned change. *Opleiding en Ontwikkeling: Tijdschrift voor Human Resource Development*, *17*, 21-24.

Vickers, M. H. and Kouzmin, A. (2001). 'Resilience' in organizational actors and rearticulating 'voice'. *Public Management Review*, *3*(1), 95–119.

Vidler, E. and Clarke, J. (2005). Creating citizen-consumers: New Labour and the remaking of public services. *Public Policy and Administration*, *20*(2), 19–37.

Virany, B., Tushman, M. L. and Romanelli, E. (1992). Executive succession and organization outcomes in turbulent environments: an organization learning approach. *Organization Science*, *3*, 72–91.

Waldersee, R. and Griffiths, A. (2004). Implementing change: matching implementation methods and change type. *Leadership and Organization Development Journal*, *25*, 424–434.

Walker, R. M. and Boyne, G. A. (2006). Public management reform and organizational performance: an empirical assessment of the UK Labour government's public service improvement strategy. *Journal of Policy Analysis and Management*, *25*, 371–394.

Walker, R. M. and Brewer, G. A. (2008). An organizational echelon analysis of the determinants of red tape in public organizations. *Public Administration Review*, *68*(6), 1112–1117.

Walker, R. M. and Enticott, G. (2004). Using multiple informants in public administration: revisiting the managerial values and actions debate. *Journal of Public Administration Research and Theory*, *14*, 417–434.

Walker, R. M., O'Toole, L. J., Jr., and Meier, K. J. (2007). It's where you are that matters: the networking behaviour of English local government officers. *Public Administration*, *85*, 739–756.

Walsh, J. P. and Weber, K. (2002). The prospects for critical management studies in the American Academy of Management. *Organization*, *9*(3), 402–410.

Walshe, K. and Higgins, J. (2002). The use and impact of inquiries in the NHS. *British Medical Journal*, *325* (19 October), 895–900.

Walton, R. A. (1985). From control to commitment in the workplace. *Harvard Business Review*, *63*(2), 77–84.

Waterman, R. H., Jr, Peters, T. J. and Philips, J. R. (1980). Structure is not organization. *Business Horizons*, *23*(3), 14–26.

Wechsler, B. (1989). Strategic management in state government. In: J. Rabin, G. J. Miller and W. B. Hildreth (eds), *Handbook of Strategic Management*. New York: Marcel Dekker.

Weick, K. E. (1995). *Sensemaking in Organizations*. London: Sage.

Weick, K. E. (2000). Emergent change as a universal in organizations. In: M. Beer and N. Nohria (eds), *Breaking the Code of Change*. Boston: Harvard Business School Press.

Weick, K. (2001). *Making Sense of Organizations*. Oxford: Blackwell.

Weick, K. E. and Quinn, R. E. (1999). Organizational change and development. *Annual Review of Psychology*, *50*, 361–386.

Weick, K., Sutcliffe, K. M. and Obsfeld, D. (2005). Organizing and the process of sensemaking. *Organization Science*, *16*(4), 409–421.

Welsh Assembly (2007). *Making Connections – Building Better Customer Service: A Framework for Improvement*, www.wales.gov.uk/makingthe connections, March 2007.

West, M. A. and Anderson, N. R. (1996). Innovation in top management teams. *Journal of Applied Psychology, 81*, 680–693.

Wheatley, M. (2001). *Leadership and the New Science*. San Francisco: Berrett-Koehler.

Whitley, R. (1989). On the nature of managerial tasks and skills: their distinguishing characteristics and organization. *Journal of Management Studies, 26*(3), 209–224.

Whittington, R. (1992). Putting Giddens into action: social systems and managerial agency. *Journal of Management Studies, 29*(6), 693–712.

Whittington, R. (2006). Completing the practice turn in strategy research. *Organization Studies, 27*, 613–634.

Wilenski, P. (1988). Social change as a source of competing values in public administration. *Australian Journal of Public Administration, 47*(3), 213–222.

Willmott, H. C. (1984). Images and ideals of managerial work: a critical examination of conceptual and empirical accounts. *Journal of Management Studies, 21*(3), 349–368.

Willmott, H. C. (1996). A metatheory of management: omniscience or obfuscation? *British Journal of Management, 7*(4), 323–328.

Willmott, H. C. (1997). Rethinking management and managerial work: capitalism, control and subjectivity. *Human Relations, 50*(11), 1329–1359.

Wilson, D. C. (1992). *A Strategy of Change*. London: Routledge.

Wischnevsky, J. D. and Damanpour, F. (2005). Punctuated equilibrium model of organizational transformation: sources and consequences in the banking industry. In: R. W. Woodman and W. A. Pasmore (eds), *Research in Organizational Change and Development*, vol. 15. New York: Elsevier.

Wischnevsky, J. D. and Damanpour, F. (2006). Organizational transformation and performance: an examination of three perspectives. *Journal of Managerial Issues, 18*, 104–128.

Worren, N., Ruddle, K. and Moore, K. (1999). From Organizational Development to change management: the emergence of a new profession. *Journal of Applied Behavioral Science, 35*(3), 273–286.

Ylijoki, O-H. (2003). Entangled in academic capitalism? A case-study on changing ideals and practices of university research. *Higher Education, 45*, 307–335.

Yukl, G. (1999). An evaluative essay on current conceptions of effective leadership. *European Journal of Work and Organizational Psychology, 8*, 33–48.

Yukl, G. and Falbe, C. M. (1990). Influence tactics in upward, downward, and lateral influence attempts. *Journal of Applied Psychology, 75*, 132–140.

Yukl, G. and Tracey, J. B. (1992). Consequences of influence tactics used with subordinates, peers and the boss. *Journal of Applied Psychology, 77*, 525–535.

Zajac, E. J. and Kraatz, M. S. (1993). A diametric forces model of strategic change: assessing the antecedents and consequences of restructuring in the higher education industry. *Strategic Management Journal, 14*, 83–102.

Zaleznik, A. (1989). *The Managerial Mystique: Restoring Leadership in Business*. New York: Harper and Row.

Zammuto, R. F., Gifford, B. and Goodman, E. A. (2000). Managerial ideologies, organization culture, and the outcomes of innovation. In: N. M. Ashkanasy, C. Wilderom and M. F. Peterson (eds), *Handbook of Organizational Culture and Climate*. Thousand Oaks, CA: Sage.

Index